KnOCK 'em DEaD

HIRING THE
BEST

—— SIXTH EDITION ——

D0951241

KnOCK em DEaD

HIRING THE BEST

— SIXTH EDITION —

Proven Tactics for Successful Employee Selection

MARTIN YATE, CPC
New York Times bestselling author

Aadamsmedia
AVON, MASSACHUSETTS

Published by
Adams Media, a division of F+W Media, Inc.
57 Littlefield Street, Avon, MA 02322. U.S.A.
www.adamsmedia.com

ISBN 10: 1-4405-6270-9
ISBN 13: 978-1-4405-6270-9
eISBN 10: 1-4405-6999-1
eISBN 13: 978-1-4405-6999-9

Printed in the United States of America.

10 9 8 7 6 5 4 3 2

Library of Congress Cataloging-in-Publication Data

Yate, Martin John.
 Knock 'em dead hiring the best : Martin Yate, CPC, *New York Times* bestselling
author. -- 6th edition.
     pages cm
  Includes index.
  ISBN-13: 978-1-4405-6270-9 (pb)
  ISBN-10: 1-4405-6270-9 (pb)
  ISBN-13: 978-1-4405-6999-9 (ebook)
  ISBN-10: 1-4405-6999-1 (ebook)
1. Employees--Recruiting. 2. Employee selection. 3. Employment interviewing. I.
Title.
  HF5549.5.R44Y37 2014
  658.3'11--dc23
                                        2013035926

This book is available at quantity discounts for bulk purchases.
For information, please call 1-800-289-0963.

ACKNOWLEDGMENTS

I would like to thank the following people for their help in bring-ing *Knock 'em Dead: Hiring the Best* to life: Karen Cooper at Adams Media for inviting me to do the book, and the erudite Peter Archer for managing the project with his usual editorial aplomb and gentle wit. William Yate for the sure editorial hand and copyediting skills that allowed us to bring in a great book with almost impossible deadlines. And last, but not least, my friend and spouse Angela Yate for her business management and people skills, which helped keep the world at bay, allowing me to concentrate on keeping Will and Peter happy.

Contents

The special considerations and questions to ask, and what to look for in the answers, when hiring for Director, VP, and C-Level positions.

Discover how to make final decisions and check references. We move from *hiring effectively* to *managing productively* and learn how to get new hires up to speed, turn around problem workers, make the most of the plodders, and keep your superstars happy.

Reviewing the building blocks of reaching good decisions. Learn how to check references and then make that final decision that leads to *hiring the best*.

How to get new hires productive fast, get the most out of your plodders, turn around troubled employees, and nurture your superstars.

PART I
THE SECRETS OF EFFECTIVE HIRING

In this section, we'll talk about the connectivity between *hiring effectively* and *managing productively*, plus look at how to create a customized Job Description, read a resume in six seconds, save time by screening with phone interviews, and structure and conduct face-to-face interview sequences.

ONE

Management—
The Path to Success

There's no question that management, with its combination of financial reward and social respect, is still the traditional icon of success. Yet there's a myth in the corporate world that can snatch that success away: the myth that on promotion into management you become mysteriously endowed with all the skills of a manager. That's magical thinking.

Successful management is an ongoing, all-too-often overlooked learning experience. This is *your* life and *your* career, and it's *your* responsibility to develop the skills that lead to survival and prosperity on the management ladder.

Getting Work Done Through Others

Management skills cover a wide range of proficiencies, but they all boil down into one simple phrase: *getting work done through others*. This is the essence of your job: You are responsible for the individual performance and collective productivity of your reports. This holds true whether you are in your first management job with just a few reports, or you're a senior manager with thousands under your guidance and command.

The Secret to Successful Management

The secret is that in order to *manage productively*, you must first *hire effectively*. If you make poor hires, the odds are that those hires will not be productive individuals or team players willing to work for the success of your department (and therefore *your* success). *Hiring effectively* is at the core of *getting work done through others*—it is the foundational skill of successful management. If you cannot *hire effectively*, you will never be able to *manage productively*, and you will fail as a manager.

The focus of *Knock 'em Dead: Hiring the Best* is to help you learn to *hire effectively* so that you can *manage productively* and have a long and successful management career. We've all heard about people whose excellent engineering or accounting or sales skills weren't enough to make them good managers. There is a big difference between the *technical skills* needed to be good at your work (the very skills that often short-list you for greater opportunity) and the *managerial* skills you need to survive and prosper on the management track.

In *Knock 'em Dead: Hiring the Best*, you will learn that employee selection isn't brain surgery. It is a series of logical steps, using the sensible strategies and practical tactics that will enable you to make consistently good hires—while simultaneously giving you skills that have ready application in other areas of your professional life where "reading people" and persuasive *communication skills* are paramount.

How to Avoid Bad Hires

U.S. Labor Department studies have consistently shown over the years that only 50 percent of new hires last more than six months in their new jobs. What happened to the other 50 percent? Even if we assume that a few of these hires were rapidly promoted, that still means a large proportion either quit or were fired. This is good news: At least decisions were made in all these instances.

What about the 50 percent who weren't promoted, and didn't quit or get fired: the 50 percent who stayed in the job more than six months? No doubt some of them were dedicated and productive professionals, but common sense tells us that their number also includes a percentage of plodders and, worse, the troubled workers who scrape by over the years, missing deadlines, getting sick, spreading discontent, or coming in two hours late in the morning and then leaving two hours early to make up for it. Every manager has made bad hires, and the cause of that bad hire can always be traced back to one of these reasons:

- Poor analysis of job functions, leading to inappropriate *recruitment* criteria
- Poor analysis of the necessary skill sets and behaviors, leading to inappropriate *selection* criteria
- Inadequate initial screening, leading to wasted time and the wrong candidates on the short list
- Inadequate *interviewing* techniques, resulting in poorer access to the facts
- Poor utilization of "second opinions," compounding all of the above errors
- Overselling of company and career/money expectations, leading to frustrated and unmotivated staff
- Not checking references, leading to troublemakers sneaking onto your payroll

What You'll Find in These Pages

You will learn a practical approach to employee selection that you can read today and use tomorrow; there's actionable advice on every page. While recruitment is probably not in your job description, every hire puts your job on the line, so in the first part of the book, we'll define the real *deliverables* of the jobs you fill (Chapter 2). Then we'll look beneath the surface of those shiny resumes (Chapter 3), and learn how and when to use the telephone as an awesomely effective time-management tool for screening candidates (Chapter 4).

After that, we'll move on to the carefully short-listed candidates you meet in person, develop the best ways to structure in-person interviews, learn how to use the most effective interviewing strategies and questioning tactics (Chapter 5), and discover how to get the maximum insight from second opinions (Chapter 6). In Chapters 8 through 15, you'll find more than 500 questions for many different situations to help you gather insights into a wide range of skills, behaviors, and values. In Chapters 16 and 17, we'll discuss final decisions, making new hires productive quickly, and how to turn around troubled workers, encourage your plodders, and keep your superstars, well . . . reaching for the stars; and you'll learn how to do all of this while staying on the right side of the law (Appendix).

Management and Your Long-Term Goals

If you've read other *Knock 'em Dead* career management books, you'll recognize the consistency and continuity with the strategies and professional advice you'll find in *Knock 'em Dead: Hiring the Best*. It is a natural extension of the overall *Knock 'em Dead* career management philosophy, which is built to support your changing needs as you navigate the twists and turns of a long career.

You might be reading *Knock 'em Dead: Hiring the Best* as a senior or midlevel manager staying on top of your game; you might have had management recently thrust upon you with no explanation of what on earth you're supposed to do next; or you may have the desire to break into management down the road and are intent on building the necessary skills. Whatever your situation, when it comes to the real guts of management—*getting work done through others*—*Knock 'em Dead: Hiring the Best* will help you develop a set of skills that will empower your career for many years to come.

TWO

DEFINING THE JOB

In Chapter 1 we talked about how important good hires are to your long-term success as a manager; but you can't make those hires without understanding the needs of each individual job. This chapter helps you develop that understanding by breaking down the job into its component *deliverables*, so that you can reassemble them into a practical Job Description (JD) that delivers a three-dimensional picture of the professional you want to hire. Put it this way: You'll never find Waldo if you don't know what he looks like.

Defining the Job

Most of the time you will have an existing JD that everyone is used to working with, but leaving your future in the hands of anonymous managers or HR recruiters would not be a smart move, as their JD could be outdated and might result in bad hires. The successful manager always uses the legally approved written JD as at least a starting point, but *only* as a starting point. Fifty percent of the success of any project is in the planning, so the first step you should take when filling a position is to generate your own JD. This will help you get the proper focus on the relative weight you should attach to *education, experience, responsibilities, deliverables*, and what I call the *transferable skills and professional values*, the foundational skills that power success in any job. Your success as a manager is rooted in the selection process and depends on how carefully you define the job in the beginning.

Responsibilities, Experience, and Deliverables

It is common sense to identify *responsibilities, experience,* and *deliverables* for the jobs you need to fill. These are the basic building blocks out of which any good JD is made.

To understand this clearly, we need to identify the three terms:

1. Responsibility: You want, for example, an accountant to deal with Accounts Receivable (A/R).
2. Experience: You determine that five years' experience dealing with A/R would be desirable. This is often as far as many job descriptions go: "Someone with X years' experience doing Y."

   But an accountant with five years' experience in Accounts Receivable who is hopeless at getting money in the door will cause his manager nothing but problems. Such an accountant's *responsibilities* and *experience* are only part of the picture; if the position's *deliverables* haven't been clearly defined as a separate issue, the performance of the chosen candidate may fall short of expectations.
3. Deliverables: What an employer expects as the tangible result of work done: The A/R accountant brought in _____ of receivables this week, representing _____ percent of outstanding receivables.

A clear-headed analysis of a job's *responsibilities, experience,* and *deliverables* (the tangible results of work done) gives you an objective way to rule out duds quickly and efficiently.

As a successful manager, defining *responsibilities, experience,* and *deliverables* helps you hire candidates based *on their real credentials, not their potential*—and that makes for better hires.

The Transferable Skills and Professional Values

Every job has a similar foundational skill set on which success is built. Whatever the job, whatever the level, in whatever profession, industry, city, and country, there are a handful of *transferable skills and professional values* that help every worker do what she does well; in other words, fulfill the job's *deliverables*. These *transferable skills and professional values* include, amongst others, *communication, critical thinking,* and *multitasking skills, determination, motivation,* and *integrity*; they are the key to your employees' success, and therefore to yours as well.

The Foundational Skills and Values That Make for Superior Employees

From that first day on your first job, when you noticed how different the world of work was from the relatively cozy life at home or school, you began to observe and emulate the more successful professionals around you.

You developed a whole slate of *transferable skills and professional values* that have helped you succeed in your professional life. These behaviors didn't always come naturally, but when you're at work, they help you do whatever it is you do well, for they are the foundation of professional success in all jobs at all levels. Now that you are responsible for hiring, you need to look for these same skills in the people you hire. You should also continue to develop them yourself for your own professional benefit.

Breakdown of the Transferable Skills and Professional Values

The following *transferable skills and professional values* are common to all professionals in the successful execution of jobs at all levels and in all professions. Read through the following outline of each and ask yourself how each one might contribute to the performance you get from your next hire.

You will become very familiar with these skills and values throughout this book and your career in management more generally: They will form the basis of job descriptions, interview questions, and performance reviews. But you need to keep in mind at all times that the *Knock 'em Dead* vocabulary used to describe these skills is not the only one. You need to be aware of variations, for example, when posting a job opening, searching a resume bank, or talking to headhunters. *Multitasking*, for instance, is still sometimes referred to as "time management and organization." I will point out these variations as we continue.

Transferable Skills
Technical
Communication
Critical Thinking
Multitasking
Teamwork and Manageability
Creativity
Leadership

Professional Values
Motivation and Energy
Commitment and Reliability, Determination, and Confidence
Productivity, Efficiency, and Profit-Orientation
Systems and Procedures
Pride and Integrity

Transferable Skills

TECHNICAL SKILLS
The *technical skills* of the job opening are the foundation of any success your new hire will achieve on the job. They speak to her *ability* to do the job, those essential skills necessary for the successful execution of her duties. These *technical skills* vary from profession to profession and do not refer to anything technical *as such* or to technology.

However, it is a given that one of the *technical skills* essential to every job is technological competence. Your candidate must be proficient in the technology and Internet-based applications relevant to his work, or at least with a plurality of the "must haves," combined with a proven ability to acquire new skills quickly. Every job today is increasingly impacted and transformed by ongoing technological innovation; so even when you are not working in a technology field, you should always consider candidates who exhibit strong technology skills and be wary of people who do not seem to have adapted to the digital age.

According to a recent study by a recruitment metrics company, 60 percent of the jobs available by 2015 will require skills held by 20 percent of the population. Technology constantly changes the nature of our jobs and the ways in which they are executed. This means you need to be a savvy manager if you want to hire good people in a competitive market.

You should look for candidates who have the *technical skills*, including the technology skills, to perform effectively on your company's operational platforms or, failing that, a proven ability to get up to speed with similar skills in a reasonable time frame.

It is also smart management to identify the new productivity-enhancement technology your company is doubtless considering, because this will give you a head start on some of the learning challenges that will be coming to your department over the next year or so. Armed with this knowledge, you can recruit candidates who already have this experience, and be prepared with an effective new hire before internal changes arrive.

CRITICAL THINKING/PROBLEM SOLVING

Employees are never added to the payroll for the love of mankind; they're added to contribute to profitability in some way. All jobs do this by helping to make money, save money, or increase productivity. Professionals accomplish this overriding mandate for every job by executing their duties reliably and conscientiously and understanding the geography of their professional world well enough to *anticipate* and *prevent problems* in their area of responsibility as they become (or even before they become) visible on the professional horizon. Additionally, they understand their professional world well enough to *solve the problems* that inevitably arise regardless of preventive measures.

Critical thinking (just as often referred to as *problem solving* or *analytical thinking*) allows a professional in any area of specialization to think through and clearly define a challenge, come up with options for a solution (carefully evaluating each one in relation to the desired outcome and its effect on all parties, including colleagues, departments, vendors, and clients), and ultimately implement the best solution given the available options.

At some level, every job is that of a *problem solver* who exists to *anticipate*, *prevent*, and *solve problems*. This applies to any job, at any level, in any organization, anywhere in the world, and it is the key to making successful hires. If there are no problems to *prevent* or *solve*, it could mean that the job has not as yet been clearly defined, or technology has advanced to the point where there is really no longer any job to fill.

Thinking about the jobs you fill in terms of their *problem identification/prevention/solution* responsibilities will clarify your focus during the selection process; it will also help with managing performance on the job after the most suitable candidate is hired. When you can identify the *problem-solving* responsibilities of a job title, you understand that job at its deepest level, and it becomes comparatively easy to identify all the other essential requirements of the position.

Once you have identified a job's areas of *responsibility*, its *deliverables*, and its *problem identification/prevention/solution* duties, it makes sense to isolate other skills that support these primary activities; for example, *multitasking*, or what used to be called *time management and organization* (see following).

COMMUNICATION

As George Bernard Shaw said, "The single biggest problem in communication is the illusion that it has taken place." Every professional job today requires *communication skills*. Good *verbal* and *listening skills* enable your team members to accurately process and share information. But when I think about the many vehicles we each possess for communication, I see it as a skill that embraces much more than just listening and speaking. In fact, within the *Knock 'em Dead* lexicon we define *communication skills* in terms of eight very different communication tools, all of which are necessary for successful communication in a professional context. So in talking about *communication skills*, I am referring to four primary skills and four supporting skills.

The primary *communication skills* are:

- Verbal skills—What does the candidate say and how does she say it?
- Listening skills—The candidate listens to understand, rather than just waiting for his turn to talk.
- Writing skills—The candidate expresses herself clearly in writing. You can assess this in resumes and cover letters, but the best candidates will keep in touch through follow-up notes throughout the hiring process, giving you more insight.
- Digital communication skills—The candidate shows mastery of e-mail, instant messaging, social and human media skills, webcasting and Skype, etc.

The four supportive *communication skills* are subtler, but nevertheless they impact every interaction you, and your staff, have with others. They are:

- Grooming and dress—These tell you who your candidate is and how he feels about himself, as well as how he will be perceived by customers, vendors, and coworkers.
- Social graces—These are demonstrated by how your candidate behaves around others, taking into account of course that she is going to be incredibly nervous because of the nature of the interactions happening at a job interview. If, for example, the job holder will be entertaining clients in restaurants or clubs, you will want to eat together and assess table manners and social graces (see Chapter 10 for more).
- Body language—Long before our species developed speech, we communicated with the silent language of the body, which displays

how we're feeling deep inside. For truly effective *communication*, what a candidate's mouth says should be in harmony with what his body says; we'll look at some useful *body language* interpretation later in the book.

- Emotional IQ—The candidate's emotional self-awareness and control in dealing with others in a wide range of professional situations.

Most of these eight aspects of *communication* are important on most jobs. For your purposes, while having them all is a distinct plus, you will need to consider with whom a particular job title will be interacting—which coworkers, departments, management ranks, and customers. In all of these areas, you need to decide which *communication skills* are needed to make a success of the job.

Ask yourself which types of *communication* occur by telephone, in person, in meetings, or at the dining table. Each of these situations can increase or decrease demands on the candidate for one or more of the *communication skills* subsets. For instance, telephone communication with other departments requires far less in the way of *body language*, *dress*, and *social graces* than do jobs requiring formal meetings and social functions with clients. If the latter is part of the job description, you might want to ask candidates to make a formal presentation, or at least discuss the tactics and pitfalls of client relations; you might even choose to do this over lunch, so you can see your top candidates functioning in an on-the-job situation. This also allows you to see whether any of the candidates wields a steak knife like a machete, berates waiters, or dabs ketchup on his face in a spontaneous fit of personal expression.

Multitasking (Time Management and Organization)

Multitasking is one of the most frequently used words in job postings. According to numerous studies, the *multitasking* demands of modern professional life are causing massive frustration and meltdowns for professionals everywhere. However, the problem is *not* multitasking *itself*, but rather understanding what "multitasking" really entails. The assumption is, all too often, that *multitasking* means being reactive to *all* incoming stimuli and therefore jumping around from one task to another as the emergency of the moment dictates. *Multitasking* such as this would of course leave you feeling as if wild horses were attached to your extremities and tearing you limb from limb.

Another problem arises when you accept candidates' assertions that they are good *multitaskers* without your personal investigation and verification.

There are two types of people in the world: the task-oriented, who let tasks expand to fill all the time allotted to them, and the goal-oriented, who organize and prioritize and strive to get all work completed in an orderly manner as quickly and efficiently as quality will allow.

Multitasking means being able to handle multiple tasks simultaneously. But it isn't based on being reactive to the most recent incoming imperative; rather, it is based on prioritizing your activities to make the maximum impact with the most economical use of your time. In other words, multitasking is based on the sound principles of *time management and organization*. There are many components to successful multitasking, and they are all based, first of all, on an understanding of the priorities of the job, and secondly, of the problems it exists to *identify, prevent, and solve*.

If your candidate is effective at *multitasking*, she almost certainly follows a Plan/Do/Review cycle every day, and follows this by creating a prioritized *To Do* list. To explain these concepts clearly we'll start with To Do list prioritization. In this process, a worker makes a list of everything that needs to be done, then designates each task as A, B, or C.

- **A:** The **As** absolutely must be done today. "A" priority activities always get her full attention; the other activities fill in around them. She knows her boss's priority is *always* an A priority.
- **B:** It would be good to get the **Bs** done today. These are the first activities a good *multitasker* fills in around her A priorities.

- **C: C** items need to get done, but they're either not urgent or are someone else's priority, not the candidate's. These fill in odd moments, unless approaching deadlines move them to B status.

The other foundational *multitasking* strategy that encourages *productivity* without increasing effort is adhering to a daily Plan/Do/ Review cycle. A good *multitasker* always sets aside time at the end of the day to review what has happened today, and based on what must happen tomorrow, creates a plan of attack for the next day. She asks:

- What went well and why?
- What didn't go so well, and what can I do about it?
- What new projects have landed on my desktop?
- What are their A/B/C priority levels?

A good *multitasker* looks at each "A" priority separately and identifies exactly where she will jump in on this project tomorrow, what she hopes to achieve, and the tools she'll need to do so. "A" priorities frequently include large and complex projects, so where will she begin? She breaks the big task into smaller action steps, things that she can get done tomorrow. This skill is at the very heart of your candidate's ability to deliver on the job's *responsibilities*. Developing *multitasking skills* enables her to do the things that have to be done based on their priority and relevance to the job's mandate.

TEAMWORK AND MANAGEABILITY

The professional world revolves around the complex challenges of making money, and this requires teams of people to provide ongoing solutions to these complex challenges. This demands that your team members work efficiently and respectfully with each other and with others who have totally different responsibilities, backgrounds, objectives, and areas of expertise—both within the department and within other departments with which yours has contact.

No one is successful in the professional world operating as a lone gun: You need people who understand their work in terms of the role it plays in contributing to the success of the department, and therefore understand the importance of getting along with others.

Teamwork asks that a *commitment* to the team and its success come first. You want people who are willing to take responsibility for their individual performances while simultaneously being willing to take on a task because it needs to be done, not because it's going to make them look good. You want to look for a candidate who:

- Cooperates
- Makes decisions based on team goals
- Keeps team members informed
- Keeps commitments
- Always shares credit, never spreads blame

Candidates who can look at *communication* from the other person's POV to achieve departmental goals, rather than turning every exchange into a competition for who is right and who is wrong, and who are genuinely concerned with what is good for the department and company, are going to add to the strength of your team; and because they are team players, they will be more *manageable*.

There isn't a manager in the world who enjoys a sleepless night caused by an unmanageable employee. You can define *manageability* in different ways: the ability to work alone; the ability to work with others toward shared goals (*teamwork*); the ability to take direction and criticism when it is carefully and considerately given; and, perhaps dearest to a manager's heart, the ability to take direction when it *isn't* carefully and considerately given, maybe because of a crisis.

Crucial to both *teamwork* and *manageability* is a willingness to work and get along with others regardless of their sex, sexual orientation, age, religion, physical appearance, abilities or disabilities, race, or national origin. To put this in terms of *communication skills*, you need employees who have the *emotional maturity* to deal with others as professional colleagues without bringing personal prejudices into the office. Of course, we will examine ways to determine the relative *manageability* and *team spirit* of your candidates as our discussion progresses.

The Complex Transferable Skills

We now come to the last two *transferable skills*, *creativity* and *leadership*, referred to as complex because they both require the interaction of the other *transferable skills* to exist as viable skills in their own right.

CREATIVITY

Creativity, like *multitasking*, is one of the most common words in job postings, but I have yet to find anyone who can define *creativity* within a professional working context in a way that can be objectively determined. This situation is one that we will now try to rectify.

There's a big difference between *creativity* and just having ideas. Ideas are like headaches: We all get them once in a while, and like headaches, they disappear as mysteriously as they arrived. *Creativity*, on the other hand, is the ability to develop those ideas with the strategic and tactical know-how that brings them to life. Someone is seen as creative when his ideas produce tangible results.

Creativity springs from the following elements:

- In a professional context, *creativity* first demands a wide and deep frame of reference for the work, the profession, and the industry, because these are the issues that define the context, the challenges, and their potential solutions. These competencies represent the healthy soil from which *creativity* grows. Without the work it takes to develop and maintain healthy soil, *creativity* cannot sprout, grow, and flourish, so the creative professional is first and foremost the candidate who is dedicated to a personal program of continual professional development.
- On top of *commitment* to professional development, *creativity* requires a consistent application of *critical thinking skills* to an area of *technical expertise*. *Technical skills* provide this knowledge of what works and what doesn't within a given field, but *technical skills* and the frame of reference they can deliver aren't always enough to come up with *creative* solutions when unusual or unprecedented problems arise; for that you need *critical thinking*.

- *Multitasking skills* allow an employee to keep pace with the events of the day and still have some time to develop ideas and work out their wrinkles. This also demands a degree of *determination*, which we'll discuss shortly.
- *Communication skills*, which allow an employee to explain her approach persuasively to others, listen to input, revise, and sell the revised approach anew.
- *Teamwork* and *leadership skills* (discussed next), which enable staff members to enlist the help of others in bringing an idea to fruition.

This wide frame of reference and integration of the other *transferable skills* enables the *committed* professional to see the *patterns* that lie behind challenges. This in turn helps them connect the dots and come up with solutions that others might have missed because they didn't have the holistic frame of reference that enabled them to step back and view the issue in its larger context.

If you're lucky enough to find people with this skill, it will be your responsibility to cultivate a working environment in which discussion of creative ideas is not penalized or treated as a threat to the status quo.

LEADERSHIP

Leadership is the most complex of all the *transferable skills*. Candidates who show leadership are people who get others to follow them because they see it as the right thing to do for team goals, departmental responsibilities, and professional advancement. Leaders accept individual responsibility for failures, but the team gets credit for success. It is a combination and outgrowth of all the other *transferable skills*:

- *Teamwork skills* give a leader the understanding of what pulls a team together and how to do it.
- *Technical expertise*, *critical thinking*, and *creativity skills* help leaders correctly define the challenges their teams face, and give them the

wisdom to guide the group toward finding solutions to complex problems.

- There's nothing more demoralizing than a leader who can't clearly articulate why you're doing what you're doing. So a leader's persuasive *communication skills* help convince the team to buy into directives and goals.
- *Multitasking skills* enable a leader to create a practical blueprint for success, and help her team take ownership of the task and deliver the expected results on time.
- *Creativity* comes from the wide frame of reference a leader has for his work and the profession and industry in which he works, enabling him to come up with previously overlooked solutions.

Leadership is a combination and outgrowth of all the *transferable skills* plus the presence of all the *professional values* we are about to discuss. Leaders aren't born, they are self-made; and just like anything else, it takes hard work. You will look for *leadership* in your employees, and develop it in yourself.

Professional Values

"Professional values" refers to the core beliefs and behaviors we bring to our interactions with the world. They reflect our feelings and belief systems, and their presence will help you make the many difficult decisions inherent in the employee selection process.

MOTIVATION AND ENERGY

It's never pleasant to work with people who cannot or will not do their jobs, or who let their tasks take up all the time allotted simply because they can. People like this sap the spirit and will of your whole team. This means every hire you make has an impact on everyone else in your work group.

Obviously, you want to hire people who are able to do the work at hand, and you also want to hire only those candidates who are motivated to do their best. Enthusiasm and a desire to make a difference, an eagerness to learn, and a willingness to take the rough with the smooth all show that a candidate is engaged in a meaningful way with her work.

As a manager, you can't succeed with players who can't or won't make an effort. You need people who will always expend that extra effort on the little things as well as more important matters.

Motivation is invariably expressed by the *energy* a candidate invests in her work. She always gives that extra effort to get the job done and get it done right. A person should be obviously healthy enough to maintain that energy over the length of the working week. This is a behavior for which posture and grooming can offer you useful input, because people who express a consistently professional and positive self-image are likely to be thoroughly engaged with their work.

In fact, when there are no other differences between two equally qualified candidates, it's best to choose the one who is most knowledgeable about the profession, the company, and the job, and who is most *intelligently enthusiastic* about joining the team. The reason is that the *motivated* employee and the *intelligently enthusiastic* worker will try harder on every assignment, be easier to work with, and ultimately will produce a better work product.

Later in this book, you will find questions specifically designed to evaluate *motivation*, but for now it's enough to know that you will find its presence expressed in the degree to which a candidate is enthusiastically engaged in her work. This *motivation* will similarly make its presence felt in the way a professionally engaged candidate changes the job interview from a one-sided examination of skills into a two-way conversation between colleagues.

It's no good to hire someone who can do the job but won't give of his best; you only want to hire the candidate who "can do" and "wants to." This order of "can do" first and "wants to" second is relevant, not only in understanding your needs and getting a three-dimensional picture of the person you want to hire, but also in prioritizing your evaluation procedures. A candidate's degree of *motivation* is only of interest once you know the person can do the work, or can learn to do the work within an acceptable time frame. This hierarchy of needs is going to affect the way you structure interview sequences and questions, as we'll see in Chapters 8–10.

COMMITMENT AND RELIABILITY

The *committed* and *reliable* professional is dedicated to his profession, and empowered by the knowledge of how his part contributes to the whole. His *commitment* expresses itself in *reliability*. The *committed* and *reliable* person doesn't come in late on Monday and then take off early on Friday afternoon to make up for it. The *committed* professional is willing to do whatever it takes to get a job done, whenever and for however long it takes to get the job done, even if that includes duties that might not appear in a job description and that might be perceived by less enlightened colleagues as beneath them.

Commitment to professional excellence is a behavior you will find expressed in a candidate's respect for the job's role and the profession. You will see it in the extra effort a candidate puts into her career via books, classes, education, and membership in professional associations. For jobs where surprises, problems, and sudden challenges are the norm, this kind of *commitment* is worth its weight in gold.

DETERMINATION AND CONFIDENCE

An employee's *determination* speaks of a resilient professional who doesn't get worn down or back off when problems or situations get tough. It's a value that marks a candidate as someone who chooses to be part of the solution rather than standing idly by and being part of the problem. The *determined* professional is someone who has decided to make a difference with his presence every day, because it is the *right* thing to do.

A *committed* and *reliable* professional is almost certainly also *determined*, and the determination results in more successes, which leads to *confidence*.

A degree of *confidence* is required in all jobs in order to look at challenges calmly, and to develop the skills and strategies necessary to fully contribute to the team's success. *Confidence* comes when a candidate has been actively engaged in her work, building a wide frame of reference for the work and its challenges. You are looking for candidates who exude *confidence* in their skills, and *confidence* in their ability to learn new skills, because they are engaged in the quest for constant improvement.

PRODUCTIVITY, EFFICIENCY, AND PROFIT ORIENTATION

Productivity-minded workers always work toward enhanced *productivity* through efficiencies of time, resources, money, and effort. Most problems have two solutions, and the expensive one isn't always the best.

Employees basically come in two flavors. First, there are the task-oriented clock watchers, who tend to let each job expand to fill the time allotted, and try to get away with the least possible effort every day. These people rarely care about *productivity*. Second, there are the goal-oriented employees, who are galvanized by a challenge and eager to bring projects to a successful conclusion. These people know that the day goes faster when you're engaged, and they want to make a difference with their presence by getting involved and making things happen. They want to be *productive* and they understand the importance of using resources, time, and materials efficiently.

A candidate like this is also likely to be *profit-aware*, and this is good news for you, because your bottom-line concerns as a manager are really quite simple: to increase productivity, and thereby profit. A *profit-oriented* candidate is someone who understands that personal and company success are functions of productivity, efficiency, and economy.

All the *transferable skills and professional values* being discussed here ultimately relate to *productivity*. *Productive* professionals are generally also *efficiency*-minded, keeping an eye open for wasted time, effort, resources, and money, and constantly looking for a better way to get the job done.

Ideas of *efficiency* and *economy* engage the goal-oriented. Companies that know how to be frugal with their resources will prosper in good times and bad, and if you know how to find workers like this, you'll do the same.

Systems and Procedures

An understanding of the role that *systems and procedures* play in supporting *profitability* is a natural result of all the other *transferable skills and professional values* evolving together. There's just no way a professional can be *committed*, *motivated*, skilled at *multitasking*, and sensitive to the *profit motive* without having concluded that *systems and procedures* are there for a reason and need to be respected.

From a practical point of view as a manager, you want employees who understand and always follow the chain of command. You don't want to hire rogue agents who implement their own "improved" procedures without consulting you, or encourage others to do so. If ways of doing things don't make sense or are interfering with *efficiency* and *productivity*, they approach you privately about the issue, and accept whatever decision you make.

Pride and Integrity

Pride and *integrity* come from having superior *technical skills* and the ability to make good on the *deliverables* of that job: to do that job well. A candidate reaches that level of professional comfort through the application of all the other *transferable skills and professional values*.

A thorough professional makes decisions in the best interests of the company, never based on personality, a whim, or personal preference. You will see that those who demonstrate *pride* and *integrity* in their professional lives are people who know what to do because they understand what is the "right" thing to do in any given situation. When you can rely on an employee's *integrity*, you have one less worry.

It is the level of attention to detail that guarantees the *integrity* of work done; an employee who takes *pride* in his work is interested in more than just getting a job onto someone else's desk. This is an extremely valuable trait to find in your employees, because in many jobs, the devil is in the details.

Together, these *transferable skills and professional values* spell long-term career success for the professional who understands and applies them, and for the manager who seeks them in potential employees and encourages their ongoing development in herself and in her team. These skills and values make for success in all jobs at all levels and across all professions—that's why they're *transferable*. They also make good topics for meetings, but that is a story for another book.

Applying the Transferable Skills and Professional Values

There's a reason we've taken the time to discuss these *skills* and *values* at such length: because possession of them is foundational to *ability*, *motivation*, *manageability*, and *teamwork*. As we progress, we'll relate them to the job for which you're hiring, and make some decisions about which attributes are most relevant to a particular position. In short, you will need to create your own Job Description (JD).

Your goal in developing a practical JD is to define each *responsibility* and the tangible results you expect (*deliverables*), and then think about which *transferable skills and professional values* are most relevant to that particular aspect of the job. Repeat this for all the *responsibilities* and *deliverables* of the job and you'll be able to prioritize which skills and values are most important in any given situation. This will give you a more comprehensive picture of the ideal candidate, and offer additional lines of investigation for your interviews.

Do Such Desirable Employees Really Exist?

A couple of years back I was in Mexico City, helping Elektra/Grupo Salsa (then a 19,000-employee conglomerate) by retraining every manager from the chairman down to the lowest first-level supervisor in every division in daylong *Knock 'em Dead: Hiring the Best* employee-selection workshops. One day, an attendee questioned whether searching for all these *transferable skills and professional values* was setting the bar too high—in the titles he hired, looking for someone who had all these desirable attributes was wishful thinking: It just wasn't going to happen.

It was a fair question, but he hadn't yet grasped two important considerations:

1. The idea that, once you create a prioritized list of *responsibilities* and their *deliverables*, you can review each *responsibility* and *deliverable* in the JD against the list of *transferable skills and professional values* in order to decide which ones are most relevant to a particular job. With this weighted list, you can make an informed judgment about which *transferable skills and professional values* are "must haves" and which are just "nice to haves."

2. You might not find someone with every *transferable skill* and *professional value* in place, but you'll know who has the most to offer and the least: If you don't know what to look for, you have no hope of finding it, and your management career suffers as a result.

One thing's certain: If you don't make the effort to look for candidates who possess the right *transferable skills and professional values*, you will never find them. "Gut feeling" just doesn't cut it, whereas prioritizing the *transferable skills and professional values* and identifying the most important ones is a great tool for objectively measuring applicants. Even if you don't find someone with everything, the candidate who fits 90 percent of your objective criteria is better than the candidate who only has 60 percent of what you are looking for. Giving up the search because no candidate is flawless is letting the perfect be the enemy of the good.

Job Deliverables Deconstruction (JDD)

Start your JD by analyzing how other companies prioritize and express their needs for this particular job.

Step #1: Collect Job Descriptions
Collect half a dozen job postings that closely match the job you need to fill, and save them in a folder with your company's official JD. The location of these jobs doesn't matter; what's important is how

others are defining and *prioritizing* their needs. If you don't have a favorite job site, try *www.simplyhired.com* or *www.indeed.com*: These are job site aggregators that will search thousands of job sites for you, making JD collection much faster.

Step #2: Create a Job Deconstruction Document

Open a new MSWord doc and title it "JDD" for Job Deliverables Deconstruction, and then specify the title; for example:

JDD—Accountant

Step #3: Prioritize the Responsibilities, Experience, and Deliverables

Add a subhead titled:

Responsibilities, Experience, and Deliverables

Look through the collection of job postings for a *single requirement* that's common to all of your job posting examples. Take the *most complete* description of that single requirement and copy and paste it into your JDD doc, putting a #6 by your entry to signify it is common to all. Then add any other words and phrases from the other job postings used to describe this same area to the bottom of the entry.

Repeat this exercise for other requirements common to all of your sample job postings. Here is an example from a JDD done for a Money Laundering Analyst working in the financial services industry:

6. Monitor customer account transactions to detect suspicious activity and make decisions on appropriate action to take.
6. Monitor and investigate money laundering, securities fraud, regulatory violations, and terrorist financing.
6. Conduct periodic internal account/customer reviews to identify potentially suspicious activity.
6. Perform various duties that include, but are not limited to, transaction look-backs, KYC file remediation projects, AML gap assessments, AML compliance monitoring, customer identification programs, AML training, and SARs review and preparation.

6. Conduct investigations of client accounts for potential suspicious behavior based on branch referrals, monitoring reports, government referrals, and other sources.

6. Review and monitor customer asset movements.

6. Conduct transactional reviews of client accounts, including historical trade/account activity reviews, to identify potential legal, regulatory, or reputational risk.

Repeat this process for requirements common to five of the jobs, and then four, and so on all the way down to those requirements mentioned in only one job posting.

When this is done you can look at your work and say, "When employers are hiring people like *this*, they prioritize their needs in *this* way and use *these* words to describe them." Doing this, you're accessing the thinking your professional peers have done to define, prioritize, and express the *deliverables* of the job you are going to fill.

Step #4: Identify Problem-Solving Responsibilities
Jobs are only ever added to the payroll for two reasons:

1. To make money or save money for the company, or otherwise increase *productivity*. How do you want this job to contribute to the success of your department and its role in helping company profitability? For example, you could be thinking, "Business is growing and we really need another accountant to help us with a growing backlog at accounts receivable."

2. To help contribute to profitability by *identifying, preventing, and solving the problems/*challenges that arise on the job and interfere with profitability.

If problems didn't occur, the job either wouldn't exist or would be done by a machine. Ultimately every one of us is hired to be a *problem solver* with a specific area of professional expertise. So sticking with the same example, you could be thinking, "So we need someone who knows the job well enough that he can *anticipate and prevent* the most common A/R problems before they crest the horizon. Also, we want someone who can get 90 percent of accounts paid within thirty days, and who knows how to prevent thirty-day overdue accounts from becoming forty-five-day overdue accounts."

Starting with the job's most common requirements, identify the problems that typically arise when a staff member is executing duties in this area. Then for each problem identify:

- How you want the next holder of this job title to execute her responsibilities in this area to prevent such problems from arising in the first place.
- How you want the next holder of this job title to solve such problems when they do occur.

Repeat the process for the rest of your identified *responsibilities*.

Step #5: Behavioral Profiles of Success and Failure

Going back to the prioritized requirements you identified in earlier steps, recall the *best* person you have ever seen do this job. Then identify what made that person stand out as a true professional. This isn't about personal fondness; it's about the employee's ability to complete the job's *deliverables* with true excellence. Think about her competency in all the *technical skills* of the job, and all her *transferable skills and professional values*; perhaps she always had a smile, listened well, and had good *critical thinking* and *multitasking skills*.

Together with the specific *technical skills* of the job you have already identified, this will give you a *behavioral profile for professional success* that you'll want to have in the back of your mind as you interview candidates.

Once the behavioral profile of the best you've seen doing this job is firmly in mind, recall the *worst* person you have ever known doing the job. Perhaps he was passive aggressive, never listened, was always late for meetings, and missed project deadlines. This will give you a *behavioral profile for professional failure* that you'll want to have in the back of your mind as you interview candidates every bit as much as your behavioral profile for professional *success*.

Creating Your Own Job Description

An effective JD—one that truly captures what it takes to do this job—will communicate your needs to recruiters (after you've cleared it through HR), and will help you identify the most relevant interview questions.

By clearly defining the *responsibilities*, *experience*, *deliverables*, *transferable skills and professional values*, and *education* required for success on the job, candidates are in no doubt about your expectations, and you have the knowledge to ask the right questions. This same knowledge will pay further dividends outside the recruitment and selection process, when it gives you the tools for successful training, motivation, and performance reviews (Chapter 17).

Step #1: Identify Responsibilities and Deliverables

Start by prioritizing the *responsibilities* and *deliverables* of the job, the tangible results of work that as a manager you have every right to expect in return for a paycheck. Using the JDD as your launch pad, list the five or so major *responsibilities* of the job opening—those areas in which the employee will spend the majority of her time every day, as determined by your JDD exercise—then add the *deliverable* expected from each of these functions: what you expect the employee to achieve while occupied with that specific activity.

For example, some of the primary *responsibilities* for an outside sales position might be:

- Clean driver's license
- Fifteen telephone sales lead calls every day
- Five face-to-face customer meetings every week

The deliverables you might expect as a tangible result of these activities might include:

- Monthly 50 percent sales quota within ninety days of start date
- Monthly 75 percent sales quota within 120 days of start date
- Four new accounts each quarter

When you define *deliverables* specifically, you develop a useful recruitment and screening tool for yourself, HR, and the recruiters. This approach will always generate better candidates—and employees—than simply going out to look for someone with a degree in communications and five years' experience in sales.

Step #2: Identify Problem-Solving Challenges

You never add employees to the payroll for the love of mankind; you add them to contribute to the bottom line. Every job and every department in every company and profession does this by helping to make money, save money, or improve productivity (which saves time and money and makes more time to make more money). There is an expectation that the challenges and problems that get in the way of making money will be *identified, prevented, and solved.* For the hiring manager, this means looking for people who:

1. Possess the *transferable skills and professional values* to *anticipate and prevent typical problems* in their area of responsibility.
2. *Solve problems* when they do arise.
3. Show consideration for colleagues who must deal with their work product.

These are the people you want to hire for any job, at any level, in any organization, anywhere in the world. Thinking about the job in terms of its *problem identification/prevention/solution* responsibilities will clarify the focus of HR and recruiters during the recruitment phase, and your own focus during the selection cycle.

When you can identify the particular *problem-solving* business a particular job title is engaged in, you have gone a long way toward isolating the additional criteria that define *ability* and *suitability*.

Step #3: Combine Deliverables and Problem-Solving Abilities

Given the importance of *problem solving/critical thinking* to each of the job's *responsibilities*, your next step is to identify the role of *problem solving* in each of the job's key *deliverables*. With each *responsibility*, identify the problems the job is meant to *anticipate* and *prevent* as a regular duty, but also the problems and challenges that naturally arise regardless of how well the job is being done, and that therefore must be *solved*, because they are inherent in the work and cannot be avoided.

Step #4: Relate Transferable Skills and Professional Values to Deliverables

Transferable skills and professional values are the foundational skills that facilitate the achievement of any job's *deliverables*. Their relative priority varies depending on the job (for example, *critical thinking skills* predominate for an auditor, while the eight *communication skills* predominate in sales and marketing), but they are all relevant to all jobs. Recognizing this, you should now review each of the job's priority *deliverables* and identify the *transferable skills and professional values* that lead to tangible results in each of these areas.

Step #5: Identify Experience Requirements

Armed with a grasp of the job's *responsibilities*, *deliverables*, relevant *transferable skills and professional values*, and the *problem-solving* territory of the job, you're now in a much better position to start thinking about necessary *experience* and *education*.

Defining *experience* is fraught with challenges. It is easy to say "five years' experience required" because you happened to have had five years of experience when you landed the job yourself, or because other people who have been successful in the position also had about five years of experience, but it is dangerous to make such criteria hard-and-fast rules.

For example, with an outside sales position, your current JD might begin with "five years' experience in outside sales." The problem with this is that some people simply repeat their first year's work experience for the rest of their lives, never learning to turn a job into a career; others come to a profession and quickly attain a level of expertise way beyond their chronological experience. I am not denying the importance of experience, but your specifications should be flexible—and be *known* to be flexible by everyone involved in your recruitment and selection team.

As an illustration, a sharp professional with three years of progressively diverse experience can often be a better bet than the ten-year seasoned pro who has in reality simply repeated one year of experience ten times, not progressing and not learning from his mistakes. It is worth pointing out that the "three years of progressively diverse experience" can apply to someone on a second or third career, just as it might to an ardent younger worker. The older worker might well bring some additional valuable assets to the table (more on this later).

Additionally, you should define exactly what you mean by "experience." Do you mean experience fulfilling the individual *deliverables* of your JD, experience in the profession, in your industry, or experience in a company of similar size and culture? To some degree, all of these considerations are relevant, but some more than others depending on your situation. For example, industry experience will come to the fore in a business-to-business marketing or an audit position, while it might have lesser importance for a customer service job where *communication skills* predominate.

Strict experience requirements can rule out good people, so you should always retain as much flexibility as possible. If you do demand "five years of solid experience," take the time to quantify what it is a candidate with five years' experience can do that a candidate with three years' experience could not. It's one thing to say that you need someone with fifteen years of manufacturing experience to relocate a facility overseas because you had fifteen years' experience when you did it; it's another to say that you need that level of experience to run a 24/7/365 four-shift operation, and simultaneously move it lock, stock, and barrel to the Philippines in eighteen months, with no downtime or failure of deliveries.

Step #6: Identify Education Requirements

Here are the opening lines from an online job posting:

Pharmaceutical Sales

Five years' experience outside sales in pharmaceutical industry and B.S. degree required.

In this instance, my concern is with "B.S. degree required." Steve Jobs and Bill Gates dropped out of college, Thomas Edison had three months of formal schooling (during which time his teacher referred to him as "addled"), and while Albert Einstein graduated from college, there have always been persistent rumors that his fiancée "helped." There you have the four greatest minds of the modern world, and not a clean degree between them.

You need to differentiate between what educational background is *necessary* to do the job and what educational background is *desirable*. Unless you or your employer regularly verifies that degree, don't put too much store in one. Exaggerating education is the single most common deception that job hunters at all levels make. When educational backgrounds do get checked, the statistics tell us that as many as three in ten resumes exaggerate educational attainments. Somehow, during the writing of the resume, the high school diploma becomes an associate's degree, the associate's degree becomes a bachelor's, and so on.

So consider being flexible here; for example, can on-the-job experience be substituted? After all, honorary degrees and accreditations are dished out to people who didn't attend those schools or sweat those books, all based on their excellence in the real world.

However, it's always wise to use educational criteria as a signpost of *commitment* and the ability to learn, which is itself an essential skill in an ever-changing workplace.

If you determine that a certain level of education or specific type of degree really is mandatory for the job, you need to make a point of credential verification as part of the selection process. If you are not going to verify education, its importance necessarily moves from a "must have" to a "nice to have." Think about it: If, say, a bachelor's degree really is a "must have," then you *have* to verify it. If that's not the case, you're just using it as an inadequate screening tool that would rule out Steve Jobs, Bill Gates, Thomas Edison, and maybe even Mr. Einstein.

Once you have created a Job Description by following these steps, it could be useful to ask for feedback from select members of your team: comments, additions, and subtractions.

Special Considerations

Almost every job you fill will have special considerations that will impact the JD. For example, if you are working toward a promotion for yourself, you might need to include succession planning in your JD. You can't move up without finding a replacement, so providing professional growth opportunity for your people—and that means grooming them for more responsibility—is good for them and marks you as a manager suitable for greater responsibilities too. We'll talk more about this issue as we leverage the selection process to do double duty as a professional development and succession-planning tool.

Finalizing the Job Description

Once you have prioritized your needs in terms of *responsibilities, deliverables*, and the *transferable skills and professional values*, you'll need to finalize the JD in a format you can use for the selection process (with HR's approval, showing respect for their front-line position in any lawsuits relating to employment). Use simple terminology that makes the performance expectations of the job easy to grasp. If you can't explain the job in simple terms, you probably don't understand it well enough yourself. Think and write in terms of the key *responsibilities*, then the *deliverables* expected in each area of *responsibility*, and the *transferable skills and professional* values that will empower an employee to do each aspect of the job well.

Include the acceptable variables of *experience* and *education* so that everyone involved in the selection cycle will have the opportunity to see and comment on your final document. When you involve your department in defining the position, you make your team stakeholders in a successful outcome, and for staff members it is an opportunity for new skill development.

Now that you know what to look for, it's time to establish a system for evaluating resumes in terms of your well-thought-out and objective JD.

Compensation

Workers are far savvier about compensation today, because they talk to peers about money and have all the tools of the Internet with which to compare their wages with regional and national norms. While pay and benefits are not *always* the number-one reason to accept or reject a job, noncompetitive offers will usually result in rejection of a job offer unless you represent a particularly high-profile company or your outfit has some other overwhelming appeal.

Your offered compensation must be competitive with other companies in the profession and within your area, and with similar jobs within your own company. It's ideal if the compensation package can incentivize for individual and group performance.

Unless you manage in a very small company, there will likely be HR and finance professionals who have already determined the salary range for this position. If your company does not have an HR department, you can still find plenty of reliable resources for compensation; you will find compensation consultants as active members in professional and management associations, the local chamber of commerce, and area employer coalitions. Headhunters can also give you a good handle on what are locally competitive salaries.

If you are not a household-name company and are unable to offer top dollar and benefits, your selection skills, as well as the skills you look for in candidates and how you go about looking for them, become even more important. The best hires don't always come from Ivy League schools and name companies; there is lots of great talent out there that you can get with even a small company's lesser bucks and bennies, as long as you know how to look for it.

Exactly what to pay is the focus of a professional field all by itself, with compensation professionals swelling the ranks of all but the smallest HR departments. *Compensation Management in a Knowledge-Based World* by Richard I. Henderson makes this complex topic accessible and is perhaps the best book on the subject.

You also have the Internet at your fingertips. Start with *www.bls .gov, www.careers.wsj.com*, and *www.salary.com*.

Performance Incentives

All jobs can be incentivized to one degree or another, although sales, technology, and management are the areas in which incentivizing is most visible. Performance incentives can increase earnings dramatically for workers in sales, where the incentive structure defines wages, and also in technology and management, where wages are often significantly enhanced through incentives.

These three particular areas of professional endeavor are more highly incentivized because individual contributions have a more direct impact on the bottom line. Consequently, if you hire in these areas, and reward for performance is not part of the package, it could be difficult for you to remain competitive. As a manager you are on the front lines of *getting work done through others,* and if you're hamstrung by lack of competitiveness, *you* will suffer before the company does.

You don't have to have the best pay, incentives, and benefits to get the best people—although that does help—but you do have to be competitive within regional norms for your profession. Also, because we typically spend more of our waking hours with our coworkers than with the people we love, you need to be able to present your department and company as a rewarding and positive environment in which hard work, competence, professionalism, and *commitment* are recognized and rewarded.

Benefits

All your potential employees will have a clear idea of the dollar value of benefits, which means that your company must be up to speed. However, this is not an area in which you are expected to be knowledgeable beyond the basics, and HR should handle it.

A Last Consideration

Sometimes managers have a perception that their best hire will be the person with 100 percent of the skills demanded by the job. However, hiring such a candidate is not always the best decision and can create problems.

Unless there is opportunity for further professional growth, a candidate with 100 percent of the required skills for the job is more likely to become demotivated because she is not challenged by the work. She is also likely to command initial compensation at or near the top of your approved salary range. This makes it difficult to provide reasonable raises, no matter how productive the person is, without promotion into another level—which isn't always possible.

This means that the person who seems most qualified may not be the best person for the job; lack of growth opportunities and increased earnings are major reasons for workers leaving one job for another. Often you will build a more effective team by hiring people who can do, say, 60 to 80 percent of the job and who are motivated by their work and the opportunity for professional growth. Such candidates can be hired lower in the approved salary range, allowing for good raises without the need for imminent promotion into another category.

THREE

How to Crack a Resume

From the hiring side of the desk, resumes are timesaving devices. Without them, you would have to interview everyone who applied for every job, and everything else would grind to a halt.

The resume is a useful screening tool, and later in the process it will act as a roadmap for interviews and as a question-generating tool. However, to be maximally effective in your selection strategies, you should also be able to interpret resumes from the job hunter's perspective.

A resume is the single most important document any working professional, including you, will ever own. Now, the Internet has dramatically changed the recruitment process, and this in turn has changed the way resumes have to be written if they are ever to be discovered and read. You need to understand these changes and how they affect your ability to screen in the contenders and screen out the rest.

What Resumes Say about the Writer

Today all commercial and most corporate databases use Applicant Tracking Systems (ATS); just as Google will search the Internet for your search terms, the ATS will search a particular database using a greater range of search terms.

A resume used to be looked on as a simple recitation of what the writer thought was important about her work, and so it was cast in the broadest possible terms.

This isn't such a bad thing, because most resumes for the job you need to fill are not worthy of your consideration. Consider this for a moment: One of the most common phrases found in all job postings is a requirement for *communication skills*, because these skills are required in just about every job; in fact, the first really important lessons you learned in the professional world required *communication skills*. Those lessons were "The customer is always right" and "Find out what the customers want and sell it to them." Most resumes never consider these issues, because their writers lack one of the job's critical *communication skills*: *listening*. For example, you can safely assume that anyone who starts a resume with "Job Objective" and then goes on to speak about what s*he* wants lacks a basic understanding of how the professional world works. So profound a lack of professional awareness is a big red flag.

Fortunately, the full-scale adoption of ATS means that, for a resume to be found in a database search, it must be focused on a particular job title (or at most two closely related titles), and it must address the key skills related to that job. In other words, the new recruitment methodologies should weed out most candidates who haven't taken the time to assess how their skills relate to your needs.

The Resume Layout Template

A resume today typically looks like the following example, because it:

- Increases ATS visibility
- Puts critical job skills up front and center
- Is visually accessible and encourages fast scanning
- Supplies all the "must haves" in the first half to two-thirds of a page

Following these "must haves," a properly constructed resume lists all the critical *skills*, *responsibilities*, and *deliverables* in the context of their development and application. This layout makes the relevant information maximally accessible to the database search engine, the recruiter, and you.

Name

Address   Telephone   E-mail address
                                                                    LinkedIn address

---

Pharmaceutical Sales

A target job title like the above example improves visibility in database searches and tells the reader what the document is about.

Brand Statement

Optional. Delivers the value proposition the writer feels she brings to the job.

Performance Profile or Career Summary

A paragraph (or paragraph and bullets) that captures the highlights of what it takes to do the job cited in the target job title.

Professional Skills/Core Competencies

A list of all the skills relevant to the target job. In this example, which we can all relate to, the writer lists the skills that might be important in a dental assistant's resume.

4-Handed Dentistry	Oral Surgery/Extraction	Emergency Treatment
Infection Control	Casts/Impressions	Radiology
Root Canals	Diagnostic X-Rays	Prosthetics/Restorations
Instrument Sterilization	Preventive Care	Teeth Whitening

Technical Skills or Competencies

An optional category depending on the professional relevance of any such skills.

Achievements or Performance Highlights

An optional category depending on experience and accomplishments.

Professional Experience

Employer's name   Dates
The company's focus
Job Title
Details of functions, responsibilities, and achievements.

Employer's name   Dates
The company's focus
Job Title
Details of functions, responsibilities, and achievements.

Employer's name   Dates
The company's focus
Job Title
Details of functions, responsibilities, and achievements.

Employer's name   Dates
The company's focus
Job Title
Details of functions, responsibilities, and achievements.

Education

Licenses/Professional Accreditations

Professional Organizations/Affiliations

Publications, Patents, Speaking

Languages

Military Service

Extracurricular Interests

Excellent references available on request

How Expert Recruiters Read a Resume in Six Seconds

It's a well known, but not (yet) clinically proven fact that if you read too many resumes in a week you will start to lose brain cells at an alarming rate—first your mind goes numb, then it begins to wander aimlessly, and before you know it an hour has passed and you've achieved nothing. You need a roadmap for reading resumes. That roadmap is not the resume, it's the Job Deliverables Deconstruction (JDD) document you created to determine exactly what qualifications would make for a good hire.

Even when a resume isn't organized in a logical and accessible way (the above example is both logical and accessible), the headings that guide a reader through a resume cover all the topics likely to be of importance in your objective evaluation of suitability for the job.

Experienced recruiters can scan a resume and within six seconds know whether to move on or give it a second, more careful read. I can't promise you six seconds, but I can show you what to scan for, and how to scan so that you catch the important information fast, without driving yourself nuts plowing through drivel.

To approximate the six-second scan, all you need is a clear understanding of the *responsibilities, deliverables,* and *transferable skills and professional values* of the job, plus a prioritization of these into "must haves" and "nice to haves." So instead of laboriously reading the resume from start to finish, you simply scan for the "must haves," and if the resume doesn't have them, you quickly move on to the next. You already have a superior understanding of these "must haves" and "nice to haves" from your own professional work experience and your JDD work.

If the six-second scan of a resume finds the appropriate "must haves," that resume stays in contention, but the next step differs from manager to manager and recruiter to recruiter. Many recruiters, knowing that this might be a viable candidate, will then give the resume a careful second reading and make a decision then and there to conduct a telephone screening interview.

Other recruiters continue their *search and scan* approach, making a pile of the possible candidates until they have a *long list* of potential candidates—usually those who have at least seventy percent of the job's required *responsibilities, deliverables,* and *transferable skills and professional values*—and this *long list* might have as many as a dozen resumes. The recruiter or manager then goes back to give each one a careful second reading, winnowing the *long list* down to a *short list* of maybe six candidates, each of whom will then be screened by a telephone interview.

From Long List to Short List

In many larger companies with well-organized recruitment functions, someone else may do the initial winnowing, while you are expected to conduct the telephone and in-person interviews. This is a wonderful bonus, if you have recruiters you can trust and who understand the job as you do. If not, you'll need to make these evaluations yourself—and even if you don't need to make them yourself with your current employer, you will have to at some point down the road, so why not develop this important skill now?

How to Read a Resume

No one likes to write resumes, and no one likes to read them, and unless you're brand new to management, it's probably a task you avoid like the plague. Nevertheless, making valid assessments of candidates based on their resumes is a useful practical management skill. Let's go through this process section by section.

Name and Contact Information

	Name	
Address	Telephone	E-mail address
		LinkedIn address

It is becoming the norm for resumes to include a link to a LinkedIn or other social media profile. Reading a social media profile may well be useful in prepping for a face-to-face or telephone interview, but it is a time waster at this point in the selection process, so skip it for now.

Target Job Titles

Pharmaceutical Sales

A resume with a relevant and clearly stated target job title gives you an immediate focus and is a good sign, quite possibly implying that the resume writer is going to focus the resume on what she feels are the important *responsibilities*, *deliverables*, and *transferable skills and professional values* for the position. It's a good omen, but nothing more at this point.

Brand Statements

Pharmaceutical Sales
Poised to outperform in pharmaceutical software sales, repeating records of achievement with major pharmaceutical companies.

Sometimes a brand statement follows the Target Job Title, though this is optional. It is meant to deliver the value proposition the writer feels she brings to the job. They are subjective and all too often reflect the way the writer would like to be seen, rather than giving an objective and accurate depiction.

Objectives, Summaries, and Profiles
Next comes a brief summary. If it is headed "Objective," you can assume that it is about what the candidate wants, including the ubiquitous "the opportunity for professional growth." At this point in

the proceedings, you don't really care what the candidate wants; the fact that he does not understand this is not a good sign.

If this section is headlined "Career Summary" or "Performance Profile," you can expect a review of what it takes to do the job. How well the resume captures the "must haves" of the job can tell you how well the candidate understands what is important and what isn't.

You are looking for an objective review of skills and perhaps achievements, so watch out for subjective claims.

Professional Skills/Core Competencies

Professional Skills/Core Competencies

4-Handed Dentistry	Oral Surgery/Extraction	Emergency Treatment
Infection Control	Casts/Impressions	Radiology
Root Canals	Diagnostic X-Rays	Prosthetics/Restorations
Instrument Sterilization	Preventive Care	Teeth Whitening

This section is a list of all the skills relevant to the target job. In this example, the writer lists the skills that might be important in a dental assistant's resume. Every word or phrase acts as a headline for a topic with which the candidate has some practical experience. Not always present, but immensely helpful when it is included, is a Professional Skills section, which helps you quickly decide whether the candidate has the hard skills you seek.

You can also learn something about the candidate's grasp of what is important in the job by the way he lists these skills. For example, the first line reads:

4-Handed Dentistry	Oral Surgery/Extraction	Emergency Treatment

But what would it tell you about this candidate's grasp of the real guts of the job if the first line had read:

Teeth Whitening	Preventive Care	Instrument Sterilization

It could mean that this candidate is not focused on what is really important in the job, or that she may not be able to differentiate essential tasks from ancillary ones.

If the skills you need are identified in this section, that's a strong plus for this person's candidacy, and even if the order of skills isn't all you could wish, it still gives you a heads-up that this candidate has skills relevant to your job opening.

Technical Skills or Competencies

This is an optional category dependent upon the job and the profession. It is common in science and technology careers, where there are so many skills to be identified that they need to be broken into two sections to increase visual accessibility and comprehension. Because of the impact of technology on all jobs, such a section is becoming increasingly common in many other jobs too.

Achievements or Performance Highlights

You won't always see this section, and it appears more often when time, experience, and seniority increase the odds of real achievement. Even if this doesn't appear as a separate section, all job hunters are told to list their achievements as a way of demonstrating how well they performed for previous employers; so if they don't show up here, in a section all their own, you can expect to see achievements and performance highlights mentioned in the Professional Experience section of the resume.

BEWARE ACHIEVEMENTS

Sometimes statements of achievement are true; at other times, they can be exaggerations of a more modest truth; and sometimes, they are outright lies. Your task as a hiring manager is to consistently separate fact from fiction. Statements of achievement almost always relate to profitability in some way: earning money, saving money, and/or increasing productivity. Subtly examining achievement claims will be part of any interview, so you'll want to make a habit of reading

resumes with your digital highlighter at the ready or, if you are looking at a print resume, with a fluorescent yellow highlighter in your
hand. When you read of achievements that seem too good to be true,
they probably are, so use your highlighter to spotlight such claims for
further examination.

APOLLO SYNDROME

Some exaggerated claims have long been wittily referred to as
"Apollo Syndrome" claims in the recruitment community, after a low-
level functionary at Cape Canaveral who claimed he "provided key
support to top scientists" during an early space mission. His actual
job? He served them coffee. He claimed they would not otherwise
have stayed awake long enough to get the ship launched successfully.
Keep an eye out for such things as:

- *Money Earned for the Company:* This junior salesman not only sold
  more peanut butter than anyone else, he also got the entire population of Maine to stand on their heads and gargle it. He would
  like to do the same for your company.
- *Money Saved for the Company:* This accountant saved her company
  from certain ruin by inventing the modern computer and reducing staffing needs in her department by 98 percent.
- *Time Saved:* This computer programmer designed a new program
  that reduced processing time by half, and that time savings is valued at $1.5 million so far this year.

Sometimes such claims are going to be real, in which case you
should be duly impressed.

However, as a rule of thumb, companies solve complex problems
for their customers, and solutions to complex problems invariably
require teams of people; consequently, little in the corporate world
is the work of one individual, and any claims that suggest otherwise
are worth investigating. At this point, just flag the word or phrase
with your highlighter as good interview fodder. A candidate who
exaggerates a little but who has nevertheless been part of successful

teams doing amazing things could still be a person you want on your team, because consistent involvement with success rubs off, and also increases the likelihood that this candidate had something real (even if intangible or hard to define) to contribute to those successes.

When Words Confuse

Sometimes, the words used in resumes will embellish the facts and confuse rather than clarify. This "painting with broad brushstrokes" technique is precisely what blurs the line between the Apollo Syndrome and a blatant falsehood, and it's used in descriptions both of skills and responsibilities and of the candidate herself.

From a management viewpoint, you should be especially alert to the fact that your definition of a given word might be very different from that of the resume writer. Verbs denote action: *achieved, streamlined, managed, implemented*, and so on. Just because such words are in front of you on a nicely laid-out resume does not make them true. It is not always so much that the writer is lying to you as it is that you cannot be certain of either your shared interpretation of that verb or the objectivity of the claim that follows.

Take verbs like *conceived, designed*, and *implemented*, and put them in a sentence, for example: "Conceived, designed, and implemented facility reorganization with resultant twenty-two percent space saving. Avoided moving to larger facility for one year." Now maybe you work at a 100,000-square-foot facility and say, "Wow, this guy must have saved his company a ton of money in rent!" On the other hand, the resume writer might work in a four-person 800-square-foot office and this could be a rather grand way of saying, "I helped shift some desks around one slow Thursday afternoon."

The point of this is not for you to pass judgment on the candidate: You will examine the claims and give credit where credit is due. The point is to be aware of—and avoid—the tendency to automatically project your situation onto the resume writer. In this context, if the claims were defensible, even though the achievement was perhaps in a smaller context than your own, the candidate still showed initiative, used his *critical thinking skills*, and made a difference with his presence—all desirable qualities, none of which should disqualify him as a candidate.

When you come across action verbs, flag them with your highlighter for further examination. You will either learn good things about the behavioral profile of your candidate, or save yourself a management headache.

As a final example, consider the word "managed." Whenever you see it in a resume, immediately highlight it and start asking yourself questions: How would this person define management? Management of a process, a project, or people? How does the candidate see the difference between management and supervision? How long has she been in management, at what level, and how many people did she manage? Did this person hire, fire, and perform salary and performance reviews? Did this person hold bottom-line fiscal responsibility? The questions that don't answer themselves in your examination of the resume are the ones for which you will frame questions at the interview, thus ensuring that you get a firm understanding of the candidate's real-world capabilities.

Professional Experience

The Professional Experience section of a resume should clearly identify employers, employment dates, job titles, responsibilities, and achievements, etc.

Employment Dates

There are a couple of options for the resume writer when addressing employment dates:

1. Month and year
2. Year only

Last-Chance Electronics 2008–2012, then *Fly-By-Night Software 2012–Present* seems like a fair progression at first glance. But what if the candidate left one company in January 2012 and did not join the next one until December 2012? You could have an employment gap of up to a year.

The job seeker has every right to use annual employment dates in a resume, but you should be alert to the fact that on occasion this could mean one less year of experience than first assumed. With the ever-increasing turbulence in the employment market, you can no longer hold gaps of employment against a candidate. In this day and age, taking months or a year or more to find a new job after getting laid off is no longer unusual, and it is absolutely reasonable: The resume writer didn't lie about employment dates, she simply positioned her between-jobs downtime effectively.

Unless you train yourself to become wary about employment dates from first glance, your tendency will be to accept them on second reading as fact. The result will be that you will ask questions that merely confirm resume content, rather than examining and question-ing it. *People respect what you inspect, not what you expect*, so a habit of inspection from the beginning of the selection process will help you set a tone for truthfulness and honest performance once the chosen candidate is on the job.

Educational Attainment
Educational claims are the most prone to exaggeration of any item on a resume. It's been said in the reference checking and credential verification communities that upward of 30 percent of all educational claims are exaggerated.

There are times when a degree or even an advanced degree really is critical to the job, most importantly in research, medicine, and the practice of law. In other instances the real need varies, and that con-versation alone could fill an entire book. In the real-world situations you face, apart from using your native savvy, there is little you can do about this conundrum. Unless you and/or your company make a habit of credential verification, you could be losing good employees by refusing to interview based solely on educational attainment. We'll talk about reference checking later.

Given the likelihood that three out of every ten candidates you evaluate aren't being entirely truthful about their educational attainments, and given also that people reach the professional heights and do good work *despite* having lied about their education (remember Einstein's fiancée), what do you do? Verify credentials if this is practical or deemed to be part of your responsibilities, but don't let it govern your screening process unless the degree requirements are truly as important as you say they are.

Beyond this, recognize that over time professional experience gradually replaces educational attainment in relative importance in your evaluations, and be careful not to confuse credentials with accomplishments. Credentials are an indicator of a certain level of awareness and *critical thinking skills*, and they promise potential, but even when verified they are not proof of superior performance. As President Calvin Coolidge once said, "Nothing in this world can take the place of persistence. Talent will not; nothing is more common than unsuccessful men with talent. Genius will not; unrewarded genius is almost a proverb. Education will not; the world is full of educated derelicts. *Persistence* and *determination* alone are omnipotent."

Licenses/Professional Accreditations/Ongoing Professional Education

Some professions require them; in others, they are simply indicators of a candidate's *commitment* to her profession. These licenses and professional accreditations can also be viewed as:

1. Proof that this applicant or her employer thought such investments of time and money worthwhile.
2. Money you don't have to spend.

Professional Organizations/Affiliations

Membership in professional organizations is one of the wisest long-term investments anyone can make in his career. It shows a *commitment* to the profession, and a candidate becomes more credible because of that *commitment*.

Publications, Patents, Speaking, Apps

Books, articles, public speaking, patents, and now software applications all take hard work and concentration over long periods of time. If they relate to the profession, any of these achievements should be regarded as an indicator of a serious professional and a candidate well worth further examination.

Languages

In an increasingly global marketplace, language abilities and cultural mindfulness can only be pluses.

Military Service

If you have a candidate who served in the military, you invariably have someone who:

- Can take direction
- Understands putting team welfare first
- Given reason, will be loyal
- Will do whatever it takes to get the job done

In my book, these are all good reasons to give such a candidate careful consideration. The best boss I ever had was a retired colonel from Airborne starting his second career, and he didn't just influence my life—I watched him impact an entire organization. Given the relevant skills and an awareness of the added flexibility and civility demanded in the civilian workplace, a military background is always a plus for someone's candidacy.

Extracurricular Interests

You don't need to be entertained by a candidate's personal interests. My collection of Prohibition Era cocktail shakers is of no relevance to any job on the planet other than a hosting gig on *Antiques Roadshow*, but that I did Ironman triathlons at fifty-three (I didn't) might say something about physical fitness and determination. These would be "nice to haves": They wouldn't make you decide or decline to interview a candidate, but along with other credentials, a fifty-plus-year-old triathlete might well be worth a look; the cocktail-shaker collector, not so much.

"Excellent references available on request"

It costs a resume writer nothing to say this, and you shouldn't give much weight to the statement. I have been writing about career management for many years and have published seventeen books. Amongst them is one of the best-selling resume books of all time, and I tell those readers exactly what I am telling you: that they should add it if they have the space, because they have nothing to lose.

Resume Length

The old rule of "one page for every ten years of experience and never more than two pages" is way out of date and should be irrelevant in your evaluation of candidates. Technology has increased the complexity of most professional jobs, and with ten or more years' experience, there are few professionals who can get that work history onto a one- or two-page resume (unless they've spent that decade sitting on their thumbs). Judgment of a resume and its author's potential fit for the job should be based on the focus of the document and the information it shares. It would be idiotic to rule a candidate out based on whether or not an outmoded page limit has been adhered to: "OMG, this otherwise perfect candidate has a three-page resume, I can't possibly interview her now!" Or, "OMG, this entry-level candidate has so many internships his resume has gone onto a second page! What a shame, I really would have liked to interview him."

Last Thoughts on the Resume Screening Process

Evaluating resumes isn't anyone's idea of a good time. After a dozen, even the strongest minds gradually turn to mush. When you are faced with shortlisting candidates for interview, work through them in batches, using the task as a break from your major duties or as a monotony-breaker when sitting in a conference room waiting for a meeting to begin. This is a priority task, but it can be fitted into stolen moments, and when you do it this way, your mind will always be alert.

While it is best to screen resumes yourself, it may well happen that at some point in your career you will be with a company where HR is in the habit of delivering screened resumes to you. It is important to have good relations with HR: Work with them to define your needs and show appreciation for their efforts. Internal HR recruiters and external headhunters have a very tough job, and when you make the effort to develop understanding and a collegial relationship, they will notice the all-too-rare civility and return your goodwill with extra effort on your behalf. When you make this effort, it helps everyone perform better in her job and everyone becomes more successful. Everyone wins and everyone forges useful alliances for the future.

Once you decide that a particular candidate is worth seeing, read through the resume again and jot down questions for any areas you feel need clarification or probing. Do it now, while your analysis is still fresh and still objective, unaffected by the impact of face-to-face familiarity. You'll be able to use these first impressions to formulate knockout questions to ask during the telephone-screening interview, which we'll cover next.

FOUR

TELEPHONE INTERVIEWS:
THE GREAT TIMESAVER

The single biggest management challenge when hiring new staff members is compensating for the huge amounts of your time consumed by screening resumes and interviewing candidates.

As a rule of thumb, for professionals as far as halfway up the corporate ladder, conducting a first interview face-to-face never takes less than thirty minutes of your time and often upward of an hour; it's longer the higher and shorter the lower the position, but even at the level of in-person servers, face-to-face interviews are time-consuming. With a telephone interview, you can be on and off the phone in as little as five to fifteen minutes, probably having gained a more objective evaluation, caused no one any offense in the process, and increased your *efficiency* and *productivity* by 50–75 percent.

For more senior professionals and management positions the "must have" skills multiply in number and complexity, and those first interviews invariably take an hour or longer. When using a telephone interview as your primary screening tool, you spend much less time on the social niceties at the beginning and end and focus on an examination of *responsibilities* and their *deliverables*. This means that learning to use telephone interviews as your first serious interaction with a candidate will enable you to gather more information faster, while increasing your *efficiency* and *productivity* with the time you save.

The Three Biggest Interviewing Mistakes

There are three major mistakes that hiring managers make in their approach to interviewing job candidates.

Mistake #1: Hiring in Your Own Image

"Only someone who went to the same schools I did, looks like me, talks like me, walks like me—in other words, someone with whom I would immediately be socially at ease—can possibly do this job." This is myopic, dumb, and illegal.

Ideally, you want a diverse team that reflects all the variety found in your customer base, because that diversity and the knowledge everyone on your staff gains about people different from themselves will give them greater insight and wisdom in dealing with clients, vendors, and coworkers who differ in gender, race, culture, and age.

Mistake #2: Hiring Overqualified Candidates

Another significant mistake is *only* looking at candidates who are 95–100 percent capable of the job. This isn't a cut-and-dried issue, and there are interesting points to be made on both sides:

- On the one hand, hiring a candidate with all the skills you are looking for and who has handled all the challenges of the job successfully before can give you a fast start but leaves you with a new employee who may quickly become bored with the lack of challenges, raises, and promotions.

  There are a few situations, however, in which this sort of candidate makes for a good hire:

  1. A more senior position, where the reward is money.
  2. A senior candidate, often someone in her fifties and early sixties, who has all the skills but got sideswiped in a merger or layoff. Many managers will pass on these candidates at the resume stage. However, you can find great candidates at later stages of their careers who can make great hires: They know the job,

they've handled the problems before, they don't panic, they can mentor, they are far less likely to job-hop, and perhaps more important, they could be the only staff members who can be trusted to stand at your back, because they aren't looking for a promotion—they are looking for a place to work and make a difference for as long as they can.

- But on the other hand, in the majority of situations not covered in the above two cases, it's better to look for someone who can do the job but who still has room for growth in the position, as the resulting "learning curve" provides challenge and enrichment to keep an employee motivated. Plus they will be cheaper, and you are likely to be able to give them raises for a year or so without title changes. As a rule of thumb, you want someone who has at least 70 percent of the job's *deliverables* and who can be brought in at the midpoint salary range or below (though obviously circumstances will vary).

Mistake #3: Skipping the Telephone Interview

The biggest mistake of all is moving from resume evaluation straight to in-person interviews, skipping the telephone interview. Even if you haven't been a manager for long, you can probably remember a time when, within thirty seconds of meeting a candidate, you knew that he couldn't spell the job title if his life depended on it and realized within three minutes that you wouldn't hire this Dumbo if he were the last person on the planet. Yet, out of a mixture of professionalism, concern for human dignity, guilt, and an instinct to protect your company's reputation in the community, you end up walking this nincompoop through his resume for fifteen minutes. Then, kicking yourself as you ask, "Do you have any questions?", you find yourself frittering away another ten minutes answering inane questions about salary, benefits, vacations, and incentive plans he is never going to receive. Finally, joy of joys, just another couple of minutes to get him out of your office, followed by another five minutes to wash away the frustration and recalibrate your focus.

Instead, why not use the telephone as the vehicle for initial screening interviews? It minimizes distractions, and lets you focus on the resume, your notes, and a few critical questions that will tell you if this person possesses those "must have" skills of the job.

Your perspective for a telephone interview is very different from an in-person interview. You are using the telephone as a time-management and screening tool, investing a few minutes to verify critical skills and improve the odds that the time you invest in face-to-face interviews will be spent with serious and qualified candidates only.

You don't need to develop all the strategies and tactics for in-person interviewing that you will learn later in the book; your goal with a "phoner" is just to assess the "must haves": "Does she understand the job?"; "Does he have the critical skills demanded by the job?" If not, "Does he have most of the critical skills demanded by the job, and bring some kind of 'special sauce' to the table?" As soon as you have answers to these questions, get off the phone.

From Phoner to Short List

You can use telephone interviews to screen your long list of candidates down to a more manageable short list of perhaps four to six candidates in whom you will invest face time.

Qualifying a candidate over the telephone allows you to move through the pleasantries in under a minute and cut to the chase more quickly. You can refer to your notes and don't have to worry about social niceties—"Would you like some water?"—or your body language: You can roll your eyes at inane comments without repercussion.

Your goal with a phone interview is *not* to decide whether to hire the person; rather, it is to decide whether she is a close enough fit to justify an in-person meeting. Once you know that the candidate in question is worth seeing, schedule an interview. If you determine that a candidate is not suitable for the position, say so, in a courteous and professional manner. Either way, when you reach a decision, pro or con, you can get off the call in under a minute. I'll show you how to bail gracefully a little later in the chapter.

The interview strategies in this chapter will help you make fast and prudent decisions about whether it's worth your time to schedule an in-person interview. Your only goal should be to determine the "must have" critical skills of the job and some of the "nice to have" requirements you have determined. You shouldn't overly concern yourself with *transferable skills and professional values*, because these only become relevant once the critical *technical skills* are unquestionably present. For the same reason—and also because it's just not possible—you should not attempt to assess the intangibles of personal chemistry over the telephone.

Using the telephone or Skype as a primary step of your screening process is also sensible when relocation is a factor and the cost of flying in any but the strongest candidates is prohibitive.

Scheduling Telephone Interviews

Arrange your telephone interviews in a manner convenient to both parties. This is especially important when dealing with employed candidates, because a phone call during business hours can cause embarrassment or worse. With an employed candidate, you might consider an e-mail suggesting a time and date to talk on the phone for a few minutes, and you must be prepared to conduct such meetings outside of business hours or perhaps at lunchtime, when the candidate has more options for privacy. When the interview is scheduled during working hours, allow the candidate to choose the time of day and, for reasons of discretion, to initiate the call.

If for whatever reason *you* initiate the call, first introduce yourself and then ask if now is a good time to talk—even with a scheduled meeting, events during work hours can be unpredictable. For all you know the candidate could be sitting across a desk from her boss. For the same reason, be sensitive to the candidate who may suddenly become limited to yes or no responses or may request that you pick up the conversation later. In such instances, it is best to suggest an evening hour convenient to you, or suggest that you communicate by e-mail to reschedule.

Questions and Techniques for Phone Interviews

Phone interviews require a little preparation if they are to gather the right information and work as a *time-management* tool. A little organization now will ensure that your evaluations are objective and your decisions logical.

Fortunately, you did the work necessary to ease the flow of your telephone interviews when you did the JDD exercise and built your own JD, so you know the priorities of the job and the skills that go with their execution. Go back to this document and identify the most highly prioritized "must have" skills necessary for delivering on the *responsibilities* of the job.

As the interviewer, you will guide the conversation, but if you say too much, the candidate will gain the time and information to tell you just what you want to hear. There is an 80/20 rule of interviewing: You should talk 20 percent of the time and listen 80 percent of the time. By sharing adequate information about the *deliverables* of the job without going into detail, you give the candidate a clear focus, but not enough information to tip him off about the response you're looking for.

Use the question examples in this section to help you plan a customized set of questions ahead of time. You'll start the conversation with a few pleasant words to set the relaxed atmosphere of a conversation between professionals, because you learn more when people are relaxed.

Pleasantries concluded, you might start the meat of the conversation with a comment like, "It's a busy day today, so let's get right to it . . . I'd like to talk with you about [*job title*], and the context in which the chosen candidate will function [*include a few details*]." And then you move directly into question time.

After a skeletal review of the job's *deliverables*—for example, "This job is responsible for consumer Accounts Receivable"—ask the candidate to give you a brief recap, not of his entire work history, but just of his understanding of the job's *deliverables*.

"What would you say are the broad responsibilities of a _____?"

This question looks at the big picture: Does this candidate understand the job's *responsibilities* and *deliverables*? As a bonus, a candidate might tell you about how the position relates to and interacts with other positions and departments.

If satisfied with the applicant's answer, you might make a note to ask this question again at the in-person meeting, this time with follow-up questions about which job titles and departments this candidate interacts with on a regular basis. We'll mention this again in later chapters; the point now is that while issues like a candidate's interaction with other professional titles are relevant to your evaluation, they only become pressing once the applicant has demonstrated possession of far more critical skills.

Always remember that a phone interview is primarily a *time-management* tool: You only need enough information to rule each candidate in or out of consideration for the face-to-face interview.

"What aspects of your work do you consider most crucial?"

With this question you are looking for insights into whether the candidate understands the job's priorities. The answer might also indicate how she prefers to spend her time at work, and you can expect to learn something from this about *motivation* and other *professional values*. In the answer, you are naturally alert for a potential mismatch. One obvious example: the personal assistant who does not regard the smoothing of your daily path as a crucial function.

After one or two questions customized from the above examples, you will be able to identify a mismatch and have enough information to bail out. If the responses so far are encouraging, you will want to narrow the focus.

"Would you tell me about your responsibilities at your current job, especially as they relate to _____ issues?"

If there is nothing in the answer that seems relevant to the needs of your job opening, share your concern with the candidate and ask about anything in her prior work history that might change your perception. If there is a mismatch, bail out.

If the current job responsibilities are in line with your needs, you will want to mark this question and answer down to be asked again if/when you meet face-to-face. In such a situation, you might start with this same question and then add follow-up questions to assess the *transferable skills and professional values* that apply to this job. However, for a telephone interview you don't need this extra detail, since you are focusing on the critical skills of the job. If a candidate does possess the most critical skills, and there are perhaps one or two more skills of almost equal importance, repeat the question with a focus on the next skill. For example, with an accounting position you might ask:

"Would you tell me about your responsibilities at your current job as they relate to payroll issues?"

This is a simple query about a "must have" skill, but for an accounting manager or controller there is much at stake here, and the answers you hear can supply a boatload of information about *ability* and *suitability* very quickly. One of the most important *responsibilities* of any job in any company is *getting money in the door to make payroll.*

The other questions in this chapter follow a logical flow, but nevertheless likely will not match your unique needs in either wording or sequence. Use them as a touchstone for your needs, then phrase and locate them in the telephone interview sequence according to your needs.

Having a set sequence of questions and asking them of every client not only gives you a more objective picture of each candidate's relative merits, it also protects you and your company from accusations of discrimination.

"Tell me about your experience with _____."

Don't ask, "How many years' experience do you have with _____?" because a bare, unadorned numerical answer can shift the focus to quantity rather than quality of experience. You want expansive answers, not a number followed by silence, and as more than one manager over the years has discovered, those ten years of experience are not always ten *progressive* years, but quite possibly just the first two years repeated five times over.

You can ask a series of these questions, each addressing a specific aspect of the critical *deliverables*/skill sets of the job, but don't waste time: Once it is clear that this person understands and can do the job—or that she doesn't and can't—you can bail out, schedule a meeting, suggest that one will be scheduled, or move on and cover new territory.

"Of all the work you have done, where have you been most successful?"

The candidate will either discuss her ability to contribute in your areas of greatest need or display inappropriate focus on less important aspects of the job. You might follow up this question with one that examines why the candidate has become successful in this area: *"Why do you think you have been able to achieve success in this area?"* The answer you receive could well address some of the *transferable skills and professional values* brought into play to help achieve that success.

"What would you say are the major qualities this job demands?"

Also:

"What would you say are the skills a competent _____ should possess?"

Every job has its pressures, and every job demands certain underlying skills to assure success. For instance, no one is successful in sales without strong *listening, critical thinking,* and *verbal skills,* along with *determination* and *resilience,* which are all part of the *transferable skills and professional values* we discussed earlier. In developing a job description with your JDD work, you will already have identified the comparative importance of each of the *transferable skills and professional values* relative to this position, so an answer that is way off base will naturally raise a red flag.

"Describe how your job relates to the overall goals of your department, and your department to those of the company."

Everyone should know that a corporation is in business to make a profit, not to run a social club aimed at keeping the feeble-minded off the streets. Consequently, the candidate who is alert to how her individual efforts fit into the bigger picture is liable to be more *productive* and conscientious than one who hasn't a clue. Specifically, this is because such awareness allows a person to become part of something bigger than herself. Additionally, when you have a worker who understands how the product of her work affects everyone else's ability to do their work, you're invariably dealing with a *team player*.

"What aspects of your job do you like best?"
Follow-Up:
"What would you change about your current job?"

These two questions are most effective when asked in a sequence. In tandem, they might reveal a candidate who likes to occupy himself with busywork, and is put off by essential *responsibilities*. No matter how qualified, someone who has problems with one of the job's primary responsibilities is obviously not suitable for your job and should be rejected now; job distraction will only lead to fast turnover, and you'll be right back in the interviewing chair again.

"What are the most repetitive tasks in your job?"
Follow-Up:
"How do you feel about these responsibilities?"
"How do you deal with them?"

With this three-part question you are looking for a candidate's real understanding of the job (all our jobs have necessary but nevertheless stinky repetitive bits), and whether his work ethic matches your carefully defined requirements.

The second part of the question asks how the candidate feels about repetition and the role it plays in the job's *deliverables*, while the third examines his appreciation of the importance of such repetitive tasks and the assiduity with which he handles them. You ask the question in stages to avoid telegraphing your intentions, which increases the likelihood of getting an honest answer. For example, if the candidate has the *technical skills* to appropriately deal with time-consuming filing responsibilities, that's a plus, but if he prefers to handle the task by building a bonfire in the break room, there might be a gap between his qualifications and his appreciation of *systems and procedures*.

"What are you looking for in your next job?"

This question fits in comfortably during a telephone interview, because identifying a mismatch early will save you both time and potential embarrassment. In the candidate's answer, you will be alert for a match between the candidate's needs for the future and what your opening can genuinely provide. A match will give the candidate job satisfaction and provide you with a motivated employee. The further apart the candidate's desires are from your ability to satisfy them, the smaller your chances of maintaining a long-term working relationship together.

"What things bother you most about your job?"

Compare the answer to this question with the job's realities. Just imagine hiring a receptionist who hated being rushed or loathed the sound of ringing bells. Again, we are looking for matches to move forward, while a series of mismatches, or a single serious mismatch like this, gives you another timesaving opportunity to bail out.

Discussing Money

This is a topic that should always be addressed first on the telephone, because it is foolhardy to waste time and money conducting a face-to-face meeting when there is a serious financial imbalance. At the same time, you should be aware that neither of you is in a position to negotiate money at this point, because:

1. You want a good employee at a competitive price who you can keep motivated over the long haul with skill development challenges and raises.
2. The candidate wants to make as much money as she possibly can. There are a number of questions you could ask here, but as neither of you is in a position to negotiate seriously, the best you can expect is to establish whether or not the candidate is in the ballpark. Usually, just one question with a considerate preamble to this important topic will suffice:

"Neither of us is in a position to negotiate salary at this point, but just to avoid wasting each other's time, how much are you looking for?"

Also:

"What salary range are you looking for?"

Follow-Up:

"How much are you making in your current/last job?"

To avoid any fudging on earnings you can add, "*I've lost really good people during the reference check and salary verification process, so I make it a point of telling everyone that I always do my best to make fair offers, and that we always check references and salary history.*" If the candidate is near the top of your salary range, tell him so—you might as well end the conversation here, unless the candidate is genuinely interested in other things more than salary. Otherwise, bail out, keeping that good candidate in mind for a more senior opportunity and letting him know that you intend to do so.

"How much money do you want?"

I really recommend you stay away from this question, unless answers to prior questions have put this person at or very near the top of your approved salary range for the job. You may get this response: "That depends on the job. How much are you paying?" If this happens, I've always found it best to be quite straightforward: "I'm not trying to negotiate with you now, John; it's just that you're already quite close to the top of my approved salary range, and I wouldn't want to waste your time or mine. Please just give me some idea of what you're looking for."

"What else should I know about your qualifications for this job?"

Also:

"What else should I know about you?"

"Is there anything else you want to tell me?"

Such questions are clear signals to the interviewee that the conversation is drawing to a close, and that it is an opportunity for the candidate to identify any strengths or relevant experience. You may even discover hidden talents that the course of the interview has not revealed. At least, you will reassure yourself that nothing valuable has been missed.

Making Decisions and Getting Off the Phone

Remembering some of my own earliest interviews from the management side of the desk, I recall them going on, and on, and on; in hindsight, this happened partly because I hadn't determined what I needed to know to make a decision, and partly because I hadn't planned a graceful exit strategy. As the interviewer, you have almost total control over the duration of any interview, and with a selection of questions like the above tailored to the specifics of your job opening (and perhaps one or two with special relevance salted in from later chapters), you should have all the information you need to decide whether or not to meet a candidate.

The Verdict

By the end of a telephone interview, you will have reached one of three conclusions:

1. *The candidate is not able to do the job.* If this is the case, you will terminate the interview as soon as you make the determination; you do not have to continue with the interview once you have determined there is a mismatch. As a common courtesy,

try to let the candidate down gently, noting that though she has good skills, you have other candidates more suitable for today's opening, but that she could be right for something else down the road. You can say, "Joan, a lot of people are interested in this job, and I have already spoken with one or two who more closely match my needs. However, you have some great skills, and I would like to keep you in mind for the future." Or, "Mark, it seems like you have some valuable skills, but I have already spoken to a couple of people who seem a little better qualified for this particular position. But we never know how our needs are going to change, and I'd like to keep your resume in my database for future reference."

2. *You are still not sure.* Tell the person how you feel—we can all handle the truth—and suggest that while you are considering the matter, the applicant may choose to send you an e-mail addressing your concerns and emphasizing her relevant strengths. You might say, "Competition is keen, and I have others to talk to. I'm not sure at this point whether you will make the short list, so I have to give it further consideration. If you are interested in the job, I'd like you to send me an e-mail detailing your strengths, and how you would compensate for your lack of experience in _____ [*some of the skills that the job demands*]." This additional test will hopefully give you more insightful information about skill match, and also help you evaluate *professional values* such as *determination*, *motivation*, and *written communication skills.*

3. *The candidate has the critical skills and seems motivated.* If this is someone you want to talk to, invite or arrange to have the candidate in for a face-to-face meeting. Agree on a mutually convenient date, time, and location to meet.

As much as the pressures of the real world allow, schedule interviews with all the short-list candidates as close together as is practical, so that you are able to objectively compare them to one another.

The end of a phone interview that is leading to an in-person meeting can also be a good time to set the ground rules for the coming meeting. State that:

- The interview will go more deeply into the candidate's *experience*, *responsibilities*, and ability to *deliver* on the particular needs of the job.
- You will treat any and all information shared with you as confidential.
- If all goes well, HR will check salary and references as a matter of policy, and you might check one or two professional references personally.

People always respect what you inspect. These statements (especially the one about checking references) will encourage honesty throughout the selection process.

Phone Interviews As Succession Training

Once your telephone interviews have helped you confirm a short list of candidates, you will want to prepare for each in-person interview, and that's where we're headed in the next chapter. Before that, though, let's look at a method for making phone interviews even more useful as a *time-management* tool for you, a skill-development opportunity for some of your better people, and ultimately a succession-planning and training exercise to empower your climb up the management ladder.

The most effective way to prepare staff members to become part of your selection team might be to get them copies of this book (we have bulk discounts for print and digital editions), then walk them through how you have customized this telephone interview chapter to your specific needs, showing them what you've marked on the resumes and why, the areas you want them to address, and maybe a list of sample questions that you use yourself. It wouldn't be a bad idea to have them role-play the entire process on the telephone with you a couple of times, taking turns playing the interviewer and the candidate.

Your only concern here is having a staff member at or near the same level engaged in any salary discussions. You need to make it clear that salary talk is off-limits: It can only cause unrest within your team, an issue over which you will almost certainly have little or no control.

This delegation might take some additional time initially while you train your chosen team members, but you are ultimately freeing management time while building the skills of your people and *motivating* them through the opportunity for further professional growth. Remember that to climb the ladder, you have to have someone to occupy the rung left open by your ascent.

FIVE

Backstage Passes: The Art and Science of Interviewing

There are two terrible places to be during an interview: sitting in front of the desk, wondering what question you are going to *be asked* next, and sitting behind the desk, wondering what question to *ask* next.

Don't panic; it's a normal reaction, especially when you are new and learning, but also when you are experienced and conscious of the outcome's importance. When learning any new skill, many people start as "unconscious incompetents"—the interviewer who *doesn't know* that he doesn't know how to interview. *Unconscious incompetence* is the first of the four stages of skill development.

Next comes, "OMG, I don't know what I'm doing, and my career depends on getting work done through others. I gotta learn to do this right!" This is the stage of *conscious* incompetence: the time of dawning awareness that you have lots of room for improvement. The logical outcome of this stage is your commitment to developing competency in this critical skill, which leads to the third stage: competence.

This third stage, conscious *competence*, which you are moving into by reading *Knock 'em Dead: Hiring the Best*, will take you to the level of the interviewer who knows what she is doing every step of the way, and who knowingly plans each action and question for the information it will yield. *In employee selection, insight is king*, and you can't get real insight without knowing what you are doing, why you are doing it, and what you hope to gain as a result.

That fourth step of competence? That's *un*conscious competence, what the philosopher Aristotle called *phronesis* or "practical wisdom."

This happens when the lessons of *conscious competence* have been thoroughly absorbed and become second nature. You reach this fourth stage of knowledge by learning the laws of your craft and then putting them into practice constantly, so that you forget the rules themselves and just know instinctively what to do. It's like learning a language. If you're like me, you can use a word in a sentence but often have a hard time defining it. You've forgotten the rules themselves, but you've internalized them so completely that you not only embody them in your every action, but can even creatively break them as the situation demands.

The same is true of *Knock 'em Dead: Hiring the Best* and the laws of effective selection. As you put these lessons into practice, you'll come back to the book as a reference—often to begin with, and then less and less as a few years go by and you come to embody the successful manager you aspire to be.

F. Lee Bailey, one of the greatest courtroom performers of modern times, talked of going into court with fifty rabbits in his hat, but never knowing which he would need to use; consequently, he had to be ready with all fifty, thoroughly prepared with multiple approaches and questioning techniques. F. Lee Bailey invariably won his cases.

You too have your day in court whenever you interview a potential new employee. Every time you interview, you are defending your livelihood and your standing as a competent manager, using all the tricks, tactics, tips, and techniques you'll find in these pages.

Your growing competency as a hiring manager begins with knowing how to structure an interview. This chapter addresses why and how to structure your interviews, offers an array of different approaches to the art of polite interrogation, and presents you with a comprehensive selection of questioning and conversational control techniques. In the following chapter, we'll move on to discuss how to structure a sequence of interviews (it's all about the complexity of the job), and how to get the best out of second opinions.

Interview Structure

When you are evaluating candidates against one another, those evaluations must be based on objective criteria. Unless you maintain consistent standards and ask largely the same set of questions of every candidate for a given job opening, you will lack consistency and objectivity. These qualities also help you stay on the right side of the law, protecting you and your company in the event of discrimination lawsuits. You can achieve this objectivity and consistency, and protect your professional integrity, by creating and following a structure for your interviews. Graphically, the steps of an interview look like this:

> Setting the Tone
> Interview Outline
> Work History
> Critical Deliverables and Transferable Skills and Professional Values

Setting the Tone

As the interviewer, you sit in the position of power, and as such you set the tone. With the right tone, a candidate feels as respected and relaxed as possible. This is your goal, because a relaxed candidate will give you more information, and a candidate who experiences an atmosphere of professional respect is more likely to accept a job.

Inexperienced interviewers often spend too much time selling the company, because they haven't thought through the right sequence of questions to ask, and instead they just talk. You can do better. In fact, selling the company too early in the process—and therefore to too many candidates—is not only bad negotiating tactics and a waste of time, but it leaves you dodging obnoxious follow-up calls from congenital imbeciles you wouldn't hire on a bet.

A job interview is uncomfortable for you, but it's far worse for the poor devil sweating across the desk. At some level, every candidate feels like the decision to be handed down is a measure of his validity as a person. You can diffuse the natural anxiety of the interview by thinking about the atmosphere that would encourage you, as a candidate, to open up during a job interview.

This isn't just for the candidate's sake: Establishing a level of comfort isn't so much part of wooing as it is part of not getting fooled. A person treated in a warm and friendly manner from the start will respond to questioning more openly and honestly than will someone whose defenses are raised.

First impressions are indelible, and you can make a positive or negative impression before you ever meet your short list of candidates. Does the front desk know you are expecting someone? How are interviewees normally treated on arrival at your company? Find out and manage the first impressions you want your candidates to receive. The tension of the occasion can be blown all out of proportion by a poor reception by the front desk: "Oh, yeah, another lamb to the slaughter, seats for the abattoir are over there, take a number." Creating the right impression means that your candidate immediately gets a picture of your company as a good place to be. If the receptionist says, "Good morning, Ms. Jones; Martin Yate told me to expect you. Good luck this morning; you'll find everyone pretty reasonable," he's creating a friendly atmosphere. Every staff member who comes in contact with potential employees should be taught to treat them as welcome guests. It is usually easy to get people on the same page once they understand that they have an important role in the process.

Some managers might not be in a position to dictate employee and receptionist behavior, but even if this is the case, you can still foster a general atmosphere of friendly relations. When a candidate or string of candidates are due, you can informally drop by the front desk and say, "Hey Carole, I know you are going to be busy today, so I brought you a cappuccino to keep your energy up. By the way, I have four candidates coming in. Think you can tell each one that I'm looking forward to meeting them? You know, make 'em feel comfortable, like you always do." A gesture like that can go a long way.

The same concept applies when meeting a candidate for the first time. It is easy to impress someone with your importance by sending a minion to lead the way to your lair—it is done all the time—but setting the right tone takes no more effort than using the same good manners you exercise when welcoming a visitor to your home. Meet the candidate in the lobby yourself if you possibly can, and offer a sincere welcome.

Look the candidate in the eye. Give a firm handshake and say, "Hi, I'm pleased to meet you, Ms. Jones, and I'm looking forward to getting to know you better." If it hasn't been done yet, offer some water or other convenient beverage. Between interview nerves and cotton mouth, your gesture will be appreciated.

Much has been written about the interview environment, including rubbish like: "Set a relaxed atmosphere. Don't interview across a desk, it sets a barrier. Instead, sit in easy chairs across a low coffee table." This is great if you have the environment to accommodate this kind of gesture; I call the advice "rubbish" only because the majority of managers don't live in such spacious elegance, but more often in burrows so small you have to step outside to change your mind.

Easy chairs, a coffee table, and good service are nice, of course, but if you can't snatch a plush office for your interview, privacy is the main thing. You need a room with a door that can be closed, and both your staff and the front desk need to know that you are not to be disturbed with telephone calls or unexpected intrusions. Very little can happen in your department during the twenty minutes to an hour needed for a typical first interview that cannot wait until its end for your attention.

In preparing for interviews, make sure you have all the relevant information about the job and the company in one master file (HR can help you set up something with all the right documentation). In the candidate's file—which you will sensibly have set up on your desktop—will be the resume and any notes from telephone conversations.

Interview Outline

Your interviews should always begin with a little small talk to relax the candidate: "How was the journey? Did you find the place easily?" This shouldn't take more than a minute.

Proceed with a nonspecific outline and benefit statement. "We are looking for a _____, and I want to learn about your experience and the strengths you can bring to our team. I don't want this to be a one-sided interrogation of your skills. We can get the best out of this by turning our meeting into a conversation between a couple of professionals, sharing information and specific examples from everyday work experience. You'll talk about your work experiences, and I'll explain a little about what we do here. I want you to know that you wouldn't be here unless I already had a good feeling that you can do the job."

Tell the candidate that her background looks interesting, that you were impressed by the way the telephone interview progressed, and that "I have lots of topics to talk with you about."

If you intend to take notes, say so! If note taking is too distracting for you, take ten minutes immediately after the interview to create a written review of the interview; do it before you get back into the daily rhythm of your department.

If there will only be one interview, you might want to briefly explain the process: that you have a number of people to interview and that with a final candidate you intend to check references and salary history prior to an offer, or that an offer will be dependent on subsequent checking of both. Making that announcement early helps to create an atmosphere of honesty; again, *people respect what you inspect, not what you expect.*

Work Experience and the 80/20 Rule

Every moment you spend talking during a job interview is lost evaluation time, so your goal is to get the candidate talking 80 percent of the time, with you asking questions 20 percent of the time and not editorializing on the answers. Every candidate is going to be nervous, so you start with nonthreatening questions about work history.

It will get you both on the same page (and the candidate's vocal cords working) to have him walk you through his work history on the resume: "I'd like to get an idea of how you got where you are today, so why don't we take just a couple of minutes for you to tell me a little about yourself as you walk me through your resume?" Early in the interview, restrict yourself to easy-to-ask, easy-to-answer questions that allow the candidate to get used to talking and to the idea that you are thorough in your analysis. Ask questions about types of tasks and projects; what the candidate liked and disliked about certain jobs (only those most closely resembling your opening are relevant) and certain managers; how past managers have gotten the best out of him; the reason for leaving the last job; and the reason for leaving the current position.

This is as far as most interviews go, but if the candidate warrants deeper consideration, your interview is just getting serious. If that isn't the case, your candidate will be quite happy with what felt like a typical interview, and you can bail out in one of two ways:

1. You can say that there are other candidates to consider and that you will be in touch. It is then professionally desirable to develop a polite rejection letter that you can use on a regular basis. The candidate might not be right for this job, but she may be perfect for another opportunity a month or a year down the line. Besides, you owe your candidates the courtesy of a gentle and considerate letdown.

2. You can reject the candidate at the end of the interview: "I've enjoyed meeting you, Carla; however, I have already interviewed a couple of people who are a little more suitable for the job. This has by no means been a waste of our time though. I have enjoyed meeting you, and with your permission I'd like to keep your resume on file for the future."

Assessment of Transferable Skills
and Professional Values

When you have a candidate who looks promising, you will move forward into the meat of the interview by more deeply examining the candidate's "must have" skills and their resulting *deliverables*, as well as the *transferable skills* and *professional values* that will empower a candidate to deliver on each of your "must have" needs.

Because you created an up-to-date and practical job description based on your JDD, you have already isolated these critical components of the job. And since you used a telephone interview for initial screening of the job's critical skills and their *deliverables*, you are assured that careful examination of these competencies is a worthwhile time investment. The hundreds of interview questions in the following chapters will help you gather the insights you need, and the following interview strategies will ensure that you get the truth and maintain control of the selection process.

The Science of Interviewing Techniques

Beyond asking a carefully sequenced series of questions to determine competency and skill levels, there are three distinct approaches to interviewing, each of which can add depth and substance to the information you gather with your questions. These are the *situational*, *behavioral*, and *stress* techniques. Each style has its strengths and weaknesses, but none of them stands entirely alone as a sole approach to candidate selection. You can learn useful techniques from each of these approaches, so let's look at them individually and then adopt facets of each and craft a comprehensive interviewing approach that you can customize to fit your specific needs.

Situational
Situational interviewing is based on the theory that the closer you can get a candidate to the real work situation, the better your

evaluation will be. You take a candidate on a tour of the workplace as an integral part of the proceedings, not just to fill in time. You also get the prospective employee to actually perform some aspect of the job. You stand by the computer with a programmer and discuss applications, then have the candidate use that application on a prepared exercise; you ask an accountant to analyze a balance sheet with procedural mistakes built into it; you put a telemarketer on the phone in another office and role-play a few typical sales calls.

As a sales and management trainer by profession, I was once surprised by being submitted to situational interviewing techniques myself. At an interview for a management-training job, I was shown around the corporate training center, and the tour finished with my interviewer and me standing by the flip charts, screen, and other presentation paraphernalia. "How do you think you'd like training here, Martin?" asked the interviewer innocently. "Fine," I said, unaware of what was to follow.

"Excellent. Then to get a feel for what it will be like, why don't you teach me something? I'll take a seat over here. Take five minutes and teach me anything you want." There I was, a top trainer, being thrown in the deep end and put through my paces (he was also throwing in a stress dimension, which we'll address shortly). Afterward, I reviewed what had happened and realized that for my particular job, no amount of probing and reference checking could give the interviewer quite the same taste for my platform skills as seeing those skills in action. It also allowed the interviewer to see whether I had a style compatible with the fabric of the corporation. As an interviewer, *situational* ploys can get you closer to real job performance than can almost any other technique. Take a few minutes to consider aspects of a job you will be filling that could be adapted to role-playing or other *situational* interviewing approaches.

Behavioral

I learned about *behavioral* techniques in the early 1980s from Dr. Paul Green, the father of behavioral interviewing. It has been integrated into the *Knock 'em Dead* approach to professional growth and career management since my first book appeared in 1985.

Behavioral or past-performance interview techniques apply the leopard-never-changes-its-spots philosophy. They base all questions in the past, requiring the candidate to give specific examples from work history. The belief that an individual will do at least as well on the new job as he has done in the past is often a reasonable assumption. Past behavior can and does predict future actions, so by asking candidates to talk about specific work experiences from the past, they will recall the details and then get into the habit of answering your questions with details of on-the-job experiences.

At the heart of *behavioral* interviewing is the identification of a skill area that you want to examine, followed by a question addressing it: "Tell me about a time when you hit a problem in this area."

Behavioral interview strategy also recognizes that there are certain *transferable skills and professional values* that allow us to do our job well, whatever we do and at whatever level. Once you have a feeling that a candidate has the essential skills of the job, asking *behavioral* questions and looking for *transferable skills and professional values* will give you a sense of whether this candidate is likely to perform as well as his resume advertised.

This effective approach should be woven into your own customized interview template. We'll discuss its applications throughout the following chapters.

Stress

If stress is a real part of the job you are filling, by all means add a *stress* dimension to the interview, and do it unexpectedly to see how the applicant processes information and handles stress in real-life situations. However, be aware that your interviewees are already in a highly stressful situation.

Every manager can regretfully tell a story of an ex-employee who "looked good on paper" but who just couldn't handle the rigors of the work. Often the problem was an inability to handle the stress that was an integral part of the job. If there is stress associated with the job you're filling, an employee who has all of the skills in place still will not be successful if he cannot function under the pressure of the problems and challenges that job throws at him every day. If there is stress on the job and a candidate lacks what Hemingway called "grace under pressure"—the ability to cope with the emotional wear of stress and yet retain the ability to function professionally—that candidate will ultimately fail, and that reflects on you.

You might even employ *stress* when applying a *situational* interview technique. Just a few pages back I told you about being asked to "teach me something." This was a perfect example of a *situational* strategy married to a *stress* technique.

Depending on the demands of a job, *stress* tactics can be useful at some point during the selection process. In speaking with the manager of a DC-based TV talk show, I heard a revealing story about just such a *stress* dimension. The story is especially valuable because it puts the stress in context: It comes at us unexpectedly.

A TV anchor position is a very stressful job; a million things can go wrong and often do, and it is the anchor's task to remain calm and collected under fire. The interviewer in this story would end each interview with a promising candidate by saying, "We really are not sure you are suitable for the job, wouldn't you agree?" One young woman, who up to that point was a sure top contender, revealed her inability to think fast and function with grace under sudden and unexpected pressure when she got up and said, "Well, I'm not sure I want to work here anyway." She showed herself to be someone who couldn't handle the pressure the job called for. She didn't remain calm, her *critical thinking skills* jammed, and she didn't listen—and so she heard a personal insult rather than an opportunity to set the record straight.

Stress questions are *not* designed for a manager to get off on newfound authority. They have to be used appropriately within the context of the job and the problems that arise within it on a regular basis.

Mix and Match Your Tactics

With these very different approaches to information gathering, it isn't a matter of choosing one or another—there will be uses for all of them in different situations. The sensible approach is to take aspects of each style and combine them to produce a comprehensive strategy for each different job it becomes your responsibility to fill. You will also need to change tactics on the spur of the moment as each interview develops. A knowledge of the different interviewing strategies and what they offer is part of what gives you the flexibility to ask a question in many different ways, along with an ability to read body language and thereby get a sense of the impact of your tactics.

Reading Body Language

As a species, we learned to read *body language* signals before we invented *verbal communication*. We master the spoken word later in life, and, in so doing, we forget the importance of nonverbal cues—but the signals are still sent and received, usually at a subconscious level. In fact, studies done at the University of Chicago found that more than 50 percent of all effective *communication* relies on *body language*. Even when a candidate isn't speaking, she is nevertheless talking to you through *body language*.

When you conduct job interviews, you will notice a candidate's bodily responses to questions. Developing awareness of these somatic "tells" is an invaluable tool for judging candidates, and it's not limited to the negative. You can use these unconscious signals not just to rule out job seekers who are withholding, feel guilty, lack *confidence*, or signal aggression, but also to assess the social graces (so necessary in many fields from the midlevel up) that become important when client and vendor interaction is part of the job.

Among the first body signals you can assess is the handshake. You will probably initiate the handshake, but how does the candidate respond? Does he look you in the eye with a smile, or does he pull back, hesitate, or give you a limp, clammy hand? Does he leave appropriate bodily space, or is he a "close talker"? Is his grip firm? Too loose, and you may have a shy, passive job seeker who lacks self-confidence—it's not a guarantee, but noticing gives you a heads-up on something to look into. Too firm, and your applicant may be an aggressive know-it-all who plans to run the place her first day on the job.

You learn even more once the candidate sits down. A chair is an opportunity for all sorts of fearful, passive, or nervous behaviors. A job hunter who slouches in his chair and crosses his arms will remind you of a petulant teen, and the resemblance may not be accidental. On the other hand, a candidate who stretches her legs out and clasps her hands behind her head may be a little bit too comfortable or displaying arrogance. Sitting upright with a slight forward tilt of the body shows interest and engagement.

When the applicant speaks, does she hold her palms open, inviting you to engage with what she's saying? Does she steeple her fingers thoughtfully when giving serious consideration to a difficult question? Or does she impatiently tap a pen or fingernail, indicating that she's tired of your description of the job's *deliverables* and impatient to get to how wonderful she is?

There are many more bodily tells you can look for (luncheon interviews are a gold mine we'll discuss later), and they all tie into the *communication skills* that are so vital in many jobs. Begin to develop a conscious awareness of these details (your subconscious is already picking up on them) and you will be that much speedier at separating the gold from the dross. For example, if a candidate leaves you uncomfortable in some undefined way, think back to his *body language* for clues.

The Art of the Question

Just as you can mix and match your interview approaches to gather information, you can supercharge questions by framing them effectively. The following ten questioning techniques will help you vary the structure of individual questions as the situation demands and ensure that you strike the right note every time. You will also be able to apply these persuasive conversational control techniques in other areas of your professional life.

These techniques will give you an almost infinite ability to customize your interview questions. As we get into the hundreds of interview questions in the coming chapters, ask yourself how you could use this or that technique to better tailor a question to your needs. You can practice by trying to rephrase each of the questions you've chosen for an interview using a different technique.

#1: The Closed-Ended Question

This is the most frequently abused questioning technique. How often have you heard an interviewer (maybe even yourself!) ask a *closed-ended question* such as, "Can you work under pressure?" The only possible answers are "yes" and "no," and who would answer "no" at a job interview? The result is little or no information, and no way of evaluating one candidate against another. But while a *closed-ended question* is inappropriate in most cases, it can also be useful.

Since the *closed-ended question* preempts a detailed response, use it when you *want* a brief answer, perhaps so you can check a box and move on to more fruitful areas of inquiry. The *closed-ended question* is a useful technique when you are looking for commitment—"Can you start on Monday?"—or when you are refreshing your memory or verifying information from earlier in the interviewing sequence: "You were with Xerox for ten years?" You can also use it to get the ball rolling with a series of questions on the same subject, as you'll see shortly.

#2: The Open-Ended Question

With an *open-ended question*, the candidate cannot get by with a monosyllabic answer; an *explanation* is inherent in the way the question is phrased. For example, "How do you respond to pressure in your work?" and "What situations arise in your job that cause pressure/problems?" are both *open-ended questions* that ask the interviewee to give a detailed answer. This style of question is preferable to *closed-ended questions*, except in the situations mentioned and still to be discussed. Since you generally want to maintain an 80/20 ratio of listening to speaking, the *open-ended question* will be your best tool to keep the interviewee talking.

Open-ended questions can begin in many ways: "I'm interested in hearing about . . ." or "I'm curious to learn . . ." or "Would you share with me . . ." They also include questions that begin with *who, what, where, when, why,* and *how,* such as, "What happened on your job the last time there was an urgent deadline?"

#3: The Past-Performance, or Behavioral, Question

This leads us to the *past-performance/behavioral questions* that are based on the premise that past actions accurately predict future behavior, and that anyone can be expected to do at least as well or as badly with a task on the new job as she did in the past. *Behavioral questions* focus on requesting specific details of past events and in the process they:

- Accustom the interviewee to answering honestly and backing up claims and statements with real-world examples.
- Inform you about the *transferable skills* and *professional values* (or lack of them) that a particular candidate has developed to effectively execute her duties.

They are usually prefaced with, "Tell me about a time when . . ." or "Share with me an experience where you had to . . ." or "Give me an example of a situation that . . ." It is wise to start asking *past-performance questions* early in the interview, so that a candidate quickly recognizes that she is expected to give detailed examples about past work situations. Doing this early in the interview cycle establishes a pattern of openness and honesty.

#4: The Negative-Balance Question

Interviewing isn't anyone's idea of fun, and as a manager you just want to fill the position and get back to business, so it is all too easy to believe that a candidate strong in one area is equally impressive in all areas. This is hardly ever the case, so when an eerie light appears around a candidate's head, it is time to get a grip and look for *negative balance.* Try, "That's very impressive. Was there ever an occasion when things didn't work out quite so well?" or the simple, "Now can you give me an example of something in this area of which you are not so proud?" *Negative-balance questions* are also useful because smart people learn as much from their mistakes as their successes, so always follow up with, "What did you learn from this?"

#5: The Negative-Confirmation Question

Sometimes the answer you receive may be disturbing enough to warrant *negative confirmation*. For example, an interviewee tells you about a time she found it necessary to go around her supervisor to achieve a goal. Because *past actions predict future behavior*, you will seek *negative confirmation* with, "You know, that's very interesting. Let's talk about another time when you had to . . ." Successive examples will help you identify someone who might become a management issue.

#6: The Reflexive Question

Reflexive questions are great topic closers and conversation forwarders, and they help you maintain control of the conversation with an overly talkative candidate. This is done by ending questions with phrases like: *Don't you? Couldn't you? Wouldn't you? Didn't you? Can't you? Aren't you?* For example: "With time so short, I think it would be valuable to move on to another area, don't you?" The candidate's natural response to such a question from an authority figure is to agree.

#7: Silence and Mirror Statements

Remember the last cocktail party you attended, when an awkward silence was broken by three people starting to talk at once? This almost universal human aversion to uncomfortable silences can be used to your advantage during an interview. You can use silence, and a smile or a nod, as a signal that you are still interested and listening, in order to encourage the candidate to continue talking.

You can also use something called a *mirror statement* to ask a candidate to expand on an answer. The technique is to mirror (paraphrase) an answer as a question and throw it back to the candidate while nodding and looking interested. For example: "So, whenever you are two hours late for work, you take off two hours early to make up for it?" Then sit quietly and listen.

#8: The Loaded Question

Loaded questions require a candidate to decide between options that are tough, and sometimes ridiculous: "Which do you think is the lesser evil, embezzlement or forgery?" For most interviewers, *loaded questions* are most commonly used when *critical thinking* and ethical behaviors are at a premium and you want to probe the candidate's decision-making processes. The most effective way to apply a *loaded question* is to recall a real-life situation in which two divergent approaches were both carefully considered. Then frame the situation as a question starting with "I'm curious to know how you would decide between two approaches where . . ." or "What would be your approach to a situation in which . . ."

#9: The Layered Question

Question *layering* helps you dig deeper into areas of interest. Let's start with a classic example: You want to know if a potential employee can work under pressure. Instead of asking a simple *closed-ended question* that will deliver little insight, take a leaf out of the journalist's notebook and layer your questions. The reporter integrates *all* these questioning techniques, peeling *layers* of truth until a topic has been examined from every angle. The journalist asks: who, what, where, when, why, and how. You can do this by using a *closed-ended question* to open a *behavioral* examination, and then follow with a number of other questioning techniques.

- *"Can you work under pressure?"*
- *"Tell me about a tight deadline when you had to work under pressure."*
- *"What do you think caused the problem that created the pressure?"*
- *"So, it was tough to meet the deadline?"*
- *"Where did the problem originate?"*
- *"How would you avoid this situation in the future?"*
- *"Who was responsible?"*
- *"What did you do?"*
- *"Where do you go for advice in these situations?"*
- *"What have you learned from the experience?"*
- *"How can you do your job in a way that prevents these types of situations from arising?"*

With question *layering* you have different angles of approach to the topic, each revealing a little more about the *technical skills*, performance, and *transferable skills and professional values*, all of which help deliver a more complete *behavioral profile* of your candidate. Nearly every one of the hundreds of interview questions in this book can be given the *layering* treatment. The technique makes the possibilities for questions endless; when you use it depends on how critical that issue is in the successful execution of the job's *responsibilities*. You are not obliged to accept a candidate's first answer to any of your questions. You have a right to look closer and to dig deeper.

#10: The "Hamburger Helper" Question

Sometimes, distractions external to the interview will make you forget who you are, what you are doing, and what this stranger in front of you is talking about. In all instances, you'll be thankful for knowing about "Hamburger Helper" questions because they help you get back on track without looking like an idiot:

1. You might say, "Give me some more detail on that. It's very interesting." Or, "Can you give me another example?" As the candidate talks, you'll have time to refocus.
2. You can also buy time to regroup by asking, "What did you learn from that experience?"
3. Perhaps the best technique for buying time to refocus and gather more information is simply to sit quietly, looking at the interviewee and saying nothing, because most people feel pressured to talk by a conversational lull.

The Art of the Conversation

It is often said that people rarely listen: They just wait for their turn to talk. From your side of the desk, this inborn narcissism can be a godsend. As you integrate all the techniques that keep the candidate talking while you evaluate their answers, your interviewing style will begin to take on the feel of a conversation.

Live by the 80/20 Rule

People like to talk, and above all things they like to talk about themselves to an appreciative audience. This works to your advantage, because you want to minimize your talking time and maximize your listening time. President Lyndon Johnson gained his most famous legislative victories through his legendary ability to read people's thoughts using this very technique. He would tell his assistants, "The most important thing a man has to tell you is what he's not telling you. The most important thing he has to say is what he's trying not to say." According to one of his speechwriters, "That's why he wouldn't let a conversation end. If he saw the other fellow was trying not to say something, he wouldn't let [the conversation] end until he got it out of him."

So whenever you interview, strive to live by the 80/20 rule: Ask questions 20 percent of the time and listen 80 percent of the time. Plan your interviews and the questions you will ask to gather the information you need to make an informed decision, and you will be able to dedicate the greater part of your time to listening and evaluation.

Many interviewers eat up valuable time by commenting on a candidate's answers. Unless you are doing it to provoke further comment, this editorializing is a waste of time. It can also show the candidate where your priorities lie and encourage answers that reflect your values, not the candidate's. While a little conversation as the interview gets going is necessary to set everyone at ease, try to remain visually and verbally neutral. In fact, *don't comment on answers at all* unless it specifically serves your purpose. Just move along with another question that shows you are deeply interested in the conversation.

Framing Questions

The candidate needs to concentrate on answering your questions, not deciphering them, so frame your questions simply. Don't string too many questions together within one larger question like this: "Tell me what kind of people you like to work with, what kind of people you don't like to work with, and how you get along with them." On the one hand, this is confusing, and on the other, it leads candidates toward a "desirable" answer: "I never met a person I didn't enjoy working with." The way you frame a question dictates the quality of the information you will gather in response.

Sequencing Themes

Try to group your questions by theme. Address performance in critical skill areas one at a time, and then move from one topic to the next, offering clear signposts so that the candidate knows what is happening. For example: "Good, now that we have established that you are a graduate of the Genghis Khan School of Management, let's talk about employee turnover." Or perhaps, more seriously, "I have a good feel for your code skills now. I'd like to move on and discuss dealing with nontechnical client needs."

Keeping the Candidate on Track

The person asking the questions controls and directs the flow of any conversation. As the interviewer, and as the candidate's possible future manager, it's smart to establish that authority from the start. Otherwise, the candidate may find ways to hide some nugget of information relevant to your evaluation. If you ask a young chemical engineer what personal qualities she thinks are necessary for success in the field, and get an answer like, "Well, you need at least three years' experience and knowledge of current chemical patents," then you've received an evasive answer, or you are facing an engineer whose ears don't work. Put the interviewee back on track by being gently persistent: "Perhaps I didn't make myself clear; I want to know what *personal qualities* are necessary for success, not what kind of experience."

Handling a Flustered Candidate

Sometimes during a job interview, your candidate will be stumped by a question, either because he does not know the answer, or due to that mind-numbing adrenaline rush we've all experienced at one time or another during a job interview. Sometimes when this happens, you might be tempted to let the candidate off the hook with, "That's all right, let's move on." This is the wrong approach. You never want to let a candidate off the hook if she is experiencing difficulty in answering your questions: It denies you essential information for decision making and sets a bad precedent for the balance of the interview and for your future management of this potential employee.

At the same time, you do want to calm the interviewee down, so when a candidate gets flustered, smile warmly and try, "That's all right, interviews makes us all nervous. Take your time to answer. I'm sure something will come." Often, it will.

But use *silence* judiciously. If you face a candidate who is completely stumped for an answer, it is advisable to move on to another topic to maintain the flow of the interview. "That's okay, Angela, everyone gets flustered at an interview. Let's move on to another topic right now, and we'll come back to this later." Remember to do so.

Getting stumped because of interview nerves, a savvy candidate might himself state that he is nervous and ask to come back to the question later. If this happens, respect the candidate's request, move on, and come back to it later. Whatever he says the second time around, the response will be telling.

Control and the Overly Talkative Candidate

When confronted with a candidate who is inebriated with his own verbosity, your challenge is not so much keeping the conversation going as guiding its flow to gather the information you need. This can easily be handled with either of these techniques:

1. Jump into the conversation with, "You know, that's very interesting. It makes me want to ask you about . . ." and then move on to the topic of your choice.
2. Start talking along with the candidate and redirect the conversation to a new area. Keep talking until the candidate shuts up, which should be in the first few seconds.

Either way, recognize that if you have difficulty controlling the candidate now, when he is arguably on his best behavior, your problem is likely to grow exponentially once he's comfortably employed and on the payroll.

If the flow of conversation is focused on the issues, that's one thing (you might have an energetic ADHD candidate who, with the right guidance, can and will move mountains for you). On the other hand, some people just need to talk, and they will latch onto any topic, expanding the range of that conversation for as long as their audience will allow. Hired, this kind of candidate (very different from the consciously focused ADHD candidate) can be a nightmare. For instance, when things go wrong (as they do in even the best-run departments) you will have a prime candidate for stirring the pot of contention rather than putting out the flames—he may even have been the genesis of the problem in the first place. Think carefully about such candidates.

Master these question and conversational control tactics, and your interviews will proceed in the direction you want and deliver the information you need to make objective decisions about job candidates at any level.

Next Steps

In this chapter we have been talking about interview structure and the tactics to manage the flow of information gathering within that structure. It's time to wind down an interview once you have completed your considered agenda of topics and questions. You can do so with, "This has been a very interesting meeting; do you have anything to add?" This gives the candidate the opportunity to add additional information that she thinks might be valuable. You could also ask, "Do you have any questions?" All too often this leads to queries about salary, vacation, and benefits; but you have to give the candidate an opportunity to ask questions. However, you are not obliged to discuss these issues until you are ready, so you can answer in the most general of terms. If salary comes up, you can reply with, "I don't think we are at the point where I am in a position to know if you are right for the job yet or what a competitive salary would be. And I don't think you know enough about the job or our company to evaluate such an offer. I'd prefer to leave it until we are a little further along." This will shut just about anyone up. With questions about benefits, refer the candidate to the appropriate party in HR.

At the end of an interview, you need to identify the next steps. If you want to see the candidate again, or have him meet with other staff members, either do it now, or schedule the next meeting (we'll address multiple interviews in the next chapter). If you do not wish to proceed further, bail out now, using the phrases we discussed earlier. Alternatively, you can have HR send a polite rejection letter (be sure to understand and follow HR procedures where they exist), or you can send the letter yourself.

SIX

MULTIPLE INTERVIEWS AND SECOND OPINIONS

Just how many interviews and interviewers does it take to make a good hire? Assuming good planning and organization, it all depends on the complexity/importance/seniority of the job. With many lower-level jobs you may be able to gather all the information necessary for an informed decision from one carefully structured interview. However, more complex and senior-level jobs will require additional interviews—and often additional interview*ers*—before you can make a sound hiring decision.

However, using multiple interviewers can be tricky. Unless the goals of each progressive interview—and the tools to reach those goals—are carefully established, you end up getting a candidate answering the same questions again and again for different interviewers.

You can make good hiring decisions on most job titles from two or three carefully structured interviews, even interviews at the VP level. C-level may run to five or six, at least one of these being the formal approval by the selection committee. We are going to talk about a three-interview cycle, because it will cover the vast number of interview situations, and because more senior positions will still be based on this three-interview foundation, with additional layers added to the end of the process as necessary.

Most interviews, like meetings, are more productive when a maximum time limit of ninety minutes is established in your mind; it keeps you focused, and besides, as the interviewer, it's your ball-game and you can always take the meeting into overtime when circumstances justify it. With self-imposed limits like these, you *decide* what to do, rather than just being carried along by events beyond your control.

Using Second Opinions

Time and again managers hear: "Will you spend a few minutes with this candidate and tell me what you think?" These additional opinions are sought at least in part because everyone is reluctant to make a wrong decision, and other opinions help spread blame and diffuse responsibility. Let's freeze the stage for a moment during a typical "multiple" interview selection cycle, walk around the desk, and think of the last few selection cycles where you were the interviewee.

1. You went to a first interview, where someone walked you through your resume and asked some questions about your skills, greatest strengths and weaknesses, why you left your last job, and why you are interested in this job. *You stumbled a bit over greatest strengths and weaknesses, why you left your last job, and why you are interested in this job.*

2. You made it to the second interview, where someone else walked you through your resume and asked pretty much the same questions about your skills, greatest strengths and weaknesses, why you left your last job, and why you are interested in this job. *You were a lot better answering questions about greatest strengths and weaknesses, why you left your last job, and why you are interested in this job.*

3. You made it to the third interview, this time perhaps with the CEO, where she walked you through your resume, asked pretty much the same questions about your skills, greatest strengths and weaknesses, why you left your last job, and why you are interested in this job. *You nailed every one of them.*

This is why requesting that your boss or a colleague give you a second opinion usually results in putting candidates through virtually the same interview repeatedly while gathering no new information.

The only way to avoid this is by giving them some insight into the information you need. This includes adequate advance notice of the interview, a detailed JD and resume, insight into the areas of examination you are interested in, and a rundown of the kind of information/questions you'd like answered.

If more than one interview is necessary, decide who should do it and why. If you still have a lot of uncharted territory to cover because of the complexity of the job, you should be conducting as many of the interviews as you need to in order to get a complete and objective picture of each real contender. In special circumstances—for instance, if you are doing succession grooming—you can train a team member to conduct the first interview of a series, particularly if you are already confident in that person's effectiveness at conducting telephone interviews.

If you do the first interview and want to get second opinions on the final two or three candidates, perhaps a good choice is another manager with whom you have a reciprocal arrangement and whose department regularly does business with yours, giving him a frame of reference for your opening from the outset. In addition, you both benefit from helping your departments work more productively together.

It's more productive if you build an interviewing team that you can use for all your department's hires, always giving participating colleagues adequate notice for interviews and confirming that they can make the time to gather the information you require. It's a given that you will conduct a briefing with each interviewer; this will include providing *copies* of your JD, resumes, application forms, and any notes about areas covered to date. You will get the best results when each interviewer has specific areas to cover (you can supply some questions) and knows what insights you expect. When you give colleagues clear expectations and the tools to deliver on them, you help them become more productive interviewers and you are more likely to get what you seek, plus you expand your professional credibility and gain influence.

Your aim is not to get a view of the candidate that merely confirms a hunch; rather you want to get different photographs from different angles taken through different lenses. When you assign specific and different topic areas to interview team members, everyone can cover different ground, and provide you with a more three-dimensional view of a candidate. This is the best way to see the candidate as a whole and make a considered judgment.

There will be times when you want your team to repeat certain questions, in order to see whether you are all getting the same answer. This is a good idea when you are uncomfortable with an answer, suspect an evasion, or find an inconsistency in the candidate's reasons for leaving jobs.

When Using Coworkers in Selection

When you involve a candidate's potential peers in the selection process, you have to be careful in clearly defining the areas you want addressed or avoided. Whereas management traditionally sticks to the same six or eight questions, peers, if left to their own devices, usually restrict themselves to three: "What's your greatest weakness?"; "How much are you making?"; and "How much do you want?" I'm exaggerating, but you get the point. Questions like these can be harmful to your team-building efforts if you make the hire. With direct reports, you can feel comfortable being specific about the questions you want them to ask and the information you expect to receive.

The Three-Interview Selection Cycle

Let's look at a schematic of what might be addressed in a selection sequence of three interviews, recognizing that this is intended merely as a guideline for you to adapt to your unique needs.

The First Interview: Ability

A first interview should focus on *ability* in critical functional areas: Are the "must have" skills of the job and their expected *deliverables* present? Do they collectively suggest that the candidate can do the job?

You will want to look for the *transferable skills and professional values* as they relate to each critical aspect of the job, as their presence will help you sort the winners from the "also rans." You want to feel comfortable about relative strengths and weaknesses in these critical areas.

Make sure you have answers to all of your knockout questions, find out why the candidate wants to leave the current job, what she knows about you, and why you are perceived as a suitable potential employer.

The first interview in a sequence becomes a major part of your winnowing process. It should be short, never more than an hour—and when you are organized, and depending on the seniority of the position, it can often be accomplished in half that time.

The Second Interview: Motivation

A second interview will continue to examine skills but should be clearly focused on *motivation*—what makes this particular candidate tick. To do this, continue to examine the *technical skills* of the job and their resulting *deliverables*, along with the *transferable skills and professional values* that empower successful execution of duties and *deliverables*. If the first interview was performed by HR or delegated to a trusted team leader, you come in at the second level to recheck any area you feel is worthy of your attention. In addition to other factors already mentioned, you might want to address how the job relates to the goals of the department and in turn the department's role in supporting the corporation's goals.

When candidates make it to the second round of interviews, they should be real contenders, and as such you begin to pay a little more attention to courtship. Now could be the time for a tour of the facility, as opposed to a walk about the immediate workplace. If your company hasn't obtained permission to check references (required under the 1970 Fair Credit Reporting Act), get it now. Normally, the permission is included in the application and granted by the candidate's signature, but you should inspect your company's forms to make sure. The end of the second round of interviews should result in only two or at most three final contenders coming back for a third and final interview.

The Third Interview: Manageability and Teamwork

The third interview should re-examine any skill issues or other unresolved questions, and present an opportunity to talk about *responsibilities* and expectations in terms of the projects with which the candidate will be involved right away. This is the time for any "rubber-stamp" meetings with higher-ups (be sure to prep them succinctly and accurately beforehand; it's an opportunity for you to gain a little bit of credibility and visibility), and gives you a chance to parade the corporate colors and dazzle the candidate with the company's eminent desirability. You want these final candidates to be ready to accept an offer if proffered.

Simultaneously, you will have mined questions about *teamwork* and *manageability* from the following chapters and will weave them into this interview. You will have gained insight on these issues from answers to questions in earlier interviews, but in this third and usually final interview you should pose some specific *team spirit* and *manageability* questions. You handle these issues last, not because they are of lesser importance but because from a time-management perspective they only become relevant once *ability* and *motivation* have been ascertained.

During the third interview there are some definite musts. Be sure that all of your remaining short-list candidates understand how your company makes money and their prospective role in the process. Explain what will be expected of the future employee during this interview, which is when candidates are likely to be most receptive. Take the time to outline the department's mission; these goals and objectives form the umbrella for the future employee's responsibilities. Your clear statement of expectations at this time will build the candidate's confidence in your leadership, the job, and the company. This is also the time when you open up and sell the pluses related to working with this company.

Multiple Interview Time Frames

Multiple interviews can take place over a day, a few days, or a few weeks. While there may be enough time to do it in one day, it is rarely practical, except at lower levels. Such a restricted time frame limits the ability of your interviewing team to give each other leads and feedback on interesting areas to examine further. Whenever multiple interviews must take place in a single day, give the candidate time to regroup every now and then in a private office with something to drink. You can use this time to caucus with your team and strategize based on the direction the interview is taking.

If you have to drag out the hiring process over an extended period, keep your short-list candidates fully informed. Otherwise, that ideal candidate will be long gone when you are ready to extend an offer. Perhaps your particular situation requires *less* than three interviews to make a prudent decision on the short-list contenders; it is, however, unlikely that it will require *more* than three when you engage in effective planning.

The Power Luncheon

It may be desirable (*social graces* are an important determinant of success) or necessary (you gotta eat sometime) that one of the interviews take place in a public setting. A luncheon or similar quasi-social meeting can be a good opportunity to gain additional information that would be difficult to obtain in the formality of most offices. You can learn much of value and gain insight into the candidate's personality while to all appearances indulging in the simple delights of the table.

Job candidates are likely to be nervous eating in front of you; throw a question-and-answer dimension in, and you have a ready-made *stress* element built in. Even without the questioning, these occasions give you the opportunity to look for the presence or absence of appropriate *social graces*.

Ordering the most expensive and exotic foods on the menu is an obvious sign of a candidate's doubtful judgment and emotional immaturity. What do you think about a person who is profligate with company money before even reaching the formality of being on the payroll? What is your travel and entertainment budget going to look like? You might also note insecurity and free-floating hostility when your guest starts returning the ice water.

The candidate is there primarily to talk and be judged, which is another reason for remembering the 80/20 rule on these occasions. That ratio lets you eat quite decently as you listen to the candidate answering your questions.

For any meal interview, you should choose a restaurant you know and at which you are known. Book a secluded table, ideally in a corner, and explain the importance of this when you make the reservation. Allow your candidate the privilege of sitting with his back to the wall, which can make him feel more secure. You might also ask whether the candidate is comfortable with the choice of restaurant; this is intended to show consideration for the candidate's privacy. You want the candidate to bare the innermost reaches of his soul, which won't happen if he feels nervous about current employers appearing. It also shows consideration for dietary restrictions: kosher, vegetarian, etc.

In vino veritas, so offer drinks; you may well have made prior arrangements for your gin and tonic to be absent the gin. To increase privacy and avoid interruptions, order all your food at the beginning of the meal. With these simple matters taken care of, you can get down to the questions.

Competent Interviewers

Becoming a competent interviewer takes time and effort, but the lessons you have to learn are logical and commonsense: To make good hiring decisions, you need a plan of attack and a structure that offers a flexible approach to understanding a candidate's *responsibilities* and *deliverables, transferable skills and professional values, motivation,* and *teamwork* and *manageability*. A structure that ensures you cover all the necessary bases, all the time, encourages objectivity in your evaluations.

We're now ready to look at the actual questions you will use to ensure that you can live by that 80/20 rule while you gather all the intelligence to make smart hiring decisions based on *ability, motivation*, and *teamwork* and *manageability*.

PART II
PRACTICAL STRATEGIES FOR EFFECTIVE SELECTION

This section breaks smart hires down into seven logical principles, then introduces a logical three-interview selection cycle that delivers on them. Each interview in the cycle addresses candidate evaluation in a specific area: *ability* to do the job, *motivation*, and finally *manageability* and *team spirit*. It is an approach that supports good *time management* and avoids duplication.

While the questions in each chapter focus on gathering insight into a particular area, many will simultaneously yield insight about a potential match or mismatch in the other areas as well. For example, when you know exactly what you are looking for, the answer to a question about *problem identification, prevention, and solution* in the *ability* chapter may well give you insights into *motivation* or *manageability*.

SEVEN

The Seven Secrets Behind Successful Hires

Before you look at the wide range of interview questions in the following chapters—questions that will fuel an effective selection process and enable you to make wise hiring decisions—let's take a moment to consolidate the information discussed so far into seven commonsense principles: the backbone of a practical and effective selection strategy.

These are the seven commonsense principles that successful hiring managers apply when hiring for any job, at any level, in every profession; and, given that *Knock 'em Dead: Hiring the Best* has stayed in print for thirty years (through six editions) and has been published in many foreign language editions, I think it is reasonable to suggest that this globally proven approach will probably work for you too.

The First Principle: Jobs Exist to Make Money

Companies come into existence to make money by delivering services or products that are beyond the scope of individual effort. Staff is added depending on the complexity of the services and products delivered, their concomitant challenges, and the company's success in surmounting them. Staff at any level is only ever added to the payroll for one reason: *to help the company make money*. Whatever the job title, however humble or exalted, you can think of that job as a small but important cog in the complex moneymaking machinery of the corporation. A job is added to the payroll only when the costs of hiring and paying someone for it are outweighed by its contribution to the bottom line, through bringing money into the company, saving time, saving money, or otherwise increasing productivity.

Each cog has a specific set of *responsibilities* and contributions to make (*deliverables*), and in doing so it must mesh seamlessly with all the other cogs, working in harmony to deliver results made possible only by their combined effort.

The Second Principle: You Must Manage Your Time

There are a number of interwoven considerations that go into your hiring decisions, but they fall into three broad categories:

1. Ability
2. Motivation
3. Manageability

They are all important, but from a commonsense and time-management perspective, a candidate's motivation is irrelevant if she does not have the ability to do the work. Taking this thought further, you obviously want to hire a candidate who is *manageable* (it's a "must have" consideration). However, from a time-management perspective, *manageability* only becomes relevant when *ability* to do the work has been established and the *motivation* to do it is evident. This prioritization of activities based on time-management principles should impact every consideration and action throughout any selection process.

The Third Principle: You Must Determine Ability and Suitability

The most vital of these considerations is *ability* and *suitability*.

1. First and foremost, a hiring manager needs to determine that the candidate has the *ability* to do the work: that a candidate possesses the *technical skills* necessary to execute the job's *responsibilities* and deliver the results that are the very reason for the job's existence (its *deliverables*). Without these *abilities*, nothing else matters.

2. If a candidate has the *ability* to do the work, you can move forward; if not, you should bail out immediately. In addition to the *technical skills* required for fulfillment of the basic *responsibilities* of the position, a *suitable* candidate ideally has industry-specific knowledge of your business sector and of the industries you interact with—or else she can get up to speed on these issues quickly.

For example, with a computer programmer, *ability* to do the job is defined by *technical skills*, specifically her *ability* to write good code for specific applications in one or more programming languages. This candidate is *able* to do a code-writing job, but in addition, she becomes more *suitable* for such a job within, say, the banking industry, if she has an understanding of *how banking works*—how and why things get done the way they do in the banking world.

A knowledge of banking isn't needed to write code, but you might get much better code if you *can* find a computer programmer who has a frame of reference for how the industry works, understands the challenges that lead to things being done in certain ways, knows how and why departments and companies interact in the ways they do, and speaks the banking jargon that has evolved to speed *communication* on these and other issues. This is why you look for *ability* first and *suitability* second.

Industry Bias

You look for *ability* and *suitability* in a candidate, but you won't always find it in the proportions you had hoped for, so how important is the mixture? You could say a computer programmer doesn't need to know banking: She can pick that up fairly quickly. It's the programming skills that are important. I don't disagree, but if you worked in banking and had to pick between two programmers with equal *technical skills, transferable skills and professional values*, and other requirements—identical, in short, except for the fact that one candidate comes from banking and the other from the oil and gas sector—which would you choose? It's a no-brainer: You'd choose the one who knows your business. Don't ignore candidates from other industries: A superior candidate from another industry is better than an inferior one from your own. Just treat *suitability* as a tiebreaker when there's little else to choose between candidates.

Suitability and Industry Bias

Every industry develops distinctive characteristics in response to the unique qualities of the service it delivers to customers. Most companies are engaged in industry-specific methodologies and challenges, and there are always idiosyncratic situations that arise from the nature of that industry's product or service. Industries naturally develop their own languages, priorities, and *ways of doing things* (*systems and procedures*) in response to the unique needs of their customer base.

Industry bias springs from your legitimate concerns about a candidate's understanding of the building blocks of commerce in your particular industry: the jargon, the myriad problems likely to crop up on the job every day, and the working relationships necessary to execute on the company's promise of an excellent service or product. A candidate who doesn't *understand the language* of your industry might not be sensitive to the specific issues and the methodologies developed to deal with them.

However, all factors being equal, if a candidate from another industry sector shows an understanding of your industry and what she must do to adapt, there is no reason she should not be a top contender. It is a well-known fact that many breakthroughs, ideas, approaches, and patents are made by people on the very periphery of an area of knowledge, because they come to old problems with fresh eyes and are unencumbered by the stultifying weight of conventional wisdom.

The Fourth Principle: Every Job Is about Problem Anticipation, Prevention, and Solution

Whatever the job title, the candidate you hire is there to *anticipate, prevent, and solve problems* within his area of expertise, and thus contribute to *productivity*. Your task at a job interview is to discover to what degree each candidate understands that the job is about *solving problems*.

There are two considerations here:

1. Does the candidate understand her professional *responsibilities* well enough to *anticipate* these problems as they lurk beyond the horizon, and execute his *responsibilities* in a manner that will often *prevent* them from arising in the first place?
2. Does the candidate understand his professional *responsibilities* well enough to *recognize* the problems that crop up every day of the week, and *solve* them when they do?

The Fifth Principle: Transferable Skills and Professional Values Are the Foundations of Professional Success

Professionalism exceeds the bounds of white- versus blue-collar work; professionals and professionalism are not determined by job title. Professionals are people who *behave* in certain predictable, effective, and honorable ways:

- Professionals have sound *technical skills* that allow them to do the job *productively*; they have good *problem-solving/critical thinking, communication*, and *multitasking skills*; and they demonstrate *leadership* in their activities—all skills that combine to encourage *teamwork* and *creativity*.
- Professionals also share certain values: They are *motivated, energetic*, and want to make a difference with their presence. They are *determined, reliable*, and *productive*; they take pride in their

work, and their personal *integrity* means they play by the rules and understand the need for *systems and procedures*.

Your task from the hiring side of the desk is to tie the relative importance of each of these *transferable skills and professional values* to the *responsibilities* and *deliverables* of the job you are hiring for and determine their presence by direct questioning and observation.

The Sixth Principle: The Best Employee Has Motivation to Do the Job—Whatever It Takes

You are looking for someone who is *committed* to his job and profession for the long haul, someone who understands the guts of the job, warts and all. *Intelligent enthusiasm* is expressed by more than smiles and a candidate saying she wants the job; it is expressed by her deep understanding and respect for the work and its challenges, her obvious relish in tackling those challenges every day, and the willingness to take the rough with the smooth that goes with every job.

This *intelligent enthusiasm*, or *motivation*, becomes visible through the candidate's degree of engagement with the work, and this can be seen in her answers, body language, and questions. Intelligent questions display a depth of understanding of the job that responses to your questions alone cannot. In a tightly run job race, when there is nothing to choose between two top candidates, the job offer should go to the most *intelligently enthusiastic* candidate.

The Seventh Principle: You Should Hire Manageable Team Players

A manageable employee is someone who is willing to work as part of a team, to get along with others regardless of their sex, sexual orientation, age, religion, physical appearance, abilities or disabilities, skin color, or national origin—in other words, someone who has the *emotional maturity* to deal with others as professional colleagues and doesn't allow negative social preconceptions to color those relationships.

Working on a team takes patience, balance, tolerance, and an ability to assert your personality without overpowering everyone else's. A good employee doesn't have to *like* everyone on his team; but he does have to make the effort to *work* with them productively. *Teamwork*, that ability to function as a productive member of a team, is critical, because many of the contributions your department must make toward the smooth running of the corporate machine are beyond the scope of individual contribution.

Putting It All Together

Organizing and executing the steps of employee selection with the *seven principles* always in mind is a way of keeping the bigger picture in focus while drilling down into those details of the candidate's experience as they relate to performing successfully in the job. Constant awareness of the *seven principles* helps you ensure that a candidate's *ability*, *suitability*, and *motivation* are supported by the appropriate *transferable skills and professional values*. The ideal candidate is aware of the *problems* the job is there to *anticipate, prevent, and solve*, and can generate viable approaches to doing so. Finally, you are looking for all these tangible assets in a person who can get along with others and take direction: a *manageable team player*. In the next three chapters you'll see it all unfold in a logical and practical manner.

EIGHT

THE FIRST INTERVIEW: ABILITY

Any first interview is concerned with determining *ability*; nothing else is relevant until the candidate proves she has the *ability* to do the job, and if *ability* is lacking, you can save time and frustration by bowing out with one of the diplomatic approaches I suggested in the telephone interview chapter.

Finding someone who can actually do the job is different from finding someone with a nice-looking resume that seems to say he can do the job. A firm grasp of the relevant *technical skills* is of course a prerequisite, but so is an *ability* and willingness to make good on the job's *deliverables*. This brings us to the problems the position exists to *anticipate, prevent, and solve*. As you walk through the questions that address a candidate's *ability*, you should keep an eye out for the *transferable skills and professional values* that are the functional underpinnings of success in that activity.

So when you ask questions to determine *ability*, you are looking for information on a number of levels: *ability* to do the job, an awareness of the professional context in which the job exists, and the capacity to *anticipate, prevent, and solve problems*. All the information you gather about a person's *ability* to do the job will be supported by her development of the relevant *transferable skills and professional values* that empower her to do it well.

In most instances, the most valuable and relevant information will come from the last seven to ten years or last three jobs, whichever comes first. The pace of technology is such that anything beyond ten

123

years ago is going to be largely irrelevant to today's workplace. Consequently, the sole aim of most questions about the distant past is to establish depth of experience.

Of course, with management hires, you will be searching for the progression that led to management and the growth and presence of the practical management skills that empower that management candidate to *get work done through others*.

Get the Candidate Used to Talking

Each hiring situation is different, so there is no set sequence to follow, no perfectly formulated set of questions to ask. The question sequences in this and all of the following chapters have been organized to proceed logically, but they are only meant to be a template that you can adapt to your unique needs and to the information-gathering style that works for you.

No two people have the same speech rhythms or vocabulary. The way you phrase a question, and the tone of voice you use in asking it, will give your questions their own range and depth, so you will naturally customize the questions to suit your particular style and the needs of the position you are trying to fill.

When you start an interview with questions that are easy to answer, it helps the candidate relax, and helps you to hit your interviewing stride: asking questions twenty percent of the time and listening for eighty percent. As the past is less threatening for the candidate than the present, begin with questions about career history and professional growth.

Basic Responsibilities

This first sequence of questions examines the candidate's *responsibilities*. These questions may help you gain insight into skills, special knowledge, and relative strengths and weaknesses. You can repeat this particular sequence as required for every job the candidate has held. The cumulative result will be a clear picture of the candidate's essential "can do" abilities. You may have asked some of these questions during the telephone interview, but it doesn't hurt to go over them again in greater detail, especially as they concern the candidate's current job.

"Tell me a little about yourself."

You want the candidate to get his vocal cords working. How he answers can tell you something about his general professional awareness. Hopefully he'll give an answer that succinctly captures his professional history and justifies his presence at the interview.

"What do you know about our company?"

The answer gives you a frame of reference for how you need to phrase ensuing questions. Some candidates will know nothing, others will know more than you do. The answer also tells you about Internet research skills and *motivation*. In a world where research is so easy, what does not knowing anything about your company say about *motivation*?

"What aspects of your work do you consider most crucial?"

All jobs exist to support profitability in some way; they generate revenue, protect assets, improve *productivity*, or perhaps combine these imperatives. By asking this question, you want to find out if the candidate understands this basic fact about the world of work and therefore grasps the reasons for the job's existence.

When you can quickly establish that a candidate understands the *responsibilities* of the job, you can move ahead to analyze her understanding of the *problems* that crop up regularly within her areas of expertise and get in the way of the job's *deliverables*. You can walk through these *deliverables* and *problem-solving activities* with reference to the candidate's previous work history with questions like:

- *"Tell me about your duties in* [specific area]. *"*
- *"What kind of problems typically cropped up in* [specific area]*?"*

- *"In what ways do you work to prevent such problems arising in the first place?"*
- *"How do you go about solving* [specific problem] *when it does crop up?"*

With all these questions you are hoping to identify candidates who understand that the heart of their *responsibilities* is not just executing their duties when all is going well, but understanding their professional landscape well enough to *identify, prevent, and solve problems* when they do occur.

Follow up questions like these with:

"What special skills or knowledge did you need to perform [this duty]?"

This follow-up question seeks to gather information about the *transferable skills and professional values* that a candidate might employ in delivering desirable outcomes on his *responsibilities*.

If, in response to questions concerning special knowledge needed to perform a specific duty, the candidate responds in terms of education, look for any courses or seminars to which a prior employer may have sent her. This kind of information is useful to you in a couple of ways: First, it tells you that the candidate, or a prior employer, felt that this education was a good investment of time and money, which is an endorsement in itself; second, it tells you that such an investment won't have to be made on your budget.

"Describe your typical day for me. What problems do you normally experience in getting things done?"

Better to ask this question rather than the common *"What is your energy level like?"*, which is asking for a reply that would put a triathlete to shame. The description of a typical workday and the problems it typically delivers will tell you about the candidate's understanding of the job's real *deliverables*, planning, *multitasking*, and, of course, *energy* . . . which, without efficient use of time, isn't a whole lot of good to anyone.

Delving Deeper Into Ability, Achievements, and Boundaries of Responsibility

Most first interviews will be a walk through each of the most important functions of the last three jobs and their resultant *deliverables* (as determined by you and your JDD, and *not* by the candidate), interspersed with follow-up questions that probe the candidate's possession of the relevant *transferable skills and professional values*. However, there are a few other questions you may wish to ask at this first meeting.

You can ask the following questions about major duties on any job, but they'll be most valuable when the duties under examination relate directly to your critical needs.

"When did you join your last company?"

This question will be followed by, *"What was your title when you joined?"* and *"What was your starting salary?"* Together, these three questions help to set a tone for the meeting. They show that you intend to get specific answers. Immediately, the candidate will realize that you are someone who expects, and has the inspection tools to get, the facts. The salary questions asked for each job—*"What was your starting salary?"*; *"How much were you making when you left?"*—show you the type of raises this person is likely to be satisfied with and the level of salary increase she is in the habit of accepting when making a job change. Sudden jumps in earnings can alert you to potential untruths. For example, when a person with a history of 5 percent increases suddenly makes a 20 percent jump, one of two things has happened: Either the individual is fudging the truth, or she has started to achieve way above prior performance levels, perhaps making a major contribution to an employer. Whichever is the case, you will want to know.

However, because just about everyone has fudged on earnings every now and then, you may want to limit the number of black marks you award; it is up to you. Many managers simply use the exercise to establish a truthful pattern in the candidate's answers, and when they come across a fudge of this nature prefer to let the candidate off the hook with some dignity by saying, "That is such a big increase that perhaps I should have made myself more clear. I am just looking for salary, not the value of your benefit package as well."

"Why did you leave [that company/that job]?"

This is one of the world's most popular—and usually least effective—interview questions. On its own, it has become ineffective through overuse; almost every job interviewee has a pat and acceptable answer ready. That's okay, because you can use this question to set up another question. The follow-up is less common and more likely to get you an honest answer:

"In what ways did/does your boss contribute to your desire to leave this/ that job?"

Now, while this question fits very neatly in the procedure of establishing work history and general *ability* to do a job, it also sheds light on potential *manageability* and *emotional maturity*.

If a candidate tells you he was laid off, it bears further examination. There are only two ways to leave a job: You either quit or get terminated. That termination might be for cause (burning down the company cafeteria) or, increasingly, due to company downsizing and offshoring; it might just be that the candidate was in the wrong place at the wrong time. Whichever it is, you need to know.

Whatever the explanation, you will want to verify it when you check references. If the candidate explains that she was fired, you'll ask, *"Why were you fired?"* and listen very carefully to the answer. Watch for the finger of blame. When we point the finger of blame we often ignore the three fingers pointing back at ourselves. Firing an employee is usually one of the most unpleasant jobs a manager will ever have to do, and because of legal ramifications it is not a decision that is ever taken lightly. If there has been a termination with cause and the candidate has taken responsibility and made changes as a result, you shouldn't necessarily rule that person out; we all make mistakes, and we can all learn from them.

Many managers have confided in me that they sometimes find that these reason-for-leaving questions throw a candidate off balance, and they want to know how best to get the interviewee back on track. This problem is neatly solved by asking, *"How did you get your last job?"* Answering this question relaxes the candidate after the difficulty of talking about unemployment or job change. The answer can also profile the candidate's *determination*, *creativity*, and the *critical thinking skills* used in *problem solving*, which are three character traits common to many successful professionals.

"What decisions or judgment calls do you have to make in your job?"
Also:
"Which of these decisions or judgment calls are most challenging?"
The answer to this question tells you about the individual's level of responsibility and the *critical thinking* processes engaged in decision making. It could be useful to know that a candidate routinely makes decisions alone that in your department would require consultation. When you identify decision-making responsibility in a candidate's background, it can be helpful to follow up with a question like, *"That's interesting. Tell me how you would approach making a decision if* [present a decision-making scenario common to the job]. *"* You can add a *situational* follow-up question here: *"Can you tell me about a time when you had to make a judgment call like this?"* You want a candidate who can discuss the root of the problem, its significance, and its potential negative impact on the department/company. She should be able to explain her solution, its value to her employer, and its difference from other possible approaches. You may need to outline these issues in follow-up questions.

"What achievements are you most proud of in this particular area?"
People are always happy to talk about their achievements, and you are happy to listen for what the answers can tell you: You want to hear about something at the core of the job and central to its success, where the candidate was part of a team working on some larger project beyond the scope of individual contribution, or where she

accepted responsibility for some dirty/ignored project that nevertheless had importance for the success of her department. Be alert for exaggerated claims, and if you sense possible exaggeration, ask about the role of others in this achievement.

You can position this question as the first part of a two-part probe, the second part being, *"Tell me about a problem you experienced in this area, something you found difficult to handle."* This is a *behavioral* question introducing a *negative balance* dimension, because whenever you give a candidate the chance to dazzle you with excellence, you should give yourself the chance to balance that view. The mettle of a candidate can often be best judged by his handling of adversity, and while your question is primarily concerned with *ability*, the answer will also tell you something about *motivation*.

If the candidate gives an answer that's a red flag, probe further with a *negative confirmation* question: *"Thank you. Now can you give me another example?"*

"Tell me about the most difficult project you've tackled."
Also:
"What is the most difficult situation you have faced?"
"Tell me about an event that really challenged you. How did you meet the challenge? In what way was your approach different from that of others?"
You want to discover:

- If the candidate has experience relative to your current projects
- How she handled difficult projects in her last job

These are *behavioral* questions, so you want specifics tied to a date and place. Encourage candidates to outline a particular project and identify its challenges (in reasonable detail), the *critical thinking* process used to isolate the causes of the *problem* and possible *solutions*, a description of the implementation of the solution, and the value it delivered to the employer.

"What are you looking for in your next job?"

Answers you *are* looking for will deal with learned and earned growth and professional fulfillment. You want someone who understands that the good things come from a *commitment* to the success of the company and the *team*. Answers you are *not* looking for: "more money, a raise, and a boss who stays off my ass." You may or may not want to hire someone whose next step up is your job, depending on whether you're working toward a promotion yourself and need to groom a successor.

"What do you spend most of your time on, and why?"

A good answer will show an understanding of the job's priorities and address the *deliverables* you targeted in your JDD work, but this question also looks at the candidate's *multitasking* abilities. Is this someone who can handle the pressure of the multiple and competing directives that are common in most professional jobs today, and who has a considered approach to *time-management and organization* issues, or is she someone likely to run from task to task in response to the loudest siren without reference to the priorities of the job? The latter type of employee is not going to be someone who turns in projects complete and on time.

"What are your special qualifications for this job?"

The candidate's understanding of the job and its priorities is the focus here. You're looking for relevant experience and possession of the *technical skills* to do the job, plus some awareness of the most applicable *transferable skills and professional values*.

"How do you stay current?"

We live in an age of technological innovation, in which the nature of every job is changing as quickly as you turn these pages. Candidates who engage in ongoing professional development activities demonstrate an awareness of this fact and a *commitment* to staying current professionally. Look for:

- Courses the candidate has taken or is planning to take
- Additional degrees pursued
- Membership in professional associations
- Subscriptions to professional journals or online professional groups
- Profession-relevant books she has read or is reading

"What are some of the problems you encounter in doing your job, and what do you do about them?"

This is a question with a trap. Remember the old saying, "A poor workman blames his tools"? When you ask this question you invite the unsuspecting candidate to do precisely that. If the trick works, pat yourself on the back for flushing out an unsuitable applicant.

A good answer will address *problem identification, prevention, and solution*, giving you examples as part of the answer.

"How do you manage your work deadlines?"

Also:

"How did you feel about your workload at that company?"
"How did you divide your time among your major areas of responsibility?"
"With all of your responsibilities, how do you plan and organize your workload?"

These questions all represent different ways of examining the *time-management and organizational abilities* that enable the ultimate holder of your job to *multitask* productively. An ideal candidate will articulate some version of the Plan/Do/Review cycle we discussed back in Chapter 2. She sets aside time at the end of every day to review that day's activities and plan tomorrow's. She prioritizes all the planned activities and sticks to those priorities to make sure the important work is attended to first.

While you may well decide to probe *multitasking* more closely later in the interview cycle, these questions will logically fit into the conversational flow at this juncture.

"What was more important on your job, written or oral communication?"

You will receive input on *verbal communication skills* throughout the interview. Though the quality of *verbal skills* can be a predictor of *writing skills*, written communication is more of a challenge. The higher up the professional ladder, the more important *written communication* becomes. The resume, cover letter, and subsequent communications that the candidate sends can give you insight here. You might request that the candidate send you a follow-up letter about his interest in the job to see *writing skills* at work, and you'll pay attention to all e-mails received during your conversations to get additional insight. You might also examine comprehension of business practices and *critical thinking skills* (and utilize some *situational* interviewing tactics) by having the candidate encapsulate a long report, or tell you which of two reports is the best and why. Nothing's better than seeing *communication* in action.

When *writing skills* are important, you can ask, *"What was the most complex report you ever had to write?"* and follow up with, *"What made this report so difficult? How did you handle it?"* Then conclude with, *"Looking back, how would you have improved it/made it easier to understand?"*

"What other functional, day-to-day activities were you involved with that we haven't discussed?"

All of the questions in this section, when tailored to your individual circumstances, will help you determine *ability*, and of course, you'll find many more in the balance of the book. As the interviewer, however, it is unwise to leave this topic of *technical skills* without throwing in this last catchall question that allows the candidate to bring up skills and attributes that may not have surfaced so far in your conversation.

How Long Will the New Employee Stay?

Hiring is usually done in the hope that you will land the perfect employee, someone who will serve faithfully down through the years as your star rises to the corporate heavens. Usually such dreams are shattered when a valued employee unexpectedly pulls up stakes and moves on. With that in mind, it is a good idea to examine all of the candidate's reasons for leaving jobs in the past. That knowledge of the past can help us predict, and therefore avoid, unpleasant problems in the future. The answers you receive will also help give you a handle on *motivation* and *manageability* issues, because you'll learn what it will take to get the best out of this person and keep her happily productive for as long as possible.

You cannot hope to hold on to employees forever without helping them achieve what they need to live successful and fulfilled lives, so it is worth noting that the Bureau of Labor Statistics says that the average staff member can be expected to stay with you for about four-and-a-half years. These numbers have held fairly steady for many years, though there are important demographic variations: Younger workers tend to move on more quickly and older workers to stay with an employer almost three times as long as the national average.

"If you went to your boss for a raise, why would you be doing it?"

This may seem like a strange place to start this line of questioning, but keep in mind that anyone who asks for a salary or performance review feels a real or perceived lack of recognition and appreciation. It's often said that loyalty is a function of appreciation.

Watch out for answers such as, "I deserve it." What you want to hear are citations of solid contributions that demonstrate that the individual has the department's interests at heart. Often, the response will lead you naturally into a discussion about the reasons behind a candidate's desire to make a job change. If not, ask:

"Why do you want to change jobs at this time?"

Acceptable reasons for job change generally fall under the LAMPS acronym:

- **L**ocation: The commute was unreasonably long.
- **A**dvancement: The candidate wasn't able to grow professionally in that position, either because there were others ahead of him or there was no opportunity for growth.
- **M**oney: The candidate was underpaid for her skills and contribution.
- **P**ride or prestige: The candidate wanted to be with a better company.
- **S**ecurity: The company was not stable.

"Why have you changed jobs so frequently?"

It costs money to hire and bring someone up to speed on a new job, so unless there are solid reasons for a candidate's job-hopping—and in today's workplace there often are—you won't want to invest valuable resources on a person who is likely to stay with you only a short while.

On the other end of the spectrum you might find that a candidate has been with one company for many years. In this case you might ask, *"Why, after all these years, are you changing jobs now?"*

The question will come as such a shock that it will give you a good read on the applicant's quick thinking and poise. You can, of course, temper the question to suit the situation, the job, and your personality.

When you have walked the candidate through her work history, you reach the first formal decision-making, or bail-out, point. You may have reached it even sooner, and if so it is perfectly okay to end the interview there. If the candidate can't do the job, or you have already seen four more who are better qualified, bail out now using the same techniques employed during the telephone interview.

Not Everyone with the Ability to Do the Job Is Equally Qualified

If the candidate passes this first hurdle, you can move on with a few more questions. You will still be examining *ability* and *suitability*, but recognize that just because a candidate can do the job doesn't necessarily mean he gets a second interview. You hope to find a number of candidates with the basic *technical skills* to do the work, so that you can pick the best of these candidates to move forward with.

"What have you learned from jobs you have held?"

Also:

"In what ways has your job prepared you to take on greater responsibilities?"

"What do you think determines progress in a good company?"

It is always good to hear an answer that indicates an ongoing pursuit of superior *technical skills*, with these skills backed up by a selection of *transferable skills and professional values* that are relevant to success in this job and profession. Look for the candidate who can outline the *technical skills* you know are required to deliver on the *responsibilities* of the job, and who then identifies the *transferable skills and professional values* that help him do the job well. (Remember that the vocabulary used to describe these skills can vary.)

A good candidate might, after talking about increased *technical skills*, say he's learned that little gets achieved without *teamwork*. He might comment that there's invariably sound thinking behind *systems and procedures*, that to get to the root of problems it's better to talk less and listen more, that you can either sit on the sidelines watching the hours go by or you can get involved and make a difference with your presence, or that time goes quicker when you're fully engaged, and besides, the relationships you build are with better people.

You are also asking this question to determine whether you've got an entitled troublemaker on your hands. Asking this question might get you more insight into the information you were looking for when you asked questions like, *"Why have you changed jobs so frequently?"* and *"Why did you leave your last job?"*

"What interests you least about this job?"

Also:

"Jobs have pluses and minuses. What were some of the minuses on this/ your last job?"

If the candidate's response includes one of the major *deliverables* of your job opening, congratulate yourself on avoiding a disastrous hire and politely end the interview. A professionally aware candidate will recall some small, tedious, repetitive task that no one but an incurable phony would ever pretend to enjoy. She will then say that although this task does not interest her, she realizes it's important and performs it conscientiously. However, there are not that many savvy candidates, and the response you get to this tough question could raise a serious red flag.

"Describe how your job contributes to the overall goals of your department and company."

Every company is in business to make a profit, and every company depends on individual initiative being harnessed to *teamwork* to perform the complex tasks that result in corporate profitability. So with this question, you're looking for a description of how the candidate's job makes its individual contribution, as well as of its role as that small but important cog in the moneymaking machinery that is your department. This cog needs to mesh with all the other cogs (the candidate's prospective colleagues) for the gears of productivity to engage and move the department toward its goals. In addition, it probes for the *technical skills* that make execution of the basic *responsibilities* possible, as well as the *critical thinking skills* that give that productive capacity focus and efficiency.

Early Decision Time

If you focus on *ability* questions first, you can end an interview whenever you determine that a particular candidate is the wrong choice for the job; there is no point in wasting your valuable time. This basic sequence of questions (and the customized sequences you build for yourself) will enable you to decide to terminate the interview or to invest more time with a promising candidate, frequently without asking all the questions we have identified here.

If you are not sure, ask some more questions about the areas of your concern. As we have already discussed, you are not necessarily looking for people who can do this job in their sleep. All that will do is give you a fast start and an employee rapidly demotivated through lack of challenge. You are looking for someone who has a good grasp of the essentials, but who will still be *motivated* and given room for professional growth as dictated by the challenges of the job.

The first interview is usually a winnowing process designed to move from a short list of six to eight candidates to three to four competitive ones. You will then examine *motivation, teamwork*, and *manageability* in a second and third interview to rank these short-list candidates.

NINE

The Second Interview:
Motivation

Now that you have established the presence of "can do," it is time to move on to establishing "will do."

Your success as a manager depends on *getting work done through others*, so just for a moment, think about the departments you've worked in, and imagine a small fire starting in the corner of the office. What would happen? Two of your coworkers would say, "That's not my job" and take a cigarette break, four people would stand back and watch how things unfold, and you and two or three others would be left to deal with the mess. Sadly, this goofy illustration accurately reflects the makeup of most departments. But your job as a manager is to build a department made up mostly of the people who strive to make a difference with their presence every day.

However, on any day, in any company and any department, you'll find the clock watchers. Year in and year out, they expend just enough effort to keep their jobs, but no more. They are the same people who were telling you to slow down and take it easy when you were on the way up. They are the ones who are long on complaints and short on solutions. They are never happy and never challenged, yet always endowed with perfect 20/20 hindsight.

The problem is that the clock watchers aren't all that easy to spot when you first meet them in the artificial atmosphere of a job interview. Most of the time, they are professionally competent; they can often actually do the work, and, after all, this is where most interviewers stop: "Hey, she can do the job, and the money is right? Fine, hire her, and let's get back to work."

This is wrong. "Can do" accompanied by "won't do if I don't like Tim" or "will only do when wind is from the south" makes for a bad hire. Don't fool yourself into thinking that your magic touch will shift someone's low-gear career into interstellar overdrive. People are largely who they want to be, and it is not your job to change them; your job is to separate the clock watchers from the candidates who intend to make a difference with their presence.

In this chapter we will look at questions that focus on *motivation*, though as always, all the non-focus skills are still examined on the periphery. *Motivation* can be thought of as the *energy* that comes from tackling exciting challenges, but it must also be considered as a willingness to take the rough with the smooth that goes with every job with the same degree of *commitment* and attention to detail. You are looking for *intelligent enthusiasm* for the work, and that comes from a holistic knowledge of the effort this job demands every day.

Understanding What It Takes

This first sequence of questions addresses self-esteem, self-awareness, understanding of the job's challenges, and what it takes to get that job done. One of your major goals is to differentiate the candidate who is going to devote herself to all of the job's critical *deliverables* from the candidate who looks for ways to shirk the less pleasant duties.

"What personal qualities do you think are necessary to make a success of this job?"
Also:
"What supporting skills and behaviors help you do your job well?"
Asking for "personal qualities" or behaviors or "special skills" is probably going to get you a better response than asking for *transferable skills and professional values*, as these latter two terms are better understood in management and HR circles than in the general public. Either way, this question is about looking for the underpinnings of success.

As you have already determined which *transferable skills and professional values* are most relevant to this particular opening, it shouldn't be difficult to weave in questions about specific *transferable skills and professional values* as they apply to other aspects of the job. For instance, in talking about client visits you might ask: *"What's your procedure for keeping track of client visits and account activity?"* The answer to this question should give you insight into attention to detail, adherence to *systems and procedures*, and *multitasking skills*. You could also ask how a candidate ranks different types of customers and how he invests his time with them as a result.

"How do you feel about your progress to date?"

This one might be referred to as a self-esteem question, and as such, you are looking for people who feel good about themselves and have *confidence* in their ability to perform.

You are looking for insights into *productivity*, professional development plans, and self-esteem. A question like this can also unmask an overinflated ego with little of substance to back up the inflation, though with younger workers you should write off some of that as enthusiasm. Having offered the candidate an opportunity to sing her own praises, you might follow up with a *negative-balance question*: *"In hindsight, in what ways could you have improved your progress?"* A candidate who takes responsibility and learns from her mistakes is someone who exhibits good judgment, objectivity, and *emotional maturity*.

"Do you consider yourself successful?"

As a *closed-ended question*, this will probably only get you a yes-or-no answer, but that's okay, because you use it as the first part of a two-part question. Follow up with the wonderful catchall, *"Why?"* or *"What professional behaviors do you think contribute to your success in the profession?"* Look for *motivation*, *multitasking skills*, and *determination*.

"How do you rank among your peers?"

This question is also designed to examine self-esteem, and you want people who justifiably have a good self-image, so you should expect a

degree of subjectivity. On the other hand, if the job itself is highly quan-
tifiable, the candidate could interpret the question as a request for a fac-
tual answer, such as, "I'm number two in the region." In most instances,
it is salespeople who will interpret your question in the latter fashion, in
which case you will remember to verify that ranking with other questions (see Chapter 13 for more), and when checking references.

"What plans do you have to improve your professional performance?"

However the prior question was answered, this logical follow-up
query does not change: You can expect any kind of answer from a con-
fused silence to a "keep on working hard" and anything in between.
You're looking for a candidate who understands the importance of
ongoing professional development.

"What have you done that you are proud of?"

There was a similar question in Chapter 8, where we were looking for *ability*, but you can also ask the question here to determine
motivation. The answer can tell you a great deal about the candidate's
understanding of the job and which areas he *thinks* are important.
Are they the same areas that you *know* are important? If there are no
accomplishments to be proud of, your candidate could be limited in
technical skills or *motivation* to achieve change with those skills, either
of which could pose a problem.

"What is your greatest strength?"

"I'm a great tax accountant" or "There isn't a CMO in the *Fortune*
1000 with my track record" are both acceptable answers, but it
isn't a particular achievement that is most interesting here; it is the
transferable skills and professional values that make such achievements
possible.

Part of the answer you hear might address, "my communication
skills," which can be a launch pad for a specific evaluation of *past performance*: *"Tell me about a time when your communication skills played
an important role in getting a difficult tax issue resolved."* You could also

ask the candidate to define *communication skills*, to see how completely she understands the eight tools of communication (see Chapter 2).

"What is your greatest weakness?"

This pair of questions about strengths and weaknesses has been used so frequently that some people think they have both lost their potency. But if you ask the one you should always look for *negative balance* by asking the other, because you never know what you'll turn up. Don't accept answers like, "I guess I work too hard"; if you get one, counter with, "What I am really looking for is what you believe to be your greatest professional weakness?"

The question is about self-awareness, but at the same time candidates don't have an obligation to hang themselves. Listen carefully to the answers you receive to both of these questions, and if they sound a little too smooth, it would be a good opportunity to practice your *layering* techniques with a series of questions examining the who, what, where, when, and why of the candidate's greatest strengths and weaknesses. In most cases, however, you are likely to learn more about the candidate's strengths and weaknesses from your whole body of questions than from just these two.

"Tell me about a responsibility/project/task you have enjoyed."

Also:

"Can you tell me about a project that really got you excited?"

Here you learn how a candidate likes to spend time. Is it in the area of the job's critical *deliverables*, or is it in the area of busywork? You might also follow up this question by asking, *"And what did you do to meet that responsibility?"* If the benefit is not immediately obvious, you could also ask, *"How did this contribute to the successful execution of your responsibilities?"*

This is another way of probing the candidate's *motivational* focus. It can be tied to follow-up questions that examine what happened to the project, how it turned out, what problems arose, how they were handled, and perhaps most important, whether the candidate's obvious enthusiasm led to any oversights or miscalculations.

It would be wise to follow this sequence of questions with, *"Now tell me about a responsibility/project/task you didn't enjoy."* Learning about what demotivates a candidate will also enlighten you about his *motivation* and how he responds to challenging situations likely to be faced in your company.

Critical Thinking and Problem Solving

We have already looked at some ways to examine a candidate's *critical thinking* and *problem-solving abilities*. However, for a candidate to have a problem-solving frame of mind, she must have the *motivation* to be challenged by difficult situations. You can learn about *critical thinking skills* and *problem-solving abilities*, *determination*, *motivation*, and, to a degree, *teamwork* and *manageability* when you ask questions about problematic situations. Here are some examples you can customize to your unique situation.

"How do you deal with complex problems in your job?"
   Also:
"What are the most difficult problems you face in your work?"
   Every job has its complexities, all the way from the Corporate Counsel dealing with the delicate maneuvers of acquisitions and mergers to the fast-food server who simultaneously has to deal with irritable customers and long lines because of the absence of a fry cook. It can be an eye opener when the candidate in front of you is unaware of the challenges of her current job. It's surprising just how many people manage to maintain a reasonably solid work history while understanding so little about the fundamental problems the job exists to solve. You might choose to follow this question with a *past-performance* question: *"Tell me about a really challenging _____ problem you had to deal with."* As appropriate, use the who, what, where, when, why, and how *layering* technique. This tactic is detailed in the next example.

"What are some of the things you find difficult to do?"

This question examines *technical skills*, but also looks at how the candidate deals with nonpreferred activities, and this tells you about *motivation*. The layered follow-up questions below examine the interviewee's *problem-solving* and *critical thinking skills* from all angles. Just as importantly, you're looking for red flags, such as a candidate who becomes grudging, resentful, or accusatory when talking about how he deals with problems that arise on the job every day.

Follow-Up:

"Why do you find this difficult?"

"How do you overcome the problem?"

"Where/to whom do you turn for help?"

"Where/when does this situation most commonly arise?"

"What have you learned from dealing with problems like these?"

"What kinds of decisions are most difficult for you?"

Here you learn about the extent of real responsibilities, but you also want to learn about why such decisions are difficult, which *critical thinking* processes led your candidate to the right decision, and indications that he has a healthy respect for *systems and procedures*. You'll also be alert for the prospective employee who rushes to judgment in his decision-making processes.

In addition, the answer can identify the areas in which an indecisive candidate will spend time dithering rather than doing. With a less experienced candidate this may be due to lack of experience and therefore indicate a growth opportunity; with a more experienced candidate, it might indicate training needs or someone who has reached the limits of his professional growth. The response to this question alone won't give you all the information you need to make such a weighty assessment, but it might inch you in the right direction. Follow up with the *layering technique* if the answer you receive doesn't include an explanation of why such decisions are difficult or how they are reached.

Staying with this theme, you could continue with, *"Tell me about a time when a difficult decision had to be made quickly."* This is a *behavioral* question focused on *past performance* to provide you with a specific real-world example. Weigh the *steps* the candidate took in coming to the decision more than the decision itself. You are not so much interested in the example of a good decision (you can't possibly expect to obtain all the extenuating factors anyway) as you are in the *critical thinking* process that led up to it. Find a candidate who has a logical approach to *problem solving* and decision making, and you have an employee who doesn't need to be watched every moment of the day.

"Tell me about an event that really challenged you. How did you meet the challenge? In what way was your approach different from that of others?"

This is a straightforward, two-part question. The first part probes the candidate's *critical thinking skills.* The second asks him to set himself apart from the herd. Look for the root of the problem, its significance, and its negative impact on the department/company. Examine the candidate's solution, its value to his employer, and how it was different from other approaches.

"Tell me about a time when you put your foot in your mouth."

The question is tricky because it asks the candidate to show herself in a poor light.

With this question you examine the candidate's ability to self-edit; it's a question about discretion, or to put it another way, about the candidate's ability to think before she speaks. Depending on the answer, this question might also give you some insight into a candidate's willingness to interact pleasantly with others.

Multitasking and Energy

Next we come to the issues of *organization, time management,* and *energy* level. These intangibles are difficult to judge, yet vital in hiring someone who is not only capable of doing the job but has the *motivation* to get out there and actually do it every day with enthusiasm and *energy.* You want to know if a candidate can break a project down into its component parts and manage those parts efficiently to complete projects successfully and on time. Such behaviors are to *motivation* what a guidance system is to a missile. Asking these questions will help you determine whether the candidate knows how to plan projects and organize and allot her time efficiently.

"How do you plan your day?"
Also:
"How do you organize yourself for day-to-day activities?"
"How many hours a week do you find it necessary to work to get your job done?"

These are all *multitasking* questions that also have a *critical thinking* dimension. Combine them with the details of the job you are filling and these questions might help you rule out a task-oriented person in favor of a goal-oriented one.

Look for individuals who have at least a basic understanding of the two essential principles of *multitasking*. The first is the Plan/Do/Review cycle discussed in Chapter 2; the second is the A/B/C prioritization performed within the Plan/Do/Review cycle. No one, especially in management, will be successful over the long haul without embodying these principles in everyday activity.

"How do you organize, plan, and execute your projects?"
Also:
"Tell me about an important project you worked on. How did you organize, plan, and execute it?"

A blank look, or even hesitancy, bodes ill for your future peace of mind, because candidates without a firm grasp of *multitasking* principles are not likely to be goal-oriented. Instead, they are likely to be people who simply let tasks expand to fill the time allotted to them. A working understanding of gap analysis (determining the current situation, the desired situation, and the actions needed to bridge the *gap* between them), good training in project planning, and evidence of the *multitasking skills* required to complete the assignment while keeping all other tasks on track, should be evident in the answer.

A good candidate will also explain how she builds a milestone schedule with commencement and completion dates for each stage, and a plan for optimum equipment and human resource utilization. You will hear how the plan is discussed with management, and how contingency plans are formed well in advance.

"Tell me about a job or project for which you had to gather information from many different sources and then create something with the information."

The answers to this *past-performance* question can be diverse, but they should all give you insight into gap analysis, milestone schedules, and *multitasking* principles, just as they did in the last question. You might also learn about *written*, *verbal*, and *digital communication skills* as well as *creativity*, *motivation*, and *energy* levels. Overall, though, you will look not so much at the project itself (apart from its applicability to your open position), but at the logical and orderly approach that the person took to define the challenge and the steps, timeline, and resources that would be required for a successful outcome.

"Do you set goals for yourself?"

Also:

"Tell me about an important goal you set recently."
"Tell me how you are going about reaching that goal."

These questions can tell you about a candidate's professional and personal priorities (or you can guide them in a specific direction by adding "professional" or "personal" to the question), and they can stand alone or be asked in order as part of a *layering sequence*. The answers can also tell you about the *professional values* that a candidate holds—*commitment*, *motivation*, and *determination*—which combine to tell you about her willingness to stretch for something deemed important; it's a question sequence that separates the dreamer from the doer.

This sequence can be continued with *"Do you always reach your goals?"* and/or, *"Do you ever have problems reaching your goals?"* Watch out for people who answer quickly without subsequently qualifying the statement. While someone who always reaches goals may be telling the truth, there are always setbacks (we are looking for evidence of setbacks and the *determination, critical thinking skills,* and *resilience* that help a person get past them). Furthermore, a person who always reaches all goals might be someone who sets low goals because she is afraid to fail. Every true professional knows that going for the ring and missing it once in a while is an integral part of professional growth and ultimately achieving success.

"Tell me about a time when you failed to reach a goal, and what you did subsequently."

One way or another, failure comes into every life, all the time. We learn more from failure than from success; a *resilient, determined,* and overall smart professional should be aware of this. Thomas Edison, the inventor of electric light (and also of movies and the phonograph), once said, "I have successfully discovered a thousand ways to *not* make a light bulb." He also said: "Negative results are just what I want. They're just as valuable to me as positive results. I can never find the thing that does the job best until I find the ones that don't."

You want to take a look at how the candidate deals with failures, how *resilient* and *analytical* she is from a practical perspective. Achieving success in most of life's endeavors is based on a person's ability to analyze the reasons for failure, accept responsibility and constructive advice, and learn and move forward. You want to know if this candidate learns from negative experiences and bounces back all the smarter for it, or merely wallows in depression, not knowing what happened, why, or how things might be done differently in the future.

"What do/did you like about your current/last job?"
Also:
"What do/did you dislike about your current/last job?"
"What was there about your last company that you particularly liked or agreed with?"
"What was there about your last company that you didn't particularly like or agree with?"

These are common questions that have lost some of their potency through overuse, but if you insert them in a sequence that includes questions that address planning, execution, outcomes, success, and failure, you can give them new life. Instead of timeworn answers, you are more likely to receive meaningful replies that can tell you how a candidate feels about the important aspects of the job such as *systems and procedures*. With answers to the "dislike" part of this sequence, follow up with a *behavioral* question about how the candidate handled those disliked aspects of a job. There are unpleasant aspects to all jobs, and that's okay as long as we recognize it and do our jobs just the same. You know that, and I know that, but you cannot assume any candidate knows that.

"How many projects can you handle at a time?"

The ability to *multitask*—to juggle conflicting priorities—is necessary in most modern jobs. This question will tell you whether a candidate prefers to work with blinders until one job is finished, or whether he can change priorities and handle conflicting project priorities without hissy fits.

You can follow this with, *"How do you organize yourself when you have equally important but conflicting priorities with deadlines?"* and then, *"How do you stay on track with multiple commitments?"* The answer will tell you what this particular candidate understands about *multitasking*. You could also follow these questions with, *"At what point do multiple projects reach the point of overload?"* It all depends on the complexity of the job, and the extent to which such issues play into the success or failure of the person you hire.

"Describe a project that required a high amount of energy over an extended period of time."

This question, followed up with, *"What did you do to keep focused and productive?"* continues to examine *commitment, determination, reliability, integrity, multitasking*, and *energy*. All jobs are marathons, but not every one requires the same degree of stamina; you always want people who can go the distance, but not every job requires an Olympic gold medalist.

An alternate question is, *"When you have a great deal of work to do that requires extra effort and time, where does your energy come from?"* This examines the same areas and can help you evaluate a candidate's approach to work and problems under pressure. Will she stay calm and get the job done? Will she fall apart and waste valuable time examining escape routes?

"Is it ever necessary to go above and beyond the call of duty in terms of effort or time to get your job done?"

Also:

"Tell me about a time when an emergency caused you to reschedule your workload/projects."

"You have a doctor's appointment arranged for noon. You've waited six weeks to get in. An unexpected emergency requires your involvement. What do you do?"

These are questions about *commitment* and *reliability*. A good candidate will understand that short of a life-threatening physical condition, you expect her to be on the job.

However, the answers to this one are always wide open, and while current corporate culture encourages burning the midnight oil, look for a sense of balance in the answers you hear. Beware of interviewees who portray themselves as martyrs who regularly miss the birth of children and get into the office at 3:00 A.M. on a Sunday. This may be true, but then again such an individual might be putting in long hours as a result of poor work habits (bad *multitasking skills*). Look for a sense of balance, sensitivity to the *profit imperative*, a high *energy* level, and a wise use of *multitasking* and planning skills.

This answer can also reveal personal flexibility, willingness to work extra hours when necessary, and—you hope—the ability to change course without nervous breakdowns. You can tag on a follow-up question—*"How did rescheduling your workload affect you/make you feel?"*—to learn about the stress a candidate experiences in such usually common circumstances. As a manager, this instantaneous realignment is probably second nature, but that isn't necessarily the case with everyone, and you have to be careful not to project your attributes onto others.

"Tell me about a system of working that you have used, and what it was like."

Follow-Up:

"What worked best with this approach?"
"What was problematic with this approach?"
"Tell me about a method you've developed for accomplishing a job. What were its strengths and weaknesses?"

These questions address *creativity, critical thinking skills,* and *multitasking.* Additionally, you can learn about the *determination* and *creativity* that a candidate might call on to create new, workable approaches to a job's challenges and problems. Listen carefully: You can sometimes pick up innovative approaches, even if you don't end up hiring the candidate.

Grace under Pressure

It is now time to look a little more closely at stress, pressure, and composure under fire. If you feel that there are never tight deadlines in your department, that everything in your company always goes according to plan, that there is never sickness or employee turnover, and that all of your people always pull their weight and never run for cover, you can skip this section. It is intended for those of us who are awake between nine and five every day.

Some of the questions in this section are similar to those suggested earlier for examining *critical thinking skills.* They work equally well when examining the ability of a potential employee to function productively under pressure, and as you become more adept as an interviewer you will learn to assess both qualities simultaneously.

"Think of a crisis situation in which things got out of control. Why did it happen, and what was your role in the chain of events and their resolution?"

Also:

"Tell me about an event that really challenged you. How did you meet the challenge? In what way was your approach different from that of others?"
"What was the most difficult situation you have faced?"

In a mining disaster, there are always those who scream against the darkness and those who light the candles and look for a way out. You probably know your preference.

In the candidate's answers, look for parallels to your department's *deliverables* and the crises that happen in your work-world. An interesting and useful variation on the first of these questions would be to pose a real-world example from your work as a hypothetical: *"What would you do in a situation where . . . ?"* For those old enough and in a position to know, this question and variations on it were how Silicon Valley grew so fast with so few prosecutions of corporate espionage: During job interviews candidates gave much of the required information of their own free will. Under the auspices of an innocent hypothetical, candidates moving from one competitor to another blithely gave away company *problem-solving* methods and *systems and procedures*.

You will be looking at the nature of the challenge and how it relates to your needs, how the challenge was analyzed, and the solution subsequently implemented. You can make a secondary probe for *creativity* and *motivation* by asking, *"How was your approach different from that of others?"*

To find out more, ask, *"Can you tell me about a departmental initiative that didn't work out well, and why in hindsight you think it panned out that way?"* You might add that you are not looking for an admission of personal culpability, but the ability to look back and learn from the mistakes of others. With this question you can gather further valuable intelligence about this candidate and information you might be able to use within your department.

"What do you do when you have a great deal of work to accomplish in a short time span and things start to spin out of control? How have you reacted?"

"If you can keep your head when all about you
Are losing theirs and blaming it on you,
If you can trust yourself when all men doubt you,
But make allowance for their doubting too . . .
Yours is the Earth and everything that's in it."
—Rudyard Kipling

You are looking for someone who can stay functional in tense situations, for someone whose *critical thinking skills*, *confidence*, and *determination* go into high gear.

"When you have been in difficult and crisis situations, which areas of your professional skills do you vow to work on further?"

Follow-Up:
"Tell me about self-improvement efforts you are currently making in this area."
"Tell me about a task you started but just couldn't seem to get finished."
"I'd be interested to hear about a time when you couldn't complete a task due to lack of support or information."

The answers you hear in response will tell you about a candidate's perceived areas of weakness far better than will responses to the question, "What's your greatest weakness?" The answers to the follow-ups will throw light on *determination* and willingness to accept responsibility for problems and for the plans that will eradicate them in the future.

"Tell me about an occasion when your performance didn't live up to your own expectations."

This is a tough one to answer. Give the candidate points for poise and honesty, and be sure to see whether he learned anything from the situation. A person who takes a concrete lesson away from a troubling experience is likely to retain the knowledge, and you will benefit from that life lesson.

"Can you recall a time when you went back to a failed project to give it another shot? Why did you do it, and what happened?"

There's a famous piece of corporate graffiti that profiles the six stages of a failed project:

1. Enthusiasm
2. Disillusion
3. Panic
4. Search for the guilty
5. Punishment of the innocent
6. Praise and honor for the survivors

Sad commentary, but often true, especially for those struggling along in more mature and institutionalized corporations. Someone who has not only experienced association with failed projects but who has subsequently gone back to give them another shot, on whatever terms, is certainly worth looking at more closely.

Some Final Questions about Motivation

Here are some final questions to help you examine *motivation*.

"What have you done to become more competent/effective in your work?"

Here you learn how important the candidate considers her career and what steps she has taken to become better at her work, perhaps building the skills that have subsequently justified a promotion. Knowing that a candidate has already taken responsibility for her success in this way can only be a good omen for her future *commitment*. Look for candidates who have gone out of their way to read books, listen to CDs, watch DVDs, and attend in-person and online training; who are members of professional associations; and who are otherwise engaged in *ongoing professional education*.

You might proceed with this line of questioning about *professional development* by asking, *"What books have had the greatest effect on your business life?"* You may be met with a blank stare (which tells you a lot) or receive a specific answer. Whatever the answer, remember that reading is nearly always done on personal time and therefore demonstrates a *commitment* to a career. Follow this up with, *"Why did this particular book have such an effect on you, and how has it changed you?"* You might go on to determine the depth of study by asking for other examples.

"How long will it take you to make a contribution?"

This is a wide-open opportunity for an interviewee to sell his candidacy. Keep your ears open for danger signals such as, "Well, I could get started with overhauling your credit and collection procedures as soon as my coat is off." No matter how competent the individual, a professional with any experience understands that it takes a while to understand the fabric of any company, and that its *systems and procedures* are invariably based on firm foundations and must be thoroughly understood before improvements of any nature are suggested. You will look for an answer that addresses the realities of joining a new company: the need to get to know peers and communication systems, the informal "way things are done here," the formal *systems and procedures*, and the brisk application of these general professional skills to everyday tasks.

"What do you think it takes to build a successful career at a new company?"

This question seeks to understand how realistic a candidate is about the *commitment*, focus, and *team spirit* necessary for professional achievement. The answer to this one can help you find out whether this particular candidate will give your job the effort you would like. You may hear some of the same information you'd hope to hear in answer to the previous question; you'll be looking for candidates who are confident in their *technical skills* and ability to deliver results, who understand the importance of building trust in relationships with coworkers in all departments, who follow *systems and procedures* yet look for opportunities to make a difference rather than wait for direct orders, who take personal responsibility for professional development, and who understand that the greater good—the department's success—sometimes requires sacrifice of personal comfort.

Last Thoughts

Once you feel comfortable with the degree of each candidate's *motivation*—and this can happen at any point—it is time to make another decision. Perhaps a candidate is *able*, but lacks the *motivation* to be a really outstanding employee, in which case you will politely bail out.

Conversely, when you feel a candidate is *technically able* to do the work and is clearly *motivated* to take the rough with the smooth that goes with every job, it's logical and now relevant to examine whether she will also be a *manageable team player* once on board.

TEN

THE THIRD INTERVIEW: TEAMWORK AND MANAGEABILITY

To be a successful manager, you need a three-dimensional picture of everyone on your short list, each candidate possessing a high level of *technical skill* coupled with a significant degree of *motivation*. Without the *technical skills* to do the job, *motivation* is irrelevant, and with the *technical skills* but without the *motivation* to take the rough with the smooth that goes with every job, who cares if a candidate is *manageable* or a *team player*?

When the final two or three candidates make it to the third interview, you should know that they are all *able* and *motivated*, and focus now on who will best complement your existing team and be most responsive to your management style.

The questions in this chapter should help you decide what it would be like to manage each of the candidates on your short list and how each of them is likely to perform as a member of the work group. Though the chapter is broken into two sets of questions, one for the *manageability* factor and one for *teamwork*, you will learn that a conscientious *team player* will invariably be *manageable*, and that a *manageable* employee will usually be a reliable *team player*.

While these questions will help you gauge the candidate's *manageability*, they cannot help you get an honest understanding of *yourself* as a manager; that is up to you. Very few of us fit the profile of the manager we read about in management books, so there is little point in hiring candidates who can only be managed by such an unrealistically ideal creature. It's important to hire only those people you can manage, and that takes self-knowledge.

As a manager, you may be the let-'em-alone type, in which case you shouldn't hire candidates whose answers fairly scream that they need constant supervision and encouragement. If, on the other end of the spectrum, you are a micromanager, you are unlikely to have a happy relationship with creative self-starters. You know yourself like no one else, and that knowledge should color the questions you ask, the way you interpret the answers, and the hiring decisions you ultimately make.

Though these questions are phrased with the current or last job in mind, there is nothing to stop you from asking similar questions as they relate to past employers. Most of the answers to these questions will not be earth-shattering on their own. You're looking for a *pattern* of *manageability* and *getting along with others* in working towards common goals.

Manageability Questions

"Who do you report to?"

This first question of the sequence gives you the name and title of the individual who will (when you check references) verify salient facts about the candidate. It is normal to follow these questions with inquiries about worker-manager relationships. *"What was your boss like?"* is a good follow-up question that offers you a lead into any of these other questions.

"How did your boss get the best out of you?"

All candidates, you'll find, will be only too happy to tell you how they like to be managed. Consequently, you can quickly learn whether or not you will be able to provide the kind of management under which the candidate functions best—and if not, of course, you can bail out.

"How did you get the best out of your boss?"

The answer will give you a different perspective on *manageability*: how likely you are to be supported and/or manipulated by the candidate. You can also ask, *"What increased responsibilities or promotions were you given on that job?"* The answer to this question could confirm or disprove the answers given to the two prior questions in your sequence.

"What do you think of your current/last boss?"

This question gives the candidate an opportunity to praise or criticize. While common sense tells even the meanest intelligence that it is unwise to criticize former employers, always ask, because some people just cannot resist the temptation to complain. An answer that states, "I would have liked more direction" is acceptable and gives you usable input when applied to your particular management style. On the other hand, if the answer is a stream of invective, remember that more of the same might be directed at you in the not-too-distant future. Other questions you can ask to gather input in this area include the following:

"Describe the best manager you ever had."
Follow-Up:
"What made her stand out?"
"How did you interact with her?"
"How did you react to feedback, instructions, and criticism she gave you?"

Then repeat the sequence in its entirety with this small change: *"Now I'd like you to describe the* worst *manager you ever had."* Both of these question sequences will tell you a great deal about what constitutes a productive work environment for the candidate and whether you can provide it for him. The responses will contribute to your effective management of the person who gets the job, and they may also be a valuable tool for your professional development as a manager.

"What are some of the things your boss did that you disliked?"

This question works for both the good and the bad manager question sequences. It gives the candidate a further opportunity to expand on the details of management styles and behaviors that will likely make her unhappy and/or a short-term employment prospect.

"In what areas could your boss have done a better job?"

The answer will tell you how the candidate *likes* to be managed as much as how he *doesn't* like to be managed.

"How well do you feel your boss rated your performance?"

While you might think that this question is by nature too subjective to gauge *technical skills* and *confidence*, you will be surprised at how truthful the answers often are, especially in those areas in which the candidate feels underrated. A good candidate will be able to answer objectively by citing performance reviews or written references.

"If you could make one suggestion to management, what would it be?"

Here you are looking for the constructive content of the answer, and the tone in which it is delivered. Over time, as you hear different candidates' answers to this question, you'll gain some useful knowledge about employee *motivation*. In my own management experience, I heard candidates answer this question often enough to register the point that they felt the walking wounded and negativists should be terminated sooner, because of the detrimental impact they had on the rest of the group. Someone even told me that because this wasn't done, better workers felt that their efforts went unrecognized and unrewarded, and so were confronted with a choice of either moving on or ceasing to make the extra effort. I subsequently hired this person.

"How do you take direction?"

Also:

"How do you accept criticism?"

There are two kinds of direction: the kind you give when you have all the time in the world, and the kind you give when the poop hits the paddle wheel. Underlying both is the desire to get a grasp on the candidate's *emotional maturity*, but you're also looking for signs of an open-minded *team player*: a low-maintenance professional who is *motivated* to ask clarifying questions about a project before beginning, and who then gets on with the job at hand, coming back with requests for direction as circumstances dictate.

If you get a pat answer, follow it up with, "*Tell me about a time when your manager was in a rush and didn't have time for the niceties.*"

"Would you like to have your boss's job?"

Listen closely! It might be your job that the candidate is talking about, and it is a rare boss who wants her livelihood taken away. On my own very first job interview, my future boss said, "Mr. Yate, it has been a pleasure to meet you. However, until you walked in my door, I wasn't out on the street looking for a new job."

If the answer is yes, ask whether the candidate feels qualified for it, and why. Such an answer is acceptable if the candidate is many years behind you in experience, and it's also an acceptable answer if you want to move up and need to do some succession planning by grooming a suitable replacement. However, someone snapping at your professional heels may not be such a good idea; and this is one of those times when hiring the older worker—who wants a home and won't stab you in the back—might be a preferable choice.

"Tell me about a time when you came up with a new method or idea. How did you get it approved and implemented?"

While hoping for *creativity* and initiative *(leadership* in this context), you are alert for attention to *systems and procedures* and personal *integrity*. You want to hear about a person who understands the development process that brings ideas to fruition, and also follows the chain of command in getting it done.

"Tell me about an occasion when you felt it necessary to convince your department to change a procedure."

Similar to the above question, but this one leans more toward the issues surrounding *systems and procedures*. What gets his goat? How strong are his convictions? How valid are they? Follow up with, *"How did you go about it, and whose feathers got ruffled?"* You need to know whether the candidate will adhere to *systems and procedures* in these circumstances, and how he will go about getting the changes made—like a diplomat, or like a bull in a china shop?

"Tell me about an occasion when there were objections to your ideas. What did you do to convince management of your point of view?"

The question examines *manageability* in connection with *determination*, and can give you insight into how far and how hard this candidate will push a thought after initial rejection.

"Tell me about an event/project for which you were criticized?"

In this instance, you want to look at the cause of criticism and how the candidate accepts and processes the input and then moves forward:

- He listened to understand.
- He confirmed his understanding.
- He asked for guidance.
- He confirmed the desired outcome.
- He reached a satisfactory resolution.
- He addressed what he learned and how the experience helped him grow.

"Tell me about a situation in which people were making emotional decisions about your project. What happened, and how did you handle it?"

Very close to the previous two questions, only with an *emotional maturity* twist to it. If you examine the question in the context of the real professional world, you will see that it is really asking, *"How did you behave, when for pragmatic reasons and in the best interests of the company a project of yours was canned or criticized? Did you act like a professional or like a spoiled brat?"*

"What are some of the things about which you and your boss disagreed?"

Remember the 80/20 rule of information gathering. You should listen, absorb, and evaluate: Could the disagreements cited in the answer foreshadow problems for you?

"How necessary is it for you to be creative in your job?"

Creativity comes into play with every job, because every job is about *identifying, preventing, and solving problems*; however, *creativity* is typically in greater demand when hiring salespeople, and *critical thinking skills* when hiring auditors. You can see that both *transferable skills* play into superior performance in both of these widely differing jobs; it's all a matter of degree. The appropriate response depends on the position you are filling.

"What do you do when there is a decision to be made and no procedure exists?"

This question is a natural follow-up to any of the last eight. Does the response tell you that in developing an appropriate procedure, the candidate sticks to established rules, or does she devise new systems without seeking input?

"Have you ever been in a situation in which people overruled you or wouldn't let you get a word in edgewise?"

The *deliverables* of the job help determine the right answer. For example, in customer service, you need someone who can be conciliatory, while in sales, you want a candidate who listens and then adds new insights and ways of looking at a situation to overcome objections.

"Give me an example of a time when you were told no. What did you do in response?"

Also:

"Describe a time when you didn't get an immediate yes from someone. What did you do?"

"When did you have to ask for something you weren't going to receive right away? How did you react?"

The answers you receive to any of these questions will give you a feeling for what to expect from a potential employee when instant gratification is denied. Emotionally immature people seek instant gratification of their desires, immediate acceptance of their ideas, and universal recognition of their talent. Such people are notorious for their inability to handle even temporary rejection and can throw hissy fits, causing unrest in an otherwise harmonious department.

"Have you ever had a supervisor who was unfair or difficult to work with? Tell me about the experience."

Not all managers are good; in fact, we both know some are certifiable. However, the goal of this question is to determine what this candidate *perceives* as "unfair" and "difficult." If the candidate's criteria match your own, you can move on with confidence; if not, you may have a potential management headache on your hands.

"What problems do you experience when working alone?"

Also:

"How much of your work was done alone in that job?"

"How do the work habits of others change when the boss is absent?"

"Tell me about a time when there was a decision to be made and your boss was absent."

"How do your work habits change when your boss is absent?"

Sequencing questions like these will tell you much more than the traditional, *"Can you work alone or do you prefer to work with others?"*, especially since most jobs today require a combination of the two. While recognizing the value of *teamwork*, we should also remember that every team is made up of individuals who need to be self-starting and self-motivating. As a manager, you cannot afford the time to crank-start each member of your team first thing every morning.

At the same time, what the mice do when the cat is away should be of concern to every manager. These questions examine both the candidate's self-reliance and his perception of his personal authority and responsibility, which tells you about his understanding of *systems and procedures*. Often, there are no specifically right or wrong answers to these questions, because so much depends on your management style and the *systems and procedures* of your particular company.

Finding the Team Players and Team Destroyers

A willingness to get along with coworkers, who spend the majority of their waking hours in your department, is a key element that is easily overlooked in the hiring cycle. You will, after all, probably be working with the chosen candidate for fifty weeks of the year.

There are those who will work for the common cause and those who are unable to see beyond their own immediate desires. You see this in the subtly disruptive influence such people can have on the general tone and productivity of your department. Most jobs today require interaction with others, so a candidate's willingness to be a *team player* can be a vital consideration in making the right hiring decision.

"How important is communication and interaction with coworkers in getting your work done?"
Follow-Up:
"What other titles and departments did you have dealings with? How do you get the best out of these interactions?"
"What are the challenges you encounter when dealing with other departments? What do you do about them?"
These questions will together establish with whom and at what levels the candidate's interactions took place and how important she thinks *communication* and sociable relations are to departmental

productivity. There are always difficulties with interdepartmental communication, so the later questions in this sequence seek to gain insight into the candidate's *communication skills*, sense of diplomacy, and understanding of *systems and procedures*.

"Can you give me an example of a project that required you to interact with different levels within the company? What was the project's goal?"
   Follow-Up:
"What was the nature of your interactions, and what were their results?"
"What types of interaction are you most comfortable/uncomfortable with?"
"What levels of management are you most comfortable/uncomfortable with?"
   This question sequence examines *problem-solving skills, communication*, and *confidence*. It seeks to understand the level of exposure the applicant has had to working in complex, multilevel business environments. The first part asks how the candidate interacts with superiors and motivates those working with—and, perhaps, for—her on the project.

"Have you ever had to make unpopular decisions?"
   This establishes whether the applicant has worked at a level at which decisions affected the well-being or comfort level of other workers—by definition more nuanced and difficult decisions to make. Any job that requires interaction with different titles, levels, and departments demands a professional with some diplomatic muscle. For these people, unpopular decisions are part of a job that demands *critical thinking, leadership, teamwork*, and *communication skills*.
   If the candidate has made this type of decision and therefore held a certain level of authority, you might proceed with a *behavioral* sequence: *"Tell me about an unpopular decision you had to make,"* and layer it with, *"Who did it affect? Why did the situation arise? How long did it take you to make the decision? How do you feel you handled it?"* Of course, this is a natural time to add at the end, *"What did you learn from this experience?"*

"Give me an example of a time when you had to convince people over whom you had no authority. What was your approach to the task?"

Apart from gauging the level of respect the candidate offers others, this is a useful question for any position in which *verbal skills* are an integral job requirement. The answer should tell you about *critical thinking*, *leadership*, and *communication skills*.

"Tell me how you became a contributing member of the team when you joined your current/last company."

Follow-Up:

"Have you worked with a group like this before?"

"What was it like?"

"How did you handle it?"

"What problems did you need to overcome?"

This sequence will tell you how this candidate will approach integration into your team.

"Tell me about a time when you needed to get an understanding of another's situation before you could get your job done. How did you get the understanding, and what problems did you encounter?"

How seriously does this person consider another's viewpoint? As well as enlightening you about an ability to get on with others, this question also looks at a candidate's *listening*, *critical thinking*, *verbal*, and perhaps *written skills*, as well as the sophistication needed to weigh individual needs against the imperatives of your department.

"In working with new people, how do you go about getting an understanding of them?"

Another question that addresses *teamwork* and *critical thinking skills*, phrased to give you insight into how the candidate will assimilate during those early days on the new job. Every new hire is expected to become a viable part of the group, which means getting an understanding of the group and its individual members. A follow-up for this is, *"Are you able to predict the behavior of others when you first meet them, and if so, how?"* This is a good question that can generate some interesting responses regarding the candidate's perception of group interaction.

"What difficulties do you have in tolerating people whose backgrounds and interests differ from yours?"

Follow-Up:

"What types of people do you get along with best?"

"What types of people do you find it difficult to get along with?"

"How do you manage to get along with these types?"

"Tell me about a difficult situation you had with one of these people, and what happened."

"What did you learn from this experience?"

This sequence looks at *teamwork* from the POV of getting along with others. Employees who cannot tolerate differences will create disharmony and an unproductive working atmosphere. Allowed to fester, this can put you in the way of a hostile work environment lawsuit.

"What is your role as a group member?"

Follow-Up:

"Tell me about a specific accomplishment you have achieved as a group member."

"What was your role?"

The thinking behind this sequence is that the first question reveals the candidate's awareness of the importance of *teamwork* and how it contributes to the company's bottom line, while the second demands a concrete example (*behavioral*), and the third completes the loop by asking the candidate to explain her role and contributions to the group.

"What titles do you typically have contact with in your work?"

Follow-Up:

"What did you do differently with each of these different types to get your job done?"

Both questions address *teamwork*. This first question identifies the different levels with whom the candidate has been involved. The second question looks at the candidate's range of response in dealing with divergent titles and personalities. Is he able to solicit and accept input, ideas, and viewpoints from a variety of sources? Does he know how to put himself in the other person's shoes and see how her attitude is informed by the demands placed upon her by her different role in the company? Does this knowledge help him respond in such a way as to maximize productivity and promote a harmonious work environment?

"Define cooperation."

This *open-ended question* examines *manageability* and asks the candidate to explain how she sees her responsibilities as a *team player*, both in taking direction and working for the overall success of her department.

"How would you define a motivational work atmosphere?"

Unfortunately, we spend the majority of our waking hours at work, and a negative atmosphere reduces *productivity* and contributes to employee turnover. The response will tell you about the candidate's preferred work environment: If the answer conflicts with the realities of your work environment, it could be a sign of trouble, either with the candidate's *suitability*, or the current working environment in your department.

Continue the sequence with, *"As a member of a department, how do you see your role as a team builder?"* If morale in your department is low for some reason, you might find out whether the candidate is a follower or a leader. Will she actively work to improve the atmosphere and build *team spirit*, passively accept the current situation, or, even worse, encourage the negative atmosphere?

"Tell me about a time when, in difficult circumstances, you pulled the team together."

Follow-Up:

"Tell me about a time when a team fell apart. Why did it happen? What did you do?"

This question is designed to identify a candidate who is willing to take responsibility for the wellbeing of the team—to take initiative and a *leadership* role in encouraging change for the better.

What efforts did the candidate make? Where was the finger of blame pointed? Remember to look for patterns in the answers you hear from a candidate. Beware of the candidate who consistently lays the responsibility for problems at others' doorsteps. She may blame others today; tomorrow, that finger of blame might just be pointed at you. If you're hiring a manager, an inability to answer convincingly could well be a black mark against the candidacy.

"Recall a time when those around you were not being as honest or direct as they should have been. What did you do?"

Use this *behavioral* question with discretion; it examines *integrity* and it is a difficult question for anyone to answer. You may only want to use it if you suspect dishonesty in the department, or the company has recently experienced the same. Of course, some industries—retail goods and services, for instance—suffer continually from petty larceny, and in those cases the question has much greater relevance.

"What is your general impression of your last company?"

Follow-Up:

"Tell me about a project for which you volunteered, and how your responsibilities increased."

"How did your attitude and the work you did affect your peers?"

These three questions have a single collective goal: to tell you about the candidate's prevailing attitudes toward management, his job, and his peers. Together, they will tell you whether this person will have a bad or a good attitude once a member of the team. People who complain invariably *like* finding things to complain about, and it has been my experience that people who complained about past employers will persist in the habit regardless of who's in charge.

"Tell me about a time when management had to change a plan or approach you were committed to. What did you do?"

This is a revealing question that tells you not only about *manageability*, but also about self-control and personal *leadership*. You'll see another version of this question restructured slightly for use when hiring managers.

Finding Flash Points

One of a manager's most important roles within the department is to maintain a work atmosphere that minimizes friction and maximizes productivity. Psychologists tell us that everyone has good days, bad days, pet peeves, and anger triggers, so it is helpful to learn whatever you can about the flash points of your candidates. This is obviously a sensitive and tricky area; coming right out and questioning what makes a candidate angry is a great way to get an unhelpful boilerplate answer. Nowhere is your tone of voice or setup of the question more important.

"Tell me about what makes you tick as a professional."

Listen to the explanation, but no matter where the conversation wanders (and it is all right to let the answer to this one wander for a minute or two), bring it back to these follow-up questions about anger:

"What are your pet peeves at work?"

"What types of people and work situations do you find most frustrating?"

"What situations can give rise to these problems?"

"Tell me about a situation that was so annoying that in hindsight you could have handled the frustration better."

The responses could reveal candidates with short fuses, and that's good for *manageability* and *teamwork* evaluation. You might also inquire about frustration and anger more directly with the next two questions.

"When was the last time you got really frustrated/angry?"

Also:

"Tell me about the last time you felt anger on the job."

It is important that whoever you hire is able to control and channel frustration. If the previous sequence doesn't quite give you all the information you need, you might try the following questions:

"What caused it?"

"What did you do about it?"

"Oh, the World Owes Me a Living"

There are few things more rewarding in a professional's life than putting out effort above and beyond the call of duty and getting recognition for a job well done. On the other hand, when an employee puts out extra effort over extended periods and these efforts are not recognized and rewarded, you lose good team members. Consequently, the prudent manager should take the time to see exactly what kinds of rewards and recognition serious candidates expect. However, you need to be sure not to make the candidate think you have now entered negotiations.

"Tell me about a time when you felt adequately recognized for your contributions."

A good answer will show *emotional maturity* and an understanding of the relevance of that contribution to the company's bottom line. Conversely, you could encounter the belief that a champagne brunch is in order every time a deadline is met.

You can follow this question with, *"What kinds of rewards are most satisfying to you?"* Ideally, you will hear that recognition and encouragement by management is most satisfying; such things are, after all, a personal validation of a person's efforts. *Layer* either of these questions with, *"How does this affect your performance?"*

"How do I get the best out of you?"

This is different from earlier questions about how prior managers got the best out of this candidate. This question is future-oriented and asks the candidate to define the ideal worker-manager relationship; it is a question that you will only ask of short-list candidates, *and you will write down the answers as they are given: partly to show that you are paying serious attention, and partly so that you have the facts in front of you, should this turn out to be the best candidate.*

What'd I Do?

One of the biggest headaches of a manager's life is the unexpected resignation. It demoralizes the troops, puts extra pressure on everybody, and makes you look bad. Time after time, people leave jobs because they do not feel appreciated for their efforts. Sometimes the one who leaves is the linchpin of the group, the person on whom you have come to rely—who in fact is so reliable that you take her for granted until it's too late. You can learn more about how bosses inadvertently cause resignations, and thereby reduce your turnover, when you ask the following questions.

"In what ways did your manager contribute to your decision to leave this/ that job?"

The answers will naturally be subjective and may once in a while rule out a particular candidate, but understanding workers' perceptions of you and your peers can be useful in honing your own management skills. You might also check out my companion career-management book for lots of ideas about how to successfully manage employees: *Knock 'em Dead in Management*, Volumes 1 and 2.

"What will your manager say when you go in to resign?"

This question can be helpful in determining how serious the candidate is about making a move. Sometimes, an employed candidate uses your job offer as leverage with a current employer, and has no real intention to leave her present situation. An ill-thought-out response to this question, or body language suggestive of discomfort, could indicate such a strategy.

Wrapping It Up

By the end of a third interview you should have gathered adequate information to determine that a candidate has the *technical skills* to do the job, is *motivated* to do a good job, is a *committed team player*, and will be *manageable* by you. In bringing this third interview to a close, you should give the candidate the opportunity to ask questions, promote his candidacy, and ask for the job: *"Are there any questions you would like to ask?"* or *"Is there anything we haven't covered that you think I should know about?"*

As we've said before, the interview is a two-way street, and the interviewee needs the chance to get information from you to make sure that your company is the right choice. After all, just as you are trying to hire the best, the candidate is also trying to hire on with the best employer for her professional future. You should be prepared to answer the candidate's questions clearly and honestly, so remember to brush up on benefits. When you have a serious candidate and cannot answer a question, arrange for her to speak to the appropriate person, either in person or on the phone, to get the question answered satisfactorily. Remember, when candidates make it to a third interview they are to be considered very serious contenders, and as such you want them ready to accept an offer should you decide to proffer it.

If you have used *stress* questions and techniques during the interview, it may be wise at this time to explain why you did so and let the candidate know that you are happy with the way she responded. A candidate will feel more comfortable accepting a job offer once he understands that there was a reason for your intermittently transforming into Attila the Hun.

After all of your short-list candidates have passed through the interview cycle, you move on to the decision-making process, perhaps scheduling a separate meeting to go over the job again, making sure that the candidate will accept your offer, and introducing her to team members and other levels of management. But first, to give you an even better handle on selection questions and techniques, we are going to look at questions for five specific titles: entry-level, administrative, sales, management, and executive. From a personal career standpoint, you should pay special attention to the questions directed at management candidates.

Restaurant Interviews

Not all interviews are conducted in your office or a conference room; they can happen in the strangest of places, and because you are a busy person who needs to fit in candidates wherever and whenever, you can find yourself conducting interviews over breakfast, lunch, or dinner.

The gesture of a meal with a job offer is never lost on a candidate as a warm and welcoming gesture, but interviews in restaurants can happen for other reasons too. Depending on the title and level of the job, *social graces* (one of the most overlooked *communication skills*) can play a significant role in the success of *all* senior positions. In fact, they are a plus in all jobs, and are only seen as unimportant by those who lack them.

Restaurant Meetings

By far the most common and useful setting for judging these issues is a restaurant. Over a meal, you get to observe a candidate's behavior in a public setting with strangers—both people with authority and those without—and his table manners, plus you gain other insights into personality that would be impossible to uncover in a formal interview setting. Besides, you have to eat sometime.

A neutral setting such as a restaurant can actually put the candidate on a quasi-equal footing with you. On the other hand, you are still in the driver's seat, and if you find yourself regularly interviewing in the same restaurants and hotel lobbies, you will be more relaxed and the unconventional setting could act as a *stress* element for the candidate, which of course has its own advantages.

As the interviewer, you get to choose the location, and it is usually a good idea to make a reservation, explaining the purpose of the meeting and asking for a secluded table. Corners are best because they tend to be quieter.

This meeting is often the final hurdle, and could include—or be the prelude to—a job offer. It is also a crucial *situational* interview test with candidates for whom table manners and conversational etiquette are primary *deliverables* of the job. It is never a good sign when candidates drink alcohol, smoke if permissible or leave the restaurant to smoke, knock over a glass, or dribble spaghetti sauce.

Here, you can ask any question you might ask in a more formal setting, plus you'll find topics impossible to address in the traditional office setting surfacing with virtually no effort on your part.

The candidate's *social graces* and general demeanor at the table can reveal as much about her as the answers to your questions. For instance:

- Drinking alcohol. This is a business meeting and alcohol relaxes and clouds judgment.
- Over-ordering food can signal poor self-discipline and a lack of budgetary concern. When you think about it, the candidate is there to talk and sell, and the eating and drinking is entirely secondary; as such, it can speak to lack of judgment and an inability to refrain from instant gratification.
- Returning food or complaining about the service, actions that, at the very least, find fault with your choice of restaurant.
- High-handed behavior toward waiters and busboys. This is insensitive, offensive to many of us, could point to personal insecurities, and reflects negatively on the candidate's ability to get along with subordinates and support staff. It also calls into judgment his *critical thinking skills*: Just who is impressed by rudeness to those who can't defend themselves?

Appropriate table manners become increasingly important the higher the rank of the job. No company needs a C-level executive who wields a dinner knife like a dagger.

By the same token, you have responsibilities in the *social graces* area too; if you offend a candidate with your own boorish manners, that candidate may start asking herself if the company you represent is the sort of place she would want to work for.

PART III
DIFFERENT JOBS, DIFFERENT QUESTIONS

All jobs are necessary; otherwise they wouldn't be on the payroll. However, some jobs are particularly testing to hiring managers. In this section we look at the issues faced when hiring workers without experience, hiring for the administrative positions that help departments run smoothly, hiring for the sales positions that bring in revenue, and hiring managers and executives.

ELEVEN

THE ENTRY-LEVEL HIRE

Hiring workers with no track record is an underappreciated challenge. You are hiring raw, untested talent with little or no real-world experience to help you judge *ability*. Corporate recruiters liken the gamble of hiring recent graduates to laying down wines for the future: Some will develop into full-bodied, excellent vintages, but others will be disappointments. When hiring professionals with work experience, you have a track record to evaluate; with recent graduates, there is little or nothing. Often, the only tangible information most interviewers have to go on is degree, SAT scores, and that ubiquitous burger-flipping job. That's not much to base a hiring decision on.

Potential *ability* to do the job is based on all facets of academic performance and whatever scant work experience you have to go on. A recent graduate who has any work experience gets points for effort, plus the experience gives you an opportunity to examine the candidate's understanding of a professional workplace. Although you have to accept that an entry-level worker must *develop* the *ability* to execute a job's *responsibilities*, the more desirable candidates will already have had some work experience, however humble, and will have started to develop the *transferable skills and professional values* that are the foundation of success in any job.

In this chapter, you will find some additional considerations and questions to give you that extra edge in determining real potential when buying "people futures." As with more senior job openings, you will customize your interview structure to each position, looking for the candidate's *motivation, manageability*, and *team spirit*, plus all the *transferable skills and professional values*.

The interview will start with general questions about education and experience to date, to get the candidate comfortable with talking. Without much work experience, educational background will obviously take on more significance. Start with an interview outline you have used for junior people in this position with little experience (or use the one at the end of this chapter), and then customize it to the entry-level situation and add any of the following questions that fit your needs.

Educational Experience

You will probably start with questions about education, and you can learn a great deal from how a candidate has handled the educational experience.

"Which of your school years was most difficult?"

This question opens a sequence that gets the candidate to focus on getting through tough experiences. You follow up with, *"Why do you feel that was the toughest year?"* or *"What were some of the toughest problems you faced?"* Then, concentrating on them one at a time, ask, *"Why was this difficult for you?"*; *"Why do you think that happened?"*; *"What did you do about it?"*; and, *"If you had to face this year/experience all over again, how would you do things differently?"*

The answers will give you insight into how the individual approaches life and its challenges: by procrastinating, laying the blame elsewhere, rushing blindly ahead, or planning and executing a considered response. Analyze the answers for pointers toward likes, dislikes, and causes of stress, as they would apply to your job.

"Do you think grades should be considered by first employers?"

Whatever the answer is, look for someone who can back up her beliefs. The question is not that valuable with a straight-A student but is very revealing with someone who may feel an understandable amount of guilt because her grades weren't perfect. With those who have perfect grades, as well as those who don't, you might ask, *"Do you feel you have anything else to learn?"* This question allows you to gain insight into potential *manageability* problems.

"So, these are the best grades you are capable of? How do we know you are good enough for our company?"

Also:

"Your grades aren't all that good. How do I know you are capable of doing the work?"

These questions on grades ask candidates to promote themselves from a defensive position. There is obviously a *stress* factor here, which is most suitable when the candidate will have to face intimidation on the job or when it is someone for whom you have high hopes. Your voice inflection plays an important role in determining the degree of *stress* you want to create: These two questions can lose much of their sting when asked in your most sympathetic voice. You should also remember that Steve Jobs and Bill Gates were dropouts, Edison never went to college, and Einstein, though he gained a degree, is long rumored to have received considerable help from a lady friend with his papers; and there you have the four greatest minds of the modern world.

"Can you put your education behind you and start from scratch in the professional world?"

This one takes a slightly different tack toward relating education to the workplace. The question usually comes as something of a shock to the candidate, so the degree of turmoil or confusion it causes can give you an indication of self-control. Occasionally, it flushes out aggression and a know-it-all-already attitude, which gives you early warning of some tiring times as a manager while you acclimate this person to the harsh realities of business.

"What college did you attend, and why did you choose it?"

The question examines the candidate's reasoning process. The college the candidate attended isn't as important as her reasoning for choosing it.

"How did you pay for college?"

Candidates who say, "Oh, Daddy handled all of that," should raise a red flag for you. Candidates who had parental assistance while carrying double majors, and maybe minors as well, were lucky to have the help and it shouldn't be held against them; interviewees who paid for their own education by working through college deserve special attention and often make the best entry-level employees, because they're clearly *motivated*, have real-world experience, and have had more opportunity to develop some of the *transferable skills and professional values* that underlie all jobs.

"We have tried to hire people from your school/your major before, and they never seem to work out. What makes you different?"

This *stress* question examines *critical thinking skills*. The point is to see whether the candidate can *think critically* and stay cool under pressure. It's often asked of candidates for sales jobs, where pressure situations demand that employees think on their feet. You might ask this of a candidate even if you've never actually had problems with employees from that school or major before. With a sales position, for example, you could be looking for a candidate whose *critical thinking skills* help him recognize that the objection cannot be overcome without first determining its cause; this candidate will ask about the problems you have experienced with such people before offering an answer.

This question not only gauges the candidate's level of understanding, but also her *motivation*. If she doesn't understand the changes happening in your profession, she's probably not *committed* to either the profession or the company, and what you have in front of you is just a young person in need of a job, rather than someone intent on launching a professional career.

"I'd be interested to hear about some things you learned in school that could be used on the job."

You want to hear about "real world" skills, and an explanation of what the experience of college taught the applicant about his profession and the professional world, rather than specific courses. You give points to candidates who can convincingly explain how college courses, the pressure of finals week, internships, or any other college experiences contributed to the development of any of the *transferable skills and professional values*.

Work Experience

If you're lucky enough to have some sort of work experience to assess, don't worry about its immediate relevance to the *deliverables* of the position. For one thing, you should be thanking your lucky stars you have *any* common ground to discuss; for another, the *transferable skills and professional values* are important precisely because they are not industry-specific: Even that burger-flipping job is an incubation tank for these skills and values, and instills a sense of why jobs exist and how a professional needs to behave at work.

"How did you spend your vacations while at school?"
Also:
"How did you get your summer jobs?"
Perhaps the greatest challenge in hiring recent graduates is that they are extremely difficult to judge due to their lack of real-world experience. It is far easier to get a fix on someone who has internship or college co-op work experience, so these candidates obviously have an edge. Nevertheless, any work experience while at school is valuable. Entry-level candidates with any work experience manage their time better, are more realistic, and are more mature. Candidates who have some work experience will stand out, because even limited experience fosters a basic understanding of the relationship between effort and money. Whether internships, co-ops, or burger-flipping jobs, the level of the job or type of experience is not as important as what and how much the candidate learned from the experience. This is where your questions should lead.

"What were your responsibilities at this job?"

Follow-Up:

"What did you learn from that job?"

"Did you ever feel bossed around? How did you react?"

"What did you like the least about the job? Why?"

"What hours did you work?"

"How many days a week did you work?"

"Do you like routine tasks/regular hours?"

"Did the job include repetitive tasks? What were they? How did you feel about each of them?"

"How did you feel about doing the same thing time and time again?"

Once you scratch the surface, no entry-level jobs are exciting. They all carry varying degrees of repetition, so understanding how the young candidate feels about regular hours and repetitive tasks, once the initial excitement has worn off, is important. The candidate's answers will tell you about *motivation* and *manageability*.

"Which of the jobs you have held have you liked least and why?"

All jobs involve a degree of repetition and drudgery, so expect immature candidates to say things like "I didn't like it because it was boring."

Follow up with, *"What did you learn from this job, if anything?"* What you're looking for is someone who shows a nascent understanding that you have to be willing to take the rough with the smooth that goes with any job, and that the less desirable aspects of the job need to be executed with the same attention to detail as the fun parts.

"What's your idea of how this profession/industry works?"

You don't want a dissertation, just the reassurance that the candidate doesn't think your profession works along the lines of a registered charity. Look for an understanding of the nuts and bolts of the services/products you deliver to your customer base, how your company brings in revenue in response to these considerations, and, ideally, an appreciation that every job exists because it contributes in some way to the company's bottom line.

"Can you take instructions without feeling upset or hurt?"

This is a *manageability* question. If the candidate takes offense eas-ily or bristles when her mistakes are pointed out, she won't last long with any company.

Reality Checks

"Are you looking for a temporary or permanent job?"

This is a good knockout question to ask at any point in the inter-view if you start to get a sneaking feeling that the candidate may not be around too long. You want reassurance that the applicant is genuinely interested in your opportunity and won't disappear in a few months.

"What have you done that shows initiative and willingness to work?"

The answer is valuable because you are giving the candidate an opportunity to share his *motivation* and the strength of his work ethic—both questionable attributes in a recent graduate. A good answer might discuss *anticipated problems* and strategies for coping with unanticipated ones.

"What kind of work interests you most, and why?"

This brings the interview back to the present and gives you an overall view of the career that the candidate feels would be fulfilling. To look into the candidate's objectivity and the degree to which she has researched your profession, you could follow with, *"What are the disadvantages of your chosen field?"* Then complete the sequence with, *"How do you think you will handle these?"*

"Why do you think you would like this type of work?"

This is a deceptive question because there is no pat answer. You ask it to see whether the candidate really understands what the specific job entails on a day-to-day basis. You can follow the response with more questions to probe this area, or you can give the candidate some information about the job that might help her decide whether she's really prepared to take on work of this kind.

"Why do you think this industry will sustain your interest over the long haul?"

Also:

"Why do you think you will shine in this profession?"

The answer should speak to the candidate's pragmatism and *motivation*.

"Do you plan on further education?"

A smart young candidate is one who understands the value of ongoing education in staying current in a rapidly changing professional world. Ask what educational goals the candidate intends to pursue, and why; you can then ask how those goals relate to a career in your profession. If the degree/courses are relevant to your business, it could be a good sign. But always be aware of that gap between dreaming and doing. This is especially true with recent graduates, who perhaps don't always understand the extra effort required to work full time and pursue academic studies.

"What are your future vocational plans?"

Also:

"Where do you want to be five years from now?"
"What type of position are you interested in?"
"What job in our company would you choose if you were free to do so?"
"What job in the company do you want to work toward?"

A candidate who has a real idea of how the profession works gets points for research and realism. These questions can help you get a feel for a candidate's sense of direction, inner strength, ambition, and *confidence*. A recent graduate may not have much practical experience, but *energy*, *commitment*, and drive can compensate. Regardless of the answer, you will find out how much the neophyte really understands about the nuts and bolts of the job and profession with questions like:

"Why that job?" and *"Tell me what you think a person in that position does on a daily basis?"*

The mistake many entry-level professionals make is to respond to questions about where they want to be in five years by saying, "In management," because they think that shows drive and ambition. It has become such a trite answer, though, that it should immediately generate a string of questions from you that, sad to say, most recent graduates can't answer:

"What is a manager's job?"

"What is a manager's prime responsibility?"

"A manager in what area?"

"How do you handle deadlines?"

You're looking for a candidate who responds with an understanding of *multitasking*. Discussion of school deadlines is quite acceptable if no work-related ones are forthcoming.

Entry-Level Interview Skeleton

There's no one sequence of questions that's perfect for every position. You may find some questions in the following skeleton that do not meet your particular needs. You may, for example, find yourself saying, "That wouldn't work for me, but if I twisted it this way or that way it would." A good plan would be to work through the *questioning techniques* discussed in Chapter 5, customizing this interview skeleton to your needs. You will find many questions here that beg for question *layering*, *past-performance*, or *situational* interviewing techniques. You will also notice that many of these questions are entry-level analogues of similar questions discussed in Chapters 8 through 10, and so you already have an understanding of the ways in which they can be adapted to the many unique hiring situations you will face in your management career.

Entry-Level Interview Skeleton

Educational Background
- Why did you enroll at your university?
- How would you describe your academic achievements?
- How did you choose your major?
- What academic subjects have you enjoyed most?
- Which school year was most difficult, and why?
- What changes would you make to your school?
- Tell me about your most rewarding college experience.
- What are your plans for further education?
- What extracurricular activities did you enjoy?
- How do you think college contributed to your overall development?
- Do you think first employers should consider college grades?
- Can you give me a sense of your capabilities?
- What have you learned from your mistakes in school?

Work History
- How would you describe your ideal job?
- What kind of work interests you most?
- What is your understanding of this job's responsibilities?
- Do you feel you still have anything to learn after all your years of academic study?
- Which summer job did you enjoy most?
- How many levels of management did you interact with?
- What was the job's biggest challenge?
- Tell me about a responsibility you have enjoyed. What has been your least valuable work experience?
- How would your references describe you?
- Are you looking for a permanent job, or do you plan to return to school?

Motivation and Leadership Potential
- If you were hiring a graduate for this position, what would you be looking for?

- What have you done that shows initiative and willingness to work?
- What would you look for in potential leaders for this organization?
- What experience have you had in leadership positions?
- As a leader, have your decisions ever been unpopular?
- When the pressure of work is high, where does your energy come from?
- Tell me about a time when unexpected events demanded that you reschedule your time.

Future Career
- Why are you interviewing with us?
- Why do you want to work here?
- Where else are you applying?
- What do you know about our company?
- What do you expect out of this job?
- What do you think you would like most about this job?
- What do you think you would like least?
- Will you go where the company sends you?
- How long will it take you to make a contribution?
- How will this job help you reach your long-term personal and career goals?
- How long will you stay with the company?
- What is more important at the start of your career, money or the job?
- What do you feel are the disadvantages of this field?
- Where do you think you could make the biggest contribution to this organization?
- What do you see yourself doing five years from now?
- How do you define a successful career?
- What can you do for us that someone else can't?
- What special characteristics do you have that I should consider?

Goals and Multitasking
- What are your long-term goals?
- How do you plan your day? Your week?

- How do you determine your priorities?
- An overwhelming, time-sensitive task has just been assigned to you. How do you plan a strategy for meeting your deadline?
- What happens when two priorities compete for your time?
- When short-term goals clash with long-term ones, which takes priority, and why?

Communication
- Getting the job done involves gathering information and input from others. How do you do this?
- What is the toughest communication problem you have faced?
- Tell me how you have verbally convinced someone of an approach or an idea.
- Tell me about a time when you have compromised successfully.
- In what situations are you inflexible?
- How do you overcome objections to your ideas?
- When have your verbal communications been important enough to follow up in writing?
- Are there situations better suited to written communication?
- What is the most difficult paper you have written?

Stress and Flexibility
- Tell me about a time when someone lost his temper with you in a business environment.
- Have you ever worked in a place where it seemed to be one crisis after another?
- What makes you tense or nervous?
- What is the most frustrating work-related experience you have faced?
- What do you do when you are being pressed for a decision?

Decision Making
- How will you evaluate the company for which you hope to work?
- What makes you think you have what it takes to be successful in this business?

- Do you take an intuitive or a logical approach to solving problems?
- What kinds of decisions are toughest for you?

Developmental Issues

- What do you see as some of your most pressing developmental needs?
- What have you been involved with that you now regret?
- What is the single biggest mistake you have made?
- What have the disappointments of life taught you?
- Tell me about an event that really challenged you. How was your approach different from that of others?
- Tell me about something you started but couldn't finish.

Teamwork

- Define cooperation.
- What is the difference between a friend and a colleague?
- Can you think of a time when you have successfully motivated friends or colleagues to achieve a difficult goal?
- How will you establish a working relationship with the employees in this company?
- How would you work with the various different opinions on a team in order to reach a goal?
- Define a good work atmosphere.
- Do you prefer working with others or alone?
- What are some of the common friction areas you watch for when working with others?

Manageability

- What qualities should a successful manager possess?
- What do you feel should be the relationship between the manager and the staff?
- Why should I hire you?
- How have past managers gotten the best out of you?
- Describe the toughest manager you ever had.
- How do you take direction?

- How do you take criticism?
- Tell me about an occasion when school or employer policies have been unfair to you.
- What have you been most frequently criticized for?
- Tell me about a time when your work or an idea was criticized.

The hiring decisions you make regarding entry-level candidates are never guaranteed. You are betting on the future with less-than-adequate information about past performance by which to judge. But as a prudent manager, with the best interests of your company and career at heart, you can reduce the long odds by careful evaluation of each candidate against the criteria addressed in this chapter.

TWELVE

THE ADMINISTRATIVE HIRE

Underpaid and underappreciated as they are, the glue that holds many departments in our companies together is the administrative staff. However, new technology is reducing their ranks, placing responsibility for self-administration more squarely on the shoulders of the individual. With more people relying on fewer administrative staff in a far more complex work environment, a superb administrative hire is a must-have for the lucky manager who can still justify one or more.

How do you make the right support/administrative hiring decision? What questions should you ask? Much administrative work can be measured in terms of functional *ability*, but a willingness to do the work is also critical, especially when that work is not "exciting." Such *motivation* often comes from the ability of a candidate to connect the job to the overall success of the department.

Anyone who has had to work with a difficult administrative assistant knows that the personal chemistry among boss, team, and support staff can make the difference between a productive and a depressing workplace, so *teamwork* and *manageability* are enormously important. You can harvest relevant questions addressing *ability*, *motivation*, and *manageability* from the other chapters as they relate to your specific needs, and then check your interview structure against the interview skeleton at the end of this chapter to make sure you have all your bases covered.

The Support/Administrative Career Path

The need for more productivity and cohesive *teamwork* is critical in all companies, but you might be hard-pressed to find an administrative assistant who will burn the midnight oil on your behalf. One of the reasons for this is that we still consider secretaries, receptionists, and general administrative assistants in their traditional role: as functionaries without the *ability* to take on increasing responsibility. However, technology places more and more responsibility for the smooth running—and therefore success—of a department in the hands of support staff. Without the opportunity for growth, and absent professional respect from the team, why would anyone stretch for an employer? So when you hire administrative staff, don't be blind to useable talent just because of the job title: Providing professional growth for your staff is very much a part of how you build loyalty and a high-performing team that will propel your own professional growth.

In the following administrative skeleton interview, there may be questions that do not meet your particular needs, but you may find that reading them generates completely new and relevant questions for your situation.

You should remember to employ the interviewing techniques discussed elsewhere in this book when building interview scripts for admin/support hires. For example, you will find many questions here that beg for question *layering*, *past-performance*, or *situational* interviewing techniques. Just like the skeleton interviews for management, sales, and entry-level positions, this skeleton is intended to be a standard against which to check your own personalized question sequences.

Notice that many of these questions are administration-focused analogues of similar questions discussed in Chapters 8 through 10, and so you already have an understanding of the ways in which they can be adapted to the many unique hiring situations you will face in your management career.

Work History
- Describe a typical workday.
- Tell me about your responsibilities.
- What skills can you bring to this position, other than the ones required in the job description?
- What accomplishments are you proudest of?
- What aspects of your job give you the most enjoyment?
- What aspects of your job cause you the most problems?

Ability and Suitability
- What would you change about your current job?
- How do you handle repetitive tasks?
- What are you looking for in your next job?
- What are the personal qualities this job demands?
- What aspects of your job do you consider the most crucial?
- How would you describe yourself in terms of your work?
- Tell me about your role in a crisis situation.
- Have you ever worked for more than one manager at a time?
- How does your job relate to the overall success of your department and your company?
- Tell me about a time when the boss was absent and you had to make a decision.
- What special responsibilities or assignments have you been given?
- Tell me about an occasion when you chose, for whatever reason, not to finish a particular task.
- Have you ever found it necessary to sacrifice personal plans in favor of your professional responsibilities?
- Are you prepared to perform duties that may not be part of your job description?
- Describe what you think a typical day would be like on this job.
- Tell me about a time when your performance did not live up to your expectations.
- Where do you see yourself six months from now?
- What kind of work interests you most?
- If you could have any job in this company, what would it be?

- How would that job help you reach your long-term personal and career goals?
- How do you define a successful career?

Motivation
- Do you ever find it necessary to go above and beyond the call of duty to get a job done?
- What role do you play in ensuring a smooth working environment when your boss is away?
- What have you done to become more effective in your career?
- If you went to your boss for a raise, why would you be doing it?

Flexibility
Support and administrative personnel must be flexible in ways not always necessary in other jobs. Here are some questions that examine this flexibility:

- How do you prioritize your responsibilities?
- Do you prefer handling one task at a time, or juggling multiple responsibilities?
- How do you handle a crisis when it is clear that priorities have to be changed?
- Have you ever found it necessary to come in early or stay late?
- In what ways do you find that work interferes with your personal life?
- Tell me about a time when you had an overwhelming number of urgent requests to handle. How did you prioritize?
- Your boss is going on vacation for a month, and although it isn't in your job description to do so, she asks you to work for another manager in her absence. What would you say and do?
- Are you prepared to fill in for someone who has different responsibilities?
- How many levels of management do you deal with?
- What types of people do you get along with best?
- How do you get along with people who you don't like?

- How necessary is it to be creative in your job?
- Describe the toughest situation you have ever faced.
- How many projects can you handle at a time?
- How do you prioritize your projects?
- When have you rescheduled your time to accommodate an unexpected workload?
- Have you ever been affected by communication problems between two managers?
- Have you ever dealt with the general public?
- Do you handle personal matters for your boss?
- When was the last time something or someone got you really upset at work?
- Tell me about a time when you put your foot in your mouth.
- The receptionist has gone home sick. Are you prepared to fill in for her, even though the job is beneath your level of responsibility?

Communication
- Tell me about the kinds of communications you type at work.
- Do you ever compose letters for others?
- How do you set up a letter? An invoice?
- What was the most complex document you ever produced?
- What forms or documents have you developed for your department?

Planning and Organization
- Describe your method for keeping track of important matters.
- How do you plan your day?
- How would you plan for a major project?
- Do you set goals for yourself?
- Tell me about a time when, despite careful planning, things got out of hand.

Teamwork and Manageability

Some of these questions are a little pointed, but they can help give you a three-dimensional picture that focuses on the indispensible functions of an administrative employee. You need someone who has the *skills* required by the job, plus the *ability* to plan, organize, prioritize, self-start, and remain flexible enough to juggle conflicting priorities. Rephrase the last sentence and you'll find it full of the *transferable skills and professional values* that we discuss throughout this book.

Reliability is a major concern when it comes to hiring admin/support staff, and this concern becomes greater as the workload and *responsibilities* increase. Poor work habits can have far-reaching repercussions. Some of these questions might help:

Teamwork
- What do you see as your role within the department?
- How do you think your job relates to the deliverables of the department?
- How do you get along with all the different personality types that are part of your daily interactions?
- What types of people are difficult for you to work with? How do you deal with them?
- Tell me about a time when you felt it better to go about a task in your own way, rather than follow established procedures.
- When have you worked on a project of little enough importance that you let it slide?
- Have you ever found it necessary to sacrifice personal plans in favor of your professional responsibilities?
- Have you ever worked with a group like this before?
- How do you establish a working relationship with new people?
- Tell me how you see your responsibilities as a group member.
- What kind of people do you like to work with?
- What kind of people do you dislike working with?
- What do you do when you have to work with these people?

- Have you ever had to stifle your normal behavior to get along with someone?
- How do you feel about people who don't like their jobs? How do you define a congenial work atmosphere?

Manageability
- How does your boss get the best out of you?
- How do you get the best out of your boss?
- What do you think of your current boss?
- Describe the best manager you ever had.
- Describe the worst manager you ever had.
- What made those managers stand out?
- How do you react to criticism?
- How do you take direction?
- Describe the toughest manager you ever worked for.
- Tell me about the kinds of rewards that make you feel adequately recognized for your contributions.
- How do your work habits change when your boss is out of the office?
- How could your boss do a better job?
- In what ways has your boss contributed to your reasons for leaving your job?

Evaluating Career Orientation

Like everyone else, many administrative professionals have career goals, which, for a good hire, have to match your realities. There's no disguising the fact that there are few promotional opportunities for administrative staff, and you want someone who understands reality—and yet is *motivated* to work hard nevertheless. These people do exist, because they have other responsibilities, obligations, and/or interests in their lives.

Many administrators are female and over fifty percent of successful entrepreneurs in this country are women, who frequently admit to being driven to entrepreneurial endeavor because their potential for growth is so consistently ignored in the traditional corporate world. Understanding the professional goals of your candidates will help you make intelligent hiring decisions and guide you in the successful long-term management of a capable and motivated employee. Here are some revealing questions that can help you define a candidate's career orientation in a professional area in which upward mobility isn't always easy.

- What are your professional goals for the future?
- Where do you see yourself six months from now?
- Where do you see yourself a year or two from now?
- What do you see as your responsibilities in achieving professional growth?
- What new skills have you developed in the last year?
- What new skills are you developing right now?
- What skills do you plan to develop in the coming year?
- What commitments do you make to your profession outside of work?
- What job would you like to work toward in our company?
- If you could have any job in our company, which would it be?
- How would this job help you reach your professional goals?
- How do you define a successful career?

The answers you get will tell you what will *motivate* each candidate over the long haul, and in the process you will also learn about his personal *commitment* to professional growth.

The hiring decision you make regarding an administrative staff member is as important as any you will ever make. Not only are these professionals responsible for the smooth flow of work in your department, they also have considerable impact on your ability to function. As a prudent manager, with the best interests of your company and your own professional success at heart, you can increase the chances of making a good hire by carefully developing the job description and not skimping on the selection process. These are important positions that have a direct impact on your future.

THIRTEEN

The Sales Hire

With turnover higher in sales than in other professions, and given the impact of the sales function on profitability, it's arguable that hiring the right sales staff is one of management's toughest jobs. The situation is further complicated by the superior *communication skills* of salespeople and their tendency to regard the interview as a sales presentation to a prospect representing the product they know best: themselves. They know how to emphasize the good points and minimize or steer clear of the others.

You already have an appreciation of interview structure and evaluation techniques, and you also have plenty of useful questions. In this chapter, you will find additional questions to give you an edge in penetrating those persuasive *communication skills* and getting to the truth of each candidate's *technical skills*, *problem-solving skills*, and other *transferable skills and professional values*.

"What do you know about our product line?"

Once you have walked a candidate through her work history (following the steps discussed earlier in the book), this can make a good opening question in the area of sales *ability*. Only an incompetent would go for a job interview in sales without a clear understanding of the company product or service line. Yet your question goes beyond this: You are looking for an understanding of how your product/service fits into the overall marketplace in which you compete.

"What steps are involved in selling your product/service?"

This question will sort out those who happen to be making a living in a good economy from those who will be able to sell regardless of the economic climate. For this, good *critical thinking skills* must accompany excellent *listening, written,* and *verbal communication skills* as well as *multitasking skills*. The answer helps give you an understanding of the candidate's grasp of the building blocks that lead to consistent sales performance.

"How do you plan your day?"

Also:

"Do you find it helpful to prioritize activities?"

The ego strength necessary for survival in sales can raise problems of *manageability*; consequently, a candidate's self-discipline and *multitasking skills* need to be examined. The Plan/Do/Review cycle is central to planning and prioritizing activities, and is nowhere more important than in successful execution of the sales process.

You need to identify candidates who understand why and how to prioritize activities and clients. Salespeople organize their day around the behavior of the industry they serve. For instance, when the hospitality industry is your field, you would never call on a client between 11 A.M. and 2 P.M.—lunchtime for the rest of us, but the busiest time of the day for restaurateurs.

In the context of examining how sales candidates deal with *time management*, you will also want to examine the mandatory non-selling activities that promote sales, such as tracking all sales activities—from e-mail to phone call to meeting—to closing ratios and all account interactions: *"How much time do you spend establishing a paper trail of your activities, their results, and other non-selling activities?"* You'll need to confirm the time of day these duties are performed, and match this information with your business's prime selling hours.

The Business of Sales

"What different types of customers do you deal with/have you called on?"
Also:
"What titles have you sold to and in what types of companies?"

Ask this question early in the interview process to tell you what experience the candidate has in dealing with the types of clients, companies, and job titles relevant to your particular customer base. The higher the ticket price of the item being sold, the longer the sales process, the more sophisticated the buyer, and therefore the more sophisticated the salesperson, including especially *critical thinking*, all eight of the *communication skills*, and *determination*.

"How many e-mails, phone calls, and in-person visits does it typically take to reach a decision maker?"
Also:
"What percentage of your sales calls result in full presentations to decision makers?"
"What are the three most common obstacles to reaching a decision maker?"
Follow-Up:
"How do you overcome each of these?"
"How do you go about identifying new customers in an old or existing market?"

This question sequence explores a candidate's ability to get through to the decision maker. It is unwise to accept any simply numerical answer as it stands—e.g., "50 percent"—because numbers and statistics are easy to fudge and difficult to remember in a long conversation; this sequence of questions will engage the candidate in a revealing discussion about her understanding of, and performance in, her market.

Watch for discrepancies in the numbers: A sales associate who claims to close one of every two sales presentations and who isn't ranked very near the top of her peers is either lying or has other performance problems such as deals falling apart because they weren't properly qualified or closed in the first place. So you can ask, *"Where do you rank in among your peers?"* and *"When you talk about a closed deal/completed sale, how would you define completion?"*

"How long does it typically take you to move from initial contact to close of sale?"

Also:

"How many phone calls/e-mails/in-person meetings does an average sale usually involve?"

Follow-Up:

"What criteria do you use to qualify a potential sale?"

"How do you establish a potential customer's needs?"

"At what point do you go for the close?"

"What techniques do you find effective in closing sales?"

Together, the answers to these questions will tell you about the candidate's grasp of selling and managing the sales process. For example, if you listen closely you'll discover whether the candidate likes to go for the close or merely jogs along, waiting until prospects make decisions of their own volition.

"How large a client base do you need to maintain sales on an even keel?"

With this question you approach one of the bigger issues for anyone working in the world of sales. As a salesperson, you have to make sales, and you want to make sales with companies who can give you repeat business, but logic tells you that all buying cycles come to an end. This is common sense, but as a hiring manager, you need to determine whether the candidate shares this awareness, and recognizes the need to build prospecting—consistent expansion of the customer base—into his everyday activities, and so maintain consistent sales in a way that also supports steady growth.

"Have you ever broken in a new territory/desk?"

"How did you approach the job?"

"How do you go about identifying and ranking customers in a new market?"

"How do you prefer to approach and secure new clients?"

"How do you turn a new client into a repeat buyer and then a regular customer?"

All of these questions address the issue of volume of activity (sales at core being a numbers game), market penetration, and market development, because these are the activities that keep the sales pipeline full. The responses give you specific information about preferred approaches, and can also tell you about the candidate's *motivation* to treat sales as a real career. You also will learn more about *creativity*, *critical thinking skills*, and *determination*.

You can repeat this whole sequence with this simple variation:

"Have you ever had to learn and introduce a new product/service to a territory?"

Also:

"Have you ever taken over an existing territory/desk?"

Follow-Up:

"How did you go about establishing rapport with existing clients?"

"What was the volume when you started? What was it when you left?"

"How did you review this territory and identify opportunities for expansion?"

These are all questions that take the focus from the individual sale to the larger picture of the business of sales; the answers to these *past-performance questions* should give you an idea of how your candidate is likely to accept and deliver on the challenges your opportunity presents. Of course, any market that has been left as it was found is eloquent testimony to a lack of skill, effort, and/or knowledge of market penetration and development techniques. Remember that any question can be rephrased as a *past-performance question* by opening with, *"Tell me about a time . . ."* and following up with questions that nail that story to a specific time and employer. Using techniques that ask sales candidates to talk about specific events helps keep them honest.

"What kind of people do you like to sell to?"

Follow-Up:

"What type of people don't you like to sell to?"
"How do you manage to sell to these people?"
"Tell me about the most difficult prospect you turned into a buyer."
"Tell me about a prospect you couldn't close."

This question sequence is designed to help you examine the candidate's ability to deal with difficult customers. You can flesh it out with *past-performance* queries—*"So tell me about a time you had to sell to someone like this."*—or by role-playing a situation: *"Perhaps I'd understand better if I put myself in the position of that customer. How will you respond when I say* [use a standard objection that your people regularly face]*?"*

"I'd be interested to hear about a difficult collection problem."

You are looking for insight into this specific challenge, but also for an understanding of how well the candidate executes the sale and thereby avoids post-sale problems. Sales go wrong after a deal is inked as well as in the sales process itself, and you can customize this question to fit your particular situation: It is, of course, most relevant if your sales force is involved with collection issues. You can follow this with, *"In hindsight, how could you have avoided this problem?"* After the answer, ask for another example of the same problem that has occurred since, to find out whether this candidate learns from his mistakes—understanding of course that collection problems are not always the fault of the account manager.

"How involved should an account manager be with individual customers and the customer base as a whole?"

You are looking for the insight that empowers a sales professional to get close to customers in order to understand and sell to their needs, while also maintaining an objective distance. Customers have buying cycles that crest and then crash, so your best candidate is one who combines a hard head with a broad client base and an intellectual understanding of these realities. So while she always pursues opportunities for further sales with an existing client, the ideal candidate is equally sensitive to the duration of this company's buying cycle.

You might follow this question with, *"All companies have buying cycles. How do you track where a company is on that continuum?"* and, *"When a company isn't buying, how do you build a relationship for when they start buying again? How much time does this take?"*

"Tell me about your most difficult sale and how you approached it."

In sales, as in other professions, you learn much about candidates' *ability* and *motivation* when you understand how they handle problems. Good sales managers know that the majority of tough, messy, or failed closes could have been avoided with better initial screening of the prospect and attention to the details along the way—that's how they got to be sales managers. The question looks for this same kind of *critical thinking ability*, and in addition uncovers areas ripe for professional development.

The answer might well highlight specific areas of interest worth probing further. For example: *"So the sale was difficult because . . ."*; *"Why do you feel that way?"*; and *"In hindsight, what could you have done earlier in the sale to prevent the problem arising in the first place?"*

"What was the most surprising objection you ever heard, and how did you handle it?"

This question is a natural segue to a sequence of *situational* questions around the sales objections common in your business, such as: *"What would you do if I said . . . ?"* A sales professional's job is dealing with objections day in and day out, so you want to know about *listening skills*, *critical thinking skills*, and poise. A good salesperson doesn't just launch into his pitch and try to steamroll over objections; he recognizes that the heart of sales is *listening* to find out what the customer wants. Only then is it time to activate *verbal communication skills*.

You might continue with, *"What are the three most common objections you run into?"* or *"What are the very toughest objections you have met in your job?"* You can also follow up with, *"How do you handle that?"* You can easily simulate real objections by using a *situational* interviewing tactic, getting the candidate to role play with you. A good way of doing it is to follow up on almost any of the questions in this sequence with, *"I think I understand, but perhaps it would be better if you showed me. If I were the customer and I said, 'It's too expensive,' what would you say?"* Short of having the candidate make a live sales presentation, *situational* techniques like this will get you closest to the candidate's real performance capabilities. Slip into the approach conversationally for best effect. The next example is a common but effective case in point.

"Sell me this pen."

This is such a wonderfully appropriate sales interview question that I'm surprised it isn't asked more frequently. At the root of every successful sale is the salesperson's ability to identify a need and subsequently demonstrate how the product will fill that need. This is commonly known as feature/benefit selling: "Here is the feature, and this is what it can do for you." This question tests your candidate's awareness of an essential sales skill and showcases his quick thinking (or lack thereof). The beauty of this question is that it abstracts from any industry-specific language and gets at the sales skills in their purest form.

"Tell me about a time when all seemed lost on an important sale. What did you do to turn it around?"

Look for a positive and *determined* attitude. There is a saying in sales that the sale isn't dead until the client is dead or has said "no" three times. That's the kind of persistence you want to see in a candidate. Since sales techniques differ with the product, service, and company, dogged persistence must be measured against company and client norms of etiquette—a question determined by the philosophy of your company's sales management team.

"Tell me about your most crushing failure."

Give the candidate all the time necessary to come up with an answer. We have all experienced defeat. You are interested in the event and circumstances, but just as much in the resilience with which the candidate handled defeat. Alternatively, you might say, *"Give me a specific example of a time when you were rejected, and how you handled it."* Ego strength and positive self-image are important components of the overachiever, which is a personality type that many believe is particularly suited to sales. Salespeople must not only be able to handle stress; it needs to be a *motivating* factor in their lives. Most important, sales professionals must be able to emerge from stressful situations with their egos firmly intact, or at least without any wounds that can't be healed by a good night's sleep; these are people who clearly understand the difference between *refusal of product* and *rejection of self.*

"Give me an example of a sale that was, for all intents and purposes, lost. How did you turn the situation around and then make the sale?"

Sales is a stressful profession, so your candidates need to be able to handle the tough questions. To keep any candidate malleable, though, you must intersperse the tough questions with easier ones. This question is easy for the candidate, but don't tune out: You just might miss a salesperson who regularly closes sales with deep discounting as the lead tool. Look for *listening skills, critical thinking skills,* and an ability to ask perceptive questions.

"All of us have failed to meet a quota at one point or another. When you don't meet your goals, how do you handle it?"

This question examines *determination* and can also be a springboard for probing where, when, how, and why the quota was missed. Because such a problem can often be one of prioritization, your next question could be, *"Why is it important to prioritize?"*

"Give me an example of a time when a sales quota period had gone sour on you and it was necessary to reach that quota in a short period of time. How did you do it?"

Every salesperson in the world has lost business and approached the end of the quota period empty-handed. You are using the question to examine whether or not the candidate can come from behind. You are also likely to get good question fodder concerning how the emergency arose in the first place—was the candidate perhaps coasting after a good quarter? You might follow up with, *"Tell me about a time when you exhibited persistence but still couldn't reach a carefully planned goal."*

"What have you been most frequently criticized for, and by whom?"

This is an *open-ended question*, and the odds of getting a straightforward answer from a salesperson are rarely good. Nevertheless, you'll never know what you might dig up if you don't ask, and the question doubles very adequately as a test of the quick thinking and poise so necessary in sales.

"How do you keep yourself going when everyone is having a bad day/is unorganized/is depressed?"

Also:

"Have you ever worked in an environment where people took advantage when management was absent? How did you handle it?"

These will tell you about *emotional maturity*, self-discipline, and *productivity*. In the sales world, someone has always just lost a sale or a client. It's all part of the territory, and can be a downer; the last thing you need on the team, however, is someone who will allow his own motivation and emotions to be affected by the negativity of others. In the responses, look for evidence of *determination* and a strong sense of self-worth. Sometimes a candidate will tell you what happens when she is having a bad day/is unorganized/is depressed. When this happens, you will of course want to probe the cause of the problem. Ask, *"What causes you to feel depressed?"*; *"How often does this happen to you?"*; and *"What have you done to be more effective in your present position?"*

Here you look for that extra effort made outside of work hours and beyond company-sponsored programs. You are hoping to find candidates who invest themselves in their professional future—perhaps a candidate who has studied the technical side of the product line, regularly attends sales seminars, or reads motivational books.

"How productive are you compared to your peers?"

Also:

"How smart are you compared to your peers?"

"How articulate are you compared to your peers?"

"How well dressed are you compared to your peers?"

"How witty are you compared to your peers?"

"How do you rank professionally compared to your peers?"

"How tenacious are you compared to your peers?"

"How well do you accept disappointment compared to your peers?"

These eight questions are all about ego strength. These are all questions that elicit subjective responses, but by the same token, you cannot possibly be expected to know the candidate's peers, so don't take the answers at face value, because all you will get is an impression of whether or not the candidate can talk a good game. Take advantage, rather, of the fact that the candidate is willing to take a position on, for example, why she is more tenacious than her peers.

Then, in the second part of the question, ask the candidate to defend the position, just as she must do in a tough sales presentation. For example, ask *"How creative are you compared to your peers?"* You might follow up with a *past-performance question*, such as: *"I'd be interested to hear about a time when you proved more tenacious than your peers."*

"What have been your highest and lowest rankings in your current/last sales force?"

All salespeople know exactly where they rank, so don't let someone off with an, "I can't remember." If that is the reply, tell the candidate to take his time—then shut up and wait. If you do have to elicit an answer in this way, and you intend to give some credence to it, be certain to verify it with a reference check. Any reticence or evasion on such an important issue for a salesperson is grounds for suspicion.

"Give me an example of a time when you surpassed what was expected of you from your employer."

Also:

"I'd be interested to hear about a specific time when you greatly exceeded the norm."

This is a chance for a candidate to brag, perhaps, but it also gives you the opportunity to find out just what this person considers exceptional performance. Of course, if no story is forthcoming, you might be in serious trouble.

"What do you dislike most about sales?"

This will test quick thinking and *creativity*. There are many odious but necessary tasks in sales, and you need to know if a specific "dislike" will preclude the candidate's doing the work necessary for success. If the answer is unhesitatingly "prospecting" or "making cold calls," it may well be the last question you have to ask—successful sales are based on making new contacts. Obviously, you'd prefer to hear that the most disliked task is record keeping and expense reports. Follow through with queries about how the candidate deals with these odious responsibilities.

"How do you feel about out-of-town/overnight travel?"

If travel or unusual hours are required to do the job, you need to know early on if personal circumstances preclude a candidate from doing the job. Where you place this question depends on the problems you experience with your team's travel schedule.

Telemarketing Skills

While not all sales jobs are done exclusively over the phone, almost all require a fair amount of time on the instrument. Here is a sequence of questions to help you evaluate the efficacy of candidates when they have to work with the telephone. Naturally, you will customize these questions to the circumstances in which the telephone is used in your sales process.

"What part of the sales process do you conduct over the telephone rather than face-to-face?"

Also:

"Have you ever sold anything over the telephone?"
"What special skills or techniques are necessary to be successful over the telephone?"

To sell on the phone—even to facilitate sales—requires a set of skills separate from face-to-face sales. Because there are no facial expressions or body language to help the salesperson, she must rely on voice inflection, highly developed *listening skills*, and advanced questioning and conversation-control techniques, very similar to the techniques we discussed in Chapter 5.

"When getting through to a sales prospect for the first time on the phone, what roadblocks can you expect?"

When telemarketing, it is necessary first of all to reach the decision-making individual. You may even want to role-play one or two of the relevant roadblocks. Follow up with, *"When you reach a potential client or decision maker on the phone for the first time, how do you establish rapport?"*

"How do you go about gathering names of new contacts on the telephone?"

The answer to this question will tell you how an intelligent sales-person can identify new prospects quickly and cost effectively with the telephone, and how prospecting (asking the right questions) is, in the right hands, an integral part of the many conversations a sales professional has during the day.

A Skeleton Interview for Sales

There's no one sequence of questions that's perfect for every position. You may find some questions in the following skeleton that do not meet your particular needs. You may, for example, find yourself saying, "That wouldn't work for me, but if I twisted it this way or that way it would." A good plan would be to work through the *questioning techniques* discussed in Chapter 5 to help customize this interview skeleton to your needs. You will find many questions here that beg for question *layering, past-performance,* or *situational* interviewing techniques. You will also notice that many of these questions are sales-focused analogues of similar questions discussed in Chapters 8 through 10, so that you already have an understanding of the ways in which they can be adapted to the many unique hiring situations you will face in your management career.

Ability and Suitability
- Why are you pursuing a career as a professional salesperson? What are your qualifications?
- Where is your experience/preference, in B2B or B2C sales?
- Of all your work in sales, where have you been more successful: in servicing clients or in developing a new territory?
- Would you prefer to sell a big- or a small-ticket item?
- When you consider your skills as a professional salesperson, what area concerns you most about your ability to sell?
- What aspects of sales do you like most?
- What do you find to be the most repetitive tasks of your job?
- What bothers you most about sales?
- How necessary is it to be creative in your job?
- What makes you think you can sell consistently?
- Tell me about your training. What have you done to become a better salesperson?
- What do you know about our company and its products?
- What do you like least about the job description?
- What special characteristics should I consider about you as a person?

Willingness
- Tell me about a sales project that really got you excited.
- What do you consider a good day's sales effort?

- Tell me about a time when you exceeded both your quota and your goals.
- When the pressure is on, where does your extra energy come from?
- How often do you find it necessary to go above and beyond the call of duty?
- Do you ever take work home?
- Give me an example of your initiative in a challenging situation.
- What are some of the things in sales that you find difficult to do?

The Indomitable Salesperson

- Tell me about a sale that was, for all intents and purposes, lost. How did you turn the situation around?
- What are the three most common objections you face?
- What would you say if the customer said, "It's too expensive"?
- Tell me about your most difficult sale. How could you have prevented problems from arising?
- Is it sometimes difficult to get an immediate "yes" from customers? What do you do in these situations?
- When do customers really try your patience?
- Tell me about a sale you couldn't close because of lack of information. What did you do?
- How do you feel when you get rejected?
- Tell me about an important sale that started to go wrong. How did you weather the storm?
- How do you react when you miss a sales quota?

Self-Image

- Do you consider yourself successful?
- What do you feel are your personal limitations?
- What sales achievement are you most proud of?
- What do you consider your greatest strength?
- How do you rank among your peers?

Communication

- What types of people do you sell to in your current job?

- Tell me how you made an "impossible" sale.
- Tell me about an occasion when your timing was good.
- Tell me about an occasion when your timing was bad.
- What do you do when you can't get a word in edgewise?
- Sell me this pen.
- How do you get a fix on people in the first few moments after meeting them?
- How do you turn things around when the initial impression you make is bad?
- Tell me about how you dealt with an angry or frustrated customer.
- How often do you prepare sales reports? How detailed are they?
- When and where in the sales process have you found silence a useful tool?
- How do you get an understanding of a customer's needs?
- What business or social situations make you feel awkward? How do you overcome this feeling?

Telephone Communication Skills
- How much time do you spend on the telephone in your job?
- What services or products have you sold over the phone?
- What special skills and techniques lead to success on the phone?
- How do you establish a rapport with a stranger on the phone?
- What kinds of roadblocks do you expect from clerical staff over the phone? How do you handle them?
- How many phone calls do you make in a day?

Multitasking
- How much time do you spend doing paperwork and non-selling activities?
- How do you organize yourself for day-to-day activities?
- Describe a typical day.
- Tell me about the planning for an important project.
- Tell me about the problems you face in getting all of the deliverables of your job completed on time.

- What are the component parts of your job, and how much time do you spend on each?
- How many accounts do you like to handle at one time?
- Do you set goals that are easy or difficult to reach?
- Tell me about some long-term working goals and how you are getting along in achieving them.

Market Penetration
- What steps are involved in selling your product?
- How long does it typically take to go from initial contact to closing the sale?
- What percentage of your sales calls result in a full presentation?
- What kind of people do you like to sell to?
- What kind of people don't you like to sell to?
- Have you ever broken in a new territory for an employer?
- How do you turn an occasional buyer into a regular buyer?
- What was the most important account you have worked on?
- Tell me about a difficult collection problem.
- What are you most proud of in your ability to develop a marketplace?

Sales Maturity
- What do you feel are the most important personal characteristics of a successful salesperson?
- What have you learned from the different sales jobs you've had?
- What aspects of your work do you consider most crucial?
- Why do people buy a product or service?
- What kinds of rewards are most satisfying to you?
- What are some of the things you have found especially motivating over the years?
- What do you dislike most about sales?

Problem Solving and Decision Making
- What kinds of problems do you have to solve as a salesperson?
- What kinds of problems do you find complex or overwhelming?
- Have you ever made a quick decision that cost you money?

- What kinds of decisions are most difficult for you?
- What is the biggest mistake you have made in your career?
- Do you discuss important decisions with anyone?

Teamwork
- Explain your role as a group member of a sales force.
- How would you define a congenial work atmosphere?
- How do you deal with disagreements with others?
- Have you ever had to change your behavior to work successfully with others?
- Have you ever been with a sales team that fell apart?

Manageability
- How does your boss get the best out of you?
- How do you get the best out of your boss?
- Describe the best manager you ever had.
- Describe the worst manager you ever had.
- Tell me about the last time you really got angry about a management decision.
- If you could make one constructive suggestion to your current management, what would it be?
- How do you take direction? How do you take criticism?
- What are some of the things your boss did that you disliked?
- What types of decisions are beyond your level of authority at your current job?
- If a coworker came to you with a complaint about the job, how would you react?
- Do you feel you are adequately recognized for your contributions?

Salespeople regard the interview as a sales presentation, and you as a hot prospect. Most salespeople know that it is easier to sell to a friend—someone who wants to speak with them in the first place—than to a stranger, and that makes your job doubly hard. Be sure to remain objective and methodical in your approaches to interviewing sales personnel, or you may get sold something that you don't really need.

FOURTEEN

The Management Hire

While all management jobs have certain responsibilities in common, not all management jobs are alike. Sometimes there is a mistaken focus on the *technical skills* of the profession rather than management competency. *Technical skills* and a wide frame of reference for the issues of the profession should be a given, but do not in themselves constitute qualifications for management. Your real concern is discovering whether the candidate can *hire effectively*, *get work done through others*, and coach staff in executing their *responsibilities* in ways that *anticipate, prevent, and solve problems* within their individual areas of responsibility. This latter mandate includes staff selection, training, *motivation*, performance reviews, discipline, troubleshooting, and termination.

You understand by now that all management jobs share a credo: *Get work done through others*. It's natural, therefore, to assume that management candidates understand this and, by extension, that they understand the art and science of interviewing. However, this is not always the case. When the people you hire must in turn hire and *get work done through others*, making the right hiring decision becomes even more important to the company and your ongoing career success.

Management Competency

With this in mind, your first sequence of questions should deal with determining general management competency and the size and scope of your candidate's job.

"How would you define your job as a _____?"
Also:
"How would you define your responsibilities?"
Over time, we all develop notions of what managers do based on our own experience, so it is all too easy to project those preconceptions onto your candidates if you don't ask for their personal definitions. You will follow up with, *"How many people do you manage and how?"* and *"What job titles are you responsible for?"* Answers to these questions will allow you to determine both the size and the scope of the individual's department and job.

"Do these people report directly and solely to you, or on a project basis?"
There is an important difference. The duties we traditionally associate with a manager are hiring, training, managing work assignments, performance and salary reviews, discipline, and terminations as necessary. However, there are other definitions that a candidate might be using. For example, project management: at its most elementary level, it could be one person managing a project for which she is solely responsible—in a flattening corporate hierarchy, the sobriquet "manager" is increasingly debased in this way—or it could mean that three employees worked under the guidance of a fourth with a similar title on a particular project. That fourth person with project responsibility becomes in some minds a manager (titles being cheaper than raises), and project management like this is indeed part of the professional growth that leads into management proper, but this person almost certainly has no fiscal responsibility, or the right to hire, fire, or administer performance reviews.

Someone with project management responsibility defined in this broad sense is not a true manager, though gaining the responsibility speaks to her worthiness in the eyes of management and is an important step along the path to management. You need to carefully determine that you and the candidate share an understanding of the term "management."

"Can you give me the titles that are your direct reports? Are you responsible for hiring these titles?"

This is a compound question, *open-ended* to elicit knowledge of the direct reports to match with your open requirement, followed by a *closed-ended* question to establish hiring responsibility. If the answer to the hiring part of this question is affirmative, you then follow with, *"What is your selection procedure, from the very beginning?"* You are looking for someone who understands the commonsense principles we have been developing and writing about throughout *Knock 'em Dead: Hiring the Best*:

- You *get work done through others*: This is one of the most important *responsibilities* of management.
- You are involved in determining the *deliverables* of the job and the *skills, experience*, and *education* necessary for that delivery.
- Your time is valuable and the entire recruitment and selection process should follow a logical flow that honors the commitment of your time.
- Wherever possible you should delegate the initial screening both as a timesaving tool and as part of a recognition and skill-building program for your more competent staff members.
- You determine the "must haves" first and understand, for example, that spending time determining *manageability* is irrelevant and a waste of precious time if you do not first determine that a candidate has the *technical skills* to do the job.

Follow up by asking, *"Are you responsible for hiring your staff?"*, *"Do you perform salary reviews on these people?"*, and *"Who terminates underperforming staff members?"* These questions will help clarify the level of management responsibility. Once you have determined an appropriate level of responsibility for the job opening, you can move logically through the building blocks of successful management.

Hiring: The First Step in Team Building

No sports coach survives by blaming poor performance on the team, and the same standards apply in your world. Because your management hires are in turn going to *get work done through others*, the direct impact they have on your own performance is magnified. Although you may know how long this person has been in management, and how many people he manages and has hired and fired, you must never mistake length of experience for competency, even though the two may be related.

"How do you plan to interview?"

Watch out for people who tell you that they "like to get to know the person," or who laugh, saying that with all of their experience, "I just know 'em when I see 'em." These are the *unconscious incompetents*: They don't even know that they don't know what they are doing. Follow this with, *"On what criteria do you base a decision to hire?"* Naturally you are looking for someone who understands the importance of defining *technical skills*, *problem-solving skills*, and *professional values* like *motivation*, *teamwork*, and *manageability*. You might ask, *"What questions do you ask when you want to know about* [for example, motivation]*?"* Then, determine what the candidate hopes to learn by asking those questions. If you get treated to responses of "What's your greatest strength/weakness?" and "Why do you want the job?" push with, *"Tell me what questions you would ask, or techniques you would use, to establish whether the person was willing to do the job."*

You can ask how the candidate structures interviews and what she hopes to discover during those interviews. You might also pick a job title that your management candidate would be hiring and ask, *"Which technical skills are most important to the success of a _____?", "Which supporting skills are most important to the success of a* _____*?"*, then follow it with a query as to why those *supporting skills* are relevant. At the end of the sequence, always be sure to ask whether your candidate checks references, and if so, the questions he typically asks of them. You might also structure questions around the number and duration of interviews necessary to make good hires, the number of second opinions that ought to be sought and why, how a decision to hire is reached, and how a dollar offer is determined and extended. Reading this book has taught you what answers you hope to receive.

"How many people have you hired?"

This reveals the extent of practical experience in this skill area, and by asking you might learn that the interviewee's first and only management job included taking over a fully staffed department with little turnover; consequently, the candidate will have only light experience in the selection area. This is occasionally the case in mature and stable companies, in which managers invariably inherit a department as a "going concern." If managers in your company are involved in the recruitment process (as distinct from the *selection* process), you may also want to examine the candidate's knowledge in this area too.

"How have you developed your skills in recruitment and selection?"

This provides an easy way to find out (a) whether the candidate has had any training, and (b) whether he has made the necessary effort to improve critical skills. The insights that come from reading this book will supply you with plenty of other questions, as will the management interview skeleton at the end of the chapter.

Orientation of a New Employee

The orientation and training of new employees can be of varying importance to a manager, depending on the role of the HR or T&D departments in the process. In all instances, though, it's the manager who is ultimately responsible for getting new employees settled in and feeling "joined up" and part of the team.

"How important do you feel orientation and training are to the success of a new employee?"

Also:

"What steps do you take to get a new employee comfortable with new ways of doing things?"

The manager who lacks sensitivity to helping new employees become productive team members PDQ is likely to lack other *team-building* and *motivational* skills as well, which can lead to high employee turnover and all that that implies for your job security.

"Have you ever had to train staff in new skills?"

This is a good opener for the area of training capabilities. It should be followed by such questions as, *"What skills have you taught?"* There is a difference between teaching and having an employee actually learn, so ask, *"How do you approach training?"* and *"What techniques did you use?"* The answers you hear should reflect this awareness and reveal a manager who is concerned with sharing needed information and skills in the fashion most conducive to enhancing the employee's learning capabilities, rather than talking to hear her own lips flap.

"How do you analyze the training needs of your department or of specific individuals?"

Training does not stop once the new employee has settled in, so you might finish the sequence with this question. It is particularly valuable because the answer will demonstrate the *critical thinking skills* used in determining training needs, and the *commitment* of the management candidate to building team competency. You may well find the good manager tying the answer into her staff performance reviews—which, incidentally, should occur more frequently than the annual performance and salary review.

Communication and Motivation

Management philosophy recognizes that *communication* and *motivation* are interrelated skills for the competent manager. Without adequate *communication skills*, staff *motivation* leaves by the early train.

"How do you keep your staff aware of information and company activities that might affect them?"

Small companies and growing companies depend largely on *verbal communication*; *written communication* comes to the fore with larger, more mature companies. Corporate turnaround stories consistently tell us that too much formality leads to communication breakdown. Watch out for the manager who prefers memoranda to personal contact—it may signify a lack of people skills elsewhere in his management style unless, of course, the memoranda are used to confirm important previous *verbal communications*.

"Have you ever had an employee suddenly start acting out of character?"

People problems—and everyone encounters them with staff at one time or another, whether they are psychological or emotional, drugs or alcohol—do intrude upon the workplace. The managers you hire have a responsibility to be alert for such issues, because they affect *productivity*, morale, and employee turnover. Appropriate help or acknowledgment of caring can go a long way toward increasing *motivation* for a valued but troubled team member. Sensitivity to *systems and procedures* is also important here; for example, a manager who, without appropriate consultation, oversteps her bounds of authority by getting a drug counselor for an employee can land your company in a heap of legal trouble. So to determine the degree of sensitivity and an awareness of *systems and procedures* you should ask, *"Would you tell me about a specific problem situation and how you approached it?"*

"Tell me about a program you introduced to improve morale."

This question can be repeated to cover subjects such as saving money; increasing efficiency; decreasing turnover, tardiness, or absenteeism; or whatever other situations are relevant to your world. *Layer* them with who, what, where, when, why, and how questions. You will gain valuable insights into the candidate, and even if you don't hire that particular applicant, you just might come up with a first-rate program that your company could use.

"How do you motivate your staff?"

The answer will tell you about the candidate's practical skills, and even a blank stare can be worth a thousand words. In the same sequence, you might ask, *"Have you ever had to meet tight deadlines?"* and then follow the unfailingly positive response with, *"Tell me about how you motivated your staff when faced with a specific tight deadline."* You are always on the lookout for the manager who uses threats or bribery as a means to meet tight deadlines, because this behavior is symptomatic of other management inadequacies.

"Tell me about a time when a team fell apart. Why did it happen? What did you do?"

This question appeared earlier in a different context. With management hires you are looking for someone who can determine root causes and takes effective remedial actions. Beware of a candidate who consistently lays the cause of problems at others' doorsteps—upper management's in particular. He may blame others today; tomorrow, things could change, and that finger of blame will be pointed at you.

"Tell me about an occasion when, in difficult circumstances, you pulled the team together."

You need a manager who is willing to take complete responsibility for the wellbeing of her team. When this question came up earlier in a different context, we noted that non-management staff members who step up to the plate in difficult circumstances could be the exception rather than the rule. In the management selection context, such skills and *motivation* need to be the norm.

"Give me an example of a time when management changed one of your projects. How did you feel, and how did you explain the change to your people?"

This is a revealing question that tells you not only about *manage-ability* but also about the candidate's *leadership skills* in the building and maintenance of a team's *productivity* when under pressure. When a candidate is promoted into the ranks of management, she becomes part of a new team and, although a manager, continues to report for directions and guidance to a more senior manager; even the CEO has a reporting relationship (the board of directors) where he must account for his performance and take direction.

Authority and Discipline

An important consideration for how a manager keeps *productivity* high and turnover low is how authority is wielded and discipline implemented. These questions will also help reveal the candidate's "management personality" and its compatibility with yours.

"What methods have you found successful in setting objectives for your reports?"

Management is a continuous coaching and nurturing process. It requires far more than directing the employee to read the proffered job description and follow directions. Look for a manager who combines both a formal approach to setting objectives and a sensitivity to understanding the need for informal coaching on an individual basis.

"Have you ever had to make unpopular decisions?"

This is a simple *closed-ended question* that sets you up for some good *layering* techniques: *"Tell me about a time when . . .", "Why did you feel this was an unpopular decision?"*, and so on. The decisions a manager must make do not always make that manager a popular person, so look for tendencies toward procrastination by asking, *"Having identified that a particular decision is necessary, how long is it before you take action?"*

Following naturally from your questions about unpopular decisions, you can ask, *"How do you maintain discipline in your department?"* and *"What issues seem to you most common with the day-to-day management of your staff?"*

The answers will shed new light on both disciplinary and management styles. *"What are the typical problems and grievances that your staff bring to you?"* and *"How do you handle them?"* can tell you a lot about the trust reports place in this manager.

"In working with other managers, how do you go about getting an understanding of them?"

An integral part of any manager's job is *communication* with other managers and their departments. You can follow this question with, *"Tell me about the other management titles you interact with on a daily/ weekly basis and the nature of those interactions."* This in turn can be followed by, *"Tell me what you can do in your interactions with these managers to make the work and information flow more smoothly between your departments."*

Attitude Toward Management

Your managers are your direct reports, and you need to know how they are likely to react to your management. Though there are questions elsewhere in this book that help you determine these aspects of an individual's *manageability*, the following few questions are particularly appropriate in evaluating management candidates.

"Tell me about a time when an emergency/directive from above caused you to reschedule your personal workload and the department's priorities."

The response can tell you about the ability to *multitask* and handle pressure, plus *communication* and *team-building skills*, and it can also reveal possible irritants and management conflicts. Teams typically react to situations in ways that reflect the feelings and displayed emotions of the leader, so probe a little deeper with, *"How did the staff react?"*

"Tell me about a time when management had to change a plan or approach you were committed to. How did you feel, and how did you explain the change to your people?"

You will be interested to find out whether the candidate explained the situation to the staff in positive, negative, or defensive terms. Ideally you'd like a candidate who explains the change of direction in terms you find easily accessible and sensible, because this would reflect how other grounded professionals would likely react. On the other hand, it is a weak manager who does not support the company's position on issues.

Employee Turnover

There are few things more costly to a manager or a company than the time and expense associated with employee turnover, and the subsequent costs of recruitment, selection, orientation, training, and the like. Remember to correlate the answers to your questions about orientation, training, and *motivation*—everything is interrelated with management.

"What has been the turnover in your department over the last couple of years?"

Is the answer above or below industry norms? As a competent interviewer you are rarely satisfied with the first snap answer to any of your questions. Instead, you use this question partly to obtain a quantitative answer but, more importantly, to give the candidate a focus for the rest of the questions in this sequence.

"What type of turnover was most frequent: termination, resignation, or downsizing?"

A history of high turnover could be a problem, but at this point you do not have enough information about the reasons. Poor interviewing and selection? Poor orientation, motivation, or training? Unsafe or hostile working conditions? The reasons are limitless, so you'll have to determine which was the cause in this case by asking these and similar questions: *"Why do you think this was the case?"* and *"What have you done about the situation?"*

"How many people have you found it necessary to terminate?"

This is another straightforward, quantitative question. It should be followed by, *"What is your most common cause for terminating an employee?"* The response—including the candidate's tone of voice—can offer insights into management style and competency.

Whatever the answer, follow it with, *"Tell me about the last time you fired someone for this reason. What led up to it?"* Then, if the information doesn't come out in the story, ask:

"When did you first notice the problem?"

"With hindsight, were there any steps you could have taken to rectify the situation?"

"What skill or behavioral coaching did you offer for the problem?"

"Did you follow a formal disciplinary procedure leading up to termination?"

"At what point were your manager and HR brought into the picture?"

"At what point did you make the decision to terminate?"

"How long was it from this decision to implementation?"

A candidate's awareness of, and adherence to, proper discipline and termination procedures minimizes lawsuits for wrongful dismissal.

"What are the most common reasons your reports give for resignation?"

It's a truism that your people are loyal when you give them a reason to appreciate you, and that's never more true than here. Pay people reasonably, recognize their contributions consistently and in different ways, give them a decent work environment and a positive atmosphere, and resignations will usually be low (see *Knock 'em Dead: Breaking Into Management* for commentary on these topics; *www.shop.knock emdead.com/Breaking-Into-Management-ebook-p/ked-bim.htm#sthash .ZnQv0eVR.dpbs*). Because a competent manager can satisfy many of these requirements for low turnover with little effort, responses to this question such as "better opportunity elsewhere" and "more money" can sometimes be cop-outs, and you'll want to examine the issue further. "*How do you keep track of an employee's relative contentment?*" and "*What signals of discontent do you look for?*" will tell you about how a manager keeps in touch with individual staff members.

You might also wish to identify when resignations typically occur: "*Within three months, six months, fifteen months, two years, four years?*" An answer in the short-term might indicate that this manager's hiring and training capabilities need closer examination; an answer in the mid-term could be cause for probing management style and judgments; and resignations after four years or more fall in line with statistical norms and aren't a cause for worry.

A manager with no turnover might speak of great management skills and a highly productive staff. However, many times over the years I have seen departments and whole divisions with superior employment longevity where at least fifty percent of the people were clock watchers and upwards of twenty percent were antagonistic and passive aggressive toward management. Interpretation of an answer is never simple, and with the complexity of hiring managers, responses to all questions must be related, in your mind, to answers to all other questions.

Day-to-Day Management Skills

Here are a handful of questions that will help you evaluate how a management candidate is likely to perform on a daily basis.

"What would you say are the major qualities a manager's job demands?"
Also:

"How would you characterize your management style?"

These questions can help you develop a deeper understanding of the management candidate. As we've seen over and over again, asking similar questions with slightly different focus delivers a three-dimensional picture that can show you someone very different from the candidate's initial presentation of herself.

"Describe the role or function of your department, and your job's contribution to the departmental function."

You might have asked this question to define *ability* to do the job, but in this context you're seeking a deeper level of professional awareness that will give you insight into the amount of education, handholding, and coaching that might be necessary. The answer should give you a picture of the management candidate at work. It will shed further light on *technical skills*, *communication*, *leadership*, *teamwork*, and *professional values*.

"What methods do you use in executing performance reviews? What are you looking for and how do you prepare?"

You are looking for a logical and consistent approach that shows the ability to track employees' performances through the year against objective, predetermined performance criteria. The answer should give you a good sense of the candidate's grasp of this key skill, and could give you insights into her management style. You will likely also learn something about the candidate's grasp of the *technical skills* of the profession and her possession of the *transferable skills and professional values* that underlie success.

"How often do you administer performance reviews?"

With a good manager, this is an ongoing process and not restricted to the annual salary review. Loyalty comes from being appreciated and recognized for a job well done just as much as it does from salary increases.

Even when feedback and positive reviews might not keep a great employee with you forever, it will keep them maximally productive in the meantime, giving you both positive memories and another good colleague. Professional life being as insecure as it is, the good relationship resulting from your nurturing may well result in an introduction or even a job for you one day when you most need it.

"How do you schedule projects, assignments, and vacations?"

Here you will learn about planning skills and will also see whether your potential manager is reactive ("Well, I just have to cover for my people if too many go away at once") or proactive ("I tell all new employees that the department must be adequately staffed at all times and that I require adequate planning notice for vacations"). More and more often, in all but the smallest companies, there is an established protocol for vacations that is implemented through Human Resources and the manager in tandem.

Projects and assignments are a different matter. You want to hear that assignments are based on *ability*, but also that wherever possible the senior project member (even if he can do the project standing on his head) has a junior on the team. This fulfills five important management functions:

1. It builds technical experience for the junior.
2. It builds leadership experience for the senior.
3. Both senior and junior feel motivated by the recognition.
4. It encourages teamwork.
5. Together, these outcomes build loyalty.

"What responsibilities do you hold in relation to other departments and the company as a whole?"

Committee involvement and interdepartmental coordinating responsibilities can be indicative of potential for increased *responsibilities*. The answer should also give you an understanding of the candidate's awareness of her role as a *team player* on the management team and how this role makes a contribution to the smooth running and *profitability* of the company.

Financial Responsibilities

These four mandatory questions examine how a management candidate handles financial responsibilities; they are obviously only relevant if the job has financial responsibilities.

"Do you hold financial or budgetary responsibility for your department?"
Also:
"What is your involvement in budgetary planning?"
"What challenges do you have staying within budget?"
"How do you go about meeting those challenges?"

The responses you get may lead you to more questions about financial skills as they relate to the applicant's level of fiscal responsibility and may have other relevance in terms of credentials versus potential.

An example is in order here. I coach senior professionals and have done so for many years. Recently, I was coaching a Sales VP who had played a significant role in growing his company from $45 to $110 million. He wanted a job with a company that had sales of at least $250 million, so that he could double it to $500 million. This may well have been possible for him, but as I explained, a company doing $250 million, which wants to reach $500 million, needs to hire a sales executive who has already managed a sales operation that generated $250 million and saw it through major growth and changes beyond that mark. *Companies hire based on credentials, not potential*, since this gives the candidate credibility and proves that he has already faced and solved the problems that accompany that kind of growth.

"What was your involvement in short-, mid-, and long-term planning?"
Budgeting and planning responsibilities go hand in hand, and the answer to this question will tell you whether your candidate is at a policymaking level. This in turn defines another nice difference in management responsibilities: There are many managers who implement, but have no input into determination of, company policy. This question lets you see which camp the candidate falls into and,

consequently, whether he will be both capable and happy in the job you are looking to fill.

"How do you quantify your results as a manager?

The question may be straightforward, but it will be intriguing to see what the candidate does with it. The effect on the bottom line, of course, is how management judges performance. Simply put, this is determined by the ability to *earn money* and to improve productivity, thus *saving money, saving time*, and *making more time in which to make more money.*

Management Interview Skeleton

There's no one sequence of questions that's perfect for every position. You may find some questions in the following skeleton that do not meet your particular needs. You may, for example, find yourself saying, "That wouldn't work for me, but if I twisted it this way or that way it would." A good plan would be to work through the *questioning techniques* discussed in Chapter 5 to help customize this interview skeleton to your needs. You will find many questions here that beg for question *layering, past-performance*, or *situational* interviewing techniques. You will also notice that many of these questions are management-focused analogues of similar questions discussed in Chapters 8 through 10, and so you already have an understanding of the ways in which they can be adapted to the many unique hiring situations you will face in your management career.

Each candidate is different, as is each company, interviewer, and position. These questions are meant to support your analysis of what is important, not to replace that analysis.

Ability
- How long have you been in management?
- How many people do you manage?
- What levels and types of people do you manage?

- How long have you held these management responsibilities?
- Do these people report directly and solely to you?
- Who hired and fired these people?
- How creative do you think the management role is?
- How do you quantify the results of your job?
- What do you perceive as the responsibilities of this job?
- How far in advance do you and management typically make specific decisions about directional changes?

Day-to-Day Management Skills

- How would you characterize your management style?
- Explain the types of decisions that are beyond your authority.
- How often do you prepare reports?
- What other departments do you deal with?
- What responsibilities do you hold in relation to other departments?
- How do you schedule projects, assignments, and vacations?
- Tell me about a recent crisis, what caused it, and how it was resolved.

Hiring

- How many people have you hired?
- How have you learned to interview?
- How do you plan to interview?
- What has been your biggest hiring mistake?

Employee Orientation

- What steps do you normally take to get a new employee settled in?
- How do you analyze the training needs of your department and of specific individuals?

Communication and Motivation

- How important is communication and interaction with the staff?
- What are some of the tasks you typically delegate?
- How do you maintain checks and balances on employee performance?

- What things cause the most friction in your department?
- Do you feel it is your responsibility to adapt to your employees, or is it their responsibility to adapt to you?
- Tell me about a time when morale was low. What did you do about it?
- When have you seen proven motivational techniques fail?
- Tell me some of the ways you have seen other managers demotivate employees.
- Have you ever become involved in an employee's personal problems?
- How do you keep the staff aware of company information and activities?
- Have you ever faced a situation with a staff member who was being less than direct with you about his activities?
- How do you organize and run department meetings?

Authority and Discipline
- How have you been successful in setting objectives for your staff?
- Have you ever had to make unpopular decisions?
- What are some of the everyday problems you face with your staff?
- Have you ever worked with a group that jointly resisted management authority?
- What management situation is personally most difficult for you?
- What sort of employee behavior makes you angry?
- What do you do when a team member breaks corporate policy?

Turnover
- How do you handle poor employee performance?
- What has been the turnover in your department over the last three years?
- How many people have you terminated?
- What steps do you take before deciding to terminate? How have you gone about forecasting manpower needs?
- Have you ever experienced problems with company pay scales when trying to attract new employees?

Fiscal Responsibility
- Do you hold budgetary responsibility in your department?
- What has been the most expensive financial mistake of your career?

Manageability
- How do you take direction?
- How do you take criticism?
- What have you been most criticized for as a manager?
- What have you and previous managers disagreed about?
- What do you do when there is a decision to be made and no procedure exists?
- How have past managers gotten the best out of you?
- Describe the best manager you ever had.
- Describe the worst manager you ever had.
- Tell me about a time when you felt that management had made an emotional rather than a logical decision about your work.
- When have you been described as inflexible?
- How does your job relate to the overall goals of the company?
- How often are you involved in making formal presentations or proposals to management or customers?
- How do you define the difference between supervision and management?
- How do you play the office politics game?
- What kinds of things bother you most?
- If you could make one constructive suggestion to management, what would it be?

In closing this chapter, remember that any manager you hire will in turn hire others, and so everything she does will reflect directly on your competency. When you pick such important players, you must leave nothing to whim or chance.

FIFTEEN

Executive Decisions

This chapter deals with selection cycles at the highest level: Director, VP, and C-level positions.

Just as professionals' needs grow and change during their professional lives, so do those of companies. Companies evolve as they cycle through different stages of growth, and your ability to make successful hires at the higher levels of management depends on your ability to identify the needs of your company at its current stage and connect these with the needs of the senior-level managers you interview.

Depending on their success and ability to reinvent themselves as part of their growth and evolution, companies can cycle through up to five stages, each with distinct needs.

The five stages are:

1. Start-up
2. Growth
3. Maturity
4. Atrophy
5. Turnaround

A company's nature and its senior management needs can change dramatically at each stage, so knowing which stage your company is at, and where it is headed next, can alert you to senior management candidates whose work experience with companies from different stages of this cycle might make them particularly desirable or undesirable.

Start-Up

The start-up company can begin on a kitchen table or in a garage, comprising just its founders as employees. The founders struggle with an idea, service, or product, its development, and its initial launch. From this point, the company may continue to struggle for survival and maintain a level of few or no employees, or it may begin to grow. At this stage, any employee may be in direct daily contact with the company owner; there is little in the way of *systems and procedures*, and the mission is relatively simple: "Pay the phone bills and the rent to stay in business while we find a market." Once a market for the product or service is found, growth begins, although the majority of start-up companies never make it to the growth phase.

Growth

The company finds its market and begins to grow. The focus is on gaining customers and then market share, rather than just struggling to keep the doors open. Staff is hired in response to overload as much as planning. At least in the early days, the founders are still involved in every aspect of the business, and *communication* is largely *verbal*. The main focus of a growth company is the sales and marketing strategies that enhance that growth. Many growth companies never grow beyond a size that the founders can manage personally, usually topping out at around 70–100 employees. An entrepreneur's inability to let go of even the tiniest detail is seen as the Achilles' heel of many growth companies: They stall out because the founder is the only individual with any authority, overseeing perhaps as many as a hundred personal assistants.

The companies that successfully pass through the growth phase to that of a mature company emerge from the "cult of the founders" by instituting a management structure and the basic *systems and procedures* common to all mature companies. This is, in fact, the rite of passage that the growth company goes through to become a viable mature company.

The Mature Company

The viable mature company is stable and at the top of its game. All *communication* necessarily becomes formal, with more emphasis on *written communication*. The company implements more and stricter *systems and procedures*; the Human Resources department moves into ascendancy; there is less room for individual *creativity*; the company is unlikely to be alone in its market; and that market may even be reaching the saturation point. A greater focus on operations replaces the aggressive investments in marketing that typify growth-cycle companies. While in earlier stages a company worried more about getting the job done and making sales, the mature company, finding it more difficult to increase sales and profit margins by increasing volume, begins to look more seriously at cost containment as a viable profit generator. Automation, downsizing, outsourcing, and offshoring of jobs and processes come to the fore.

Even with flatter corporate hierarchies, a company's larger size necessitates more levels of management. It becomes possible for careers to flourish simply by avoiding mistakes, and as the mature company relies more on committee than on individual initiative, such avoidance becomes easier. This means less initiative and risk taking, partly because now any risk is so much greater, and partly because of the depressing effect on *creativity* and initiative of ever-more-burdensome *systems and procedures* (sometimes dubbed "analysis paralysis") resulting from the stultifying effect of ever-growing numbers of managers and administrators. The once-vibrant concern has become a bureaucracy, sluggish with overhead. It behaves like an institution, a legend in its own mind, blind to maladies that it believes to be strengths. Under all these pressures, the mature company eventually begins to stagnate.

Atrophy

Hence the onset of the decay stage of the corporate life cycle. Early signs are an acceptance of excuses that the market, the economy, or the numbers of competitors now flooding the field make it impossible for anyone to make a living, as well as complaints about the lack of competent employees. The cash-flow crises that occur with increasing frequency in this stage now accentuate the emphasis on cost cutting and layoffs. The finger of blame points outward, and no one sees where the other three digits on the hand are pointing.

Turnaround

The fifth stage is recognition of atrophy, and sustained, concerted action to achieve turnaround. Consultants are everywhere, turnaround experts are brought on board, and the focus is on returning to the Edenic vibrancy of the start-up and growth-phase psychology.

Hiring and the Life-Cycle Challenge

Now let's apply this concept of a corporate life cycle to senior-level management hiring decisions. At the higher levels, the *suitability* of a candidate for a position depends in part on the *ability*, *motivation*, *manageability*, and *team spirit* of that candidate, and in part on the corporate life cycle suitability of the candidate. A candidate from one phase of the cycle may, or may not, be appropriate for a company in another phase. Consequently, the lesson you learned about selection at the lower levels applies in the upper echelons too: *The most objectively qualified person you can find may not be the best person for the job.*

Take the example of a young Silicon Valley company at the start of its high-growth phase of the cycle, looking to bring on its first PR director. Its ultimate choice was one of the top people in the industry—he headed the publicity department of a *Fortune* 500 company. He had wanted a new challenge, and a start-up company in the field seemed the answer to his prayers. The company principals were pinching themselves to make sure they weren't dreaming. Who would have thought they could land one of the best in the business?

The honeymoon lasted six weeks, and the marriage six months, before the "resignation" was accepted. Our top man was used to managing an established team—the best money could buy—and controlling multimillion-dollar budgets, while at the new company, his budget was loose change and his staff even smaller. Although no one was better at driving the train once it was out of the station, this particular PR executive had neither the skills, the desire, nor the drive to stoke the corporate engine from a cold start. His skills had passed many years ago from those of a doer to those of a delegator.

Now while these are complex and important executive skills, the life cycle demands of the company required an executive who still wanted—and had the *ability*—to roll up his sleeves and climb down into the trenches. The moral is that what you see isn't always what you get. There needs to be a match between the company's level of development and the candidate's understanding and credentials in delivering at that stage of development. A different lesson could be taken from the selection of a senior sales or marketing executive for that same growth company. Say, for example, that your company does a very respectable $50 million a year and you are poised to double that volume. In hiring the next senior sales or marketing executive, you don't want a sales or marketing executive who has done $50 million; ideally, you want one who has done $70 million (or more), who understands and can *anticipate, prevent, and solve the problems* associated with such growth.

How This Applies to Your Company

Start-ups will frequently benefit most from executives who have seen their prior employers through the growth phase. Growth-stage companies, on the other hand, benefit from executives who can introduce the *systems and procedures* that will encourage growth through this phase and into the more predictable waters of maturity: for example, an HR executive who can create an HR department with all its *systems and procedures* from scratch, facilitate steady growth, and stop the cash drain that comes with high-growth companies lacking adequate HR functions.

Later growth-stage companies benefit from a combination of executives with experience in that stage and those who have overseen the successful transition into maturity and are able to inculcate a corporate culture conducive to a successful transition.

Companies in the fourth (Atrophy) and fifth (Turnaround) stages need fresh blood, executives who can raise the dead and have a track record of rejuvenating mature operations. The ideal candidate is an executive from a mature company who also has successful start-up and growth experience, or experience and a reputation as a turn-around expert (rare birds who often have experience throughout all the different stages).

The problem with bringing executives from start-up and growth companies into a mature or atrophying organization is that sometimes they just cannot fit into the cultural "way we do things here" of the company. The bureaucracy drives them crazy, and they upset everyone else on the train. Of course, that is often the reason they were hired in the first place, but unless they are to have autonomy in growing a (perhaps new) endeavor or turning around a troubled purchase, they aren't always *manageable* or sophisticated in the ways of the established corporate institution.

The essence of what we are addressing here is credentials versus potential. Ideally, you want someone who has already, "been there, done that," rather than the guy who is ready for a new challenge. An experienced manager's credentials for successfully delivering on the job can be verified, and that makes for a more circumspect hire, especially at higher levels, where his work product is of such critical importance.

Finding someone who has successfully operated in all these phases is rare indeed, as each demands different approaches and skills. While a senior-level professional may, over the course of years, have practical experience with a number of different corporations—each in a different phase of development—it is more common to find senior people whose experience has been entirely with companies within one phase of the corporate life cycle.

For companies in transition from one phase to the next, broad corporate life-cycle experience can be eminently desirable. On the other hand, an individual with a track record in companies from a single phase may have become indoctrinated by the behavior patterns common to that phase and bring special knowledge and skills to such companies. This is by no means always the case, but being aware of this possibility will lead you to fruitful areas of inquiry during the selection process.

This means that in the selection of VP and C-level candidates, you need to be aware of where your company stands in its evolutionary cycle, where it is headed, and how the background of each short-list candidate has prepared her for the challenges your company is facing on its own evolutionary path:

- When you are in start-up mode, the challenge is two-fold: to find the skills you need at a price you can afford. The more skills a candidate brings to the table and the more hats he can wear in your organization, the better. This makes more mature workers from the steps in the cycle ahead of you enormously attractive, assuming they can adapt to the ways, pay, and benefits of a start-up or growth company.

- In the growth phase, you are wise to look for someone who comes from a similar cultural environment of hustle and full-speed ahead—but at the same time, your strong growth is tilting you toward the need for order and organization that typifies the mature company, and you need to be attuned to candidates who can put your company on the firm foundations it needs for growth. Again, this makes more mature managers, perhaps from the steps ahead of you, enormously attractive.

- The mature company, with its ability to attract the best talent with pay, opportunity, and benefits, will look for candidates who have already performed well in such an environment.

- If your company is approaching transition from one phase to another, you may well benefit from someone grounded in the next phase of the corporate life cycle.

- If your company is in a state of atrophy or turnaround, you will want turnaround experts and candidates from the earlier stages of growth and maturity to prune and re-energize.

None of this means that you should reject otherwise qualified candidates out of hand just because their professional background is in a different step of the corporate life cycle; but it does mean that you are likely to make more productive hires when:

1. You know where your company stands on the continuum, and therefore the type of management you need and where it is likely to come from
2. You are able to identify the life-cycle stages of companies with which a candidate has experience

Once you do this, you can examine the areas of possible mismatch together, openly and frankly—a good senior candidate will always be open to a serious talk about serious issues.

To identify where a candidate's company lies on the continuum, you should find out how long the candidate's company has been in business; its recent and projected growth rates; its dollar volume and number of employees in relation to management ranks; its ratio of administrative assistants to management; and whether the company prefers *verbal* or *written communication*. Its approaches to planning and project management can also indicate matches, mismatches, or long learning curves. But most of all, open conversation about the issues with mature and intelligent short-list candidates is the best way to get the answers you need.

It can be effective to discuss these issues over food and drink, and this also gives you an opportunity to evaluate the social graces so important in a successful executive.

Here are some questions that will help you examine these areas and avoid hitching yourself to a star from the wrong universe.

"What is the size and role of the HR department in your present company?"

Human Resources becomes increasingly powerful as companies grow and mature, so the answer will give you a general idea about the stage of the corporation. Knowing the responsibilities of Human Resources can lead you into fruitful discussions about the extent of influence of HR as it affects the day-to-day operations of your candidate's company.

"Describe in detail your impression of the day-to-day responsibilities of this job."

In the context of senior management selection this question can catch catastrophic misconceptions before they cost either of you time, money, or reputation. The earlier example of the top PR executive in the young growth company in Silicon Valley might never have occurred if the answers to this question had not been taken for granted. This question is a must in every final interview, so that even the smallest misunderstanding is cleared up.

"What interests you least about these responsibilities?"

You have both confirmed the day-to-day *responsibilities* and *deliverables* of the job. This is a check on the candidate's perception of the job's realities and her *suitability* to your daily routine.

"What kinds of management rub you the wrong way?"

An awareness of the corporate life cycle might make the candidate's people skills worthy of some revaluation. For instance, to put a successful bureaucrat among the entrepreneurial types common in start-ups or the rough autocrats they often need to become in growth companies is to ask everyone to suffer needless frustrations. Follow the subsequent conversation to its natural conclusion.

"What was the least relevant/fulfilling job you have held?"

The response will tell you how clearly the candidate sees the sum of his experience. If the "least relevant" job turns out to be one from, say, a company in the growth stage, and your company is about to enter that stage, you have gained some valuable information.

"Wouldn't you feel happier in another company?"

Also:

"I'm not sure that you're suitable for the job."

Earlier in the book, we addressed the judicious use of *stress* questions to test poise and quick thinking. Here, you are using the query in a far more straightforward manner. When you notice a life-cycle and/or attitudinal misfit between the candidate and your needs, you might want to discuss it frankly and openly with the candidate. The ensuing conversation should help you both reach consensus on whether and why there is a mismatch.

The issues dealt with in this chapter are only of concern when you are hiring at the highest levels. Only here do you need to give serious consideration to the fit between your company's place in the life cycle and your candidate's experience with related stages. Proper attention to these nuances will save you and the candidate from professional embarrassment, and lead you to a successful hire.

PART IV
THE BIG PICTURE: HIRING EFFECTIVELY AND MANAGING PRODUCTIVELY

Building a successful managerial career requires seeing the connections between everything we've discussed and making this knowledge second nature. In this section we examine final decisions and reference checking, then move on from *hiring effectively* to *managing productively*, and learn how to get new hires up to speed, turn around problem workers, make the most of the plodders, and keep your superstars happy.

SIXTEEN

Hiring the Best

When your job's primary responsibility is *getting work done through others*, making the right hiring decisions has a direct impact on your success on the job and your career as a whole. In this chapter, we'll revisit the building blocks that lead to consistently successful hires.

The Job's Deliverables

Good hires always depend on a clear understanding of the *responsibilities* and the day-to-day *problems* that need to be *anticipated, prevented, and solved* for the successful candidate to deliver tangible results—the *deliverables* you expect in return for steady employment. Without this understanding, you cannot develop a short list of suitable candidates or the right questions to ask them during the ensuing selection cycle.

You know that all jobs are at some level the same: *problem-solving* jobs, each doing its small part in meeting the ongoing challenges that every corporation shares—making money, saving money, and improving *productivity*, the last of which is the double whammy that both saves money and makes time to make more money. Tying each job to its specific *problem-solving responsibilities* and identifying its role in the bigger picture is the most critical step in *hiring effectively*—the essential first step if you hope to *manage productively*.

You then match the job's *responsibilities* and *deliverables* to the most relevant *transferable skills and professional values* (addressed in

Chapter 2) in order to identify the foundational skills that the right candidate will need to do his job well.

Motivation

Given the skills to do the job, a good hire requires a candidate who has the *motivation* to do whatever it takes, no matter what it takes. You want a candidate who looks forward to the challenges of her chosen profession.

Manageability and Teamwork

The reality is that we spend more waking hours with our coworkers than our loved ones, so it only makes sense to hire someone both you and the rest of your team can bear to work with for fifty weeks of the year. This means determining the degree to which each candidate is *manageable* and a *team player,* willing to work—and, when necessary, sacrifice—for the common good. This final aspect of candidate assessment is vital to all good hires, but from a *time-management* perspective, you are only interested in *manageability* and *teamwork* once you have verified *ability* and *motivation.*

Efficient Candidate Screening

You only want to invest time with in-person interviews for candidates you are reasonably certain can fulfill the essential *deliverables* of the job. You can weed out many unsuitable candidates at the resume-screening stage, more through the judicious use of telephone interviews, and yet more through the gradual delegation of these tasks. (This delegation in turn motivates your superstars with professional development opportunities, and helps you with succession planning.)

Once the face-to-face interviews commence, you are ready with a logical approach to sequentially determining *ability, motivation, team spirit,* and *manageability*. Based on the unique needs of each new opening, you create a structured interview format that guarantees you will compare apples to apples by developing a slate of questions that enable you to fairly judge each candidate against the others.

You determine *ability* first, and if a candidate cannot do the job, you bail out, because your interviews are objective, businesslike, and sensitive to needless time wasting. Once *ability* is proven, you move on to *motivation*, because you know that all-important *ability* isn't enough without the willingness to tackle the job's challenges, problems, and constant headaches every day. Only then, once you have determined a candidate's *ability* and *motivation*, is it worth your time to examine a candidate's *manageability* and *team spirit*.

Depending on the complexity of the job, you invite the shrinking number of short-list candidates back for second, third, and perhaps (to formally extend offers or when a choice between top candidates is difficult) even fourth interviews. You may employ others to give second opinions, prepping them with a clear picture of what you are looking for. In narrowing down the final contenders, you will naturally lean toward those who have the most experience, but you will also be aware that someone with all the skills of the job is likely to come in at the higher end of your approved salary range, and that if there is no room for professional or financial growth through further skill development, raises and promotions become difficult. Sometimes, when there is clearly no room for such growth—and unless this is an older worker who has greater stability—you might consider the candidates who come in a little lower down on the experience and salary scales.

Final Decisions

It's easy to make errors in judgment at decision time. When the *technical skills, motivation,* and *teamwork/manageability* factors allow, it is a good idea to look for balance and strive to add depth to the team, because the more your department mirrors your employer's customers, the more connected you will be to those customers, and the better the job you will deliver as a team.

With this in mind, a team dominated by one particular sex or race should make you push for diversity. One staffed with Young Turks should look for maturity, and hire people who can share with new generations the practical solutions and know-how that experience can bring.

When There Are Two Top Contenders

This logical approach to selection will usually deliver one clearly superior candidate, but unfortunately, "usually" isn't "always." Occasionally you may need to decide between two evenly matched final contenders. If this happens, conduct another interview with each of the finalists—within twenty-four hours of one other—to address any outstanding issues.

To come to a decision between such top contenders when there is little or nothing to distinguish between them, you need to consider not only what they say but also how they say it, the questions they ask, and the understanding of the job such questions display. You are looking for an undercurrent of *intelligent enthusiasm* about the profession, and *motivation* about the job and the company. This will come out in an energized conversation between professionals sharing a common interest, rather than a one-sided examination of skills burdened by stilted professionalism.

When not one but two top candidates emerge and all things seem equal, you break the tie by determining which of these two equal contenders is the most *intelligently enthusiastic* about the job, because the most *intelligently enthusiastic* candidate will work harder, turn in a better work product, be a better *team player*, and be easier to *manage*.

Offer Time

You might assume that every candidate is desperate for the privilege of coming to work for you; after all, they did apply for the job. However, a prudent manager will be interested in a candidate's motivations for applying, because that knowledge helps you make offers only to candidates who will actually accept them: Making offers that get rejected every now and then happens to everyone, but regular rejections can become a career growth impediment.

With final candidates, even if you have done so before, you should always carefully review performance *responsibilities* and expectations during the final interview, when the candidates are likely to be most receptive. Clear expectations from you at this time will build the candidate's confidence in your leadership. You will find that the candidates you hire using this approach want to succeed, and want to work for managers who they feel can lead them to success. The fact that you know where the troops are heading and why, and how you are going to reach your destination, breeds confidence in your followers and attracts people to your banner.

Final Considerations

Earlier, in discussing work history, we talked about determining starting and leaving salary for all jobs to determine salary progression. Now, as we come to offer time, these insights become useful again, because they can show you the sort of offer (percentage increase) that a candidate is likely to accept. In extending an offer, you will follow company guidelines, but it certainly helps to ask, *"How much money are you looking for?"* or *"What are you looking for in an offer?"* in order to get an idea of salary requirements.

Background and Reference Checks

Background checks conducted by third-party companies allow you to verify a person's educational history, criminal record, credit history, driving record, and so on. This is not only a sensible precaution, but, depending on the job, can also provide protection in the event of lawsuits. For example, when a moving company didn't do background checks, and one of its employees with a violent crime history raped a customer in her home, the moving company was held liable. Background checks could have prevented both the crime and the ensuing liability.

In all instances, the privacy of the individual whose background and references you are checking must be respected. This privacy is protected under the Fair Credit Reporting Act of 1970, which essentially says that in order for you to check background and references, you need written approval. This is usually covered when an employee fills out the application form and signs the bottom, above a paragraph that grants such authority.

Many companies have a formal policy about background and reference checks; in these instances, HR usually implements it. If corporate policy permits, I recommend that you become personally involved in checking references with past managers; this is an important last step in making sure that you are hiring the best. If your company uses a third-party company to check references, ask for a rundown of the questions to be asked, amending that list with appropriate questions of your own.

In preparing your reference-check questions, you will first go back to the job's performance analysis and recall the specific *deliverables*, *technical skills*, and *transferable skills and professional values* that you determined to be important to success in this job, and ask questions related to the skills that underwrite the job's *deliverables*. The time invested in reference checking helps you make the right hiring decision, while simultaneously expanding your own professional network.

The following are some of the questions you could ask when you check references. Customize the list to your needs so that, if you only get a few minutes with a past manager, you can spend the time talking about performance and *manageability* issues rather than attendance record: "How would you rank _____'s skills in _____?" You will repeat this question to cover all the relevant areas of performance.

- "How would you rate _____'s motivation?"
- "How would you rate _____ as a team player?"
- "As a manager, how did you get the best out of _____?"
- "What would you say was _____'s greatest strength?"
- "What would you say was _____'s greatest weakness?"
- "How would you say _____ took direction?"
- "What management problems, if any, did _____ cause you?" If necessary, follow up with, "How did you resolve these issues?"
- "What parts of the job did _____ have the most problems with?"
- "What was _____'s attitude toward developing necessary new skills?"
- "How adept was _____ at developing new skills?"
- "Would you describe _____ as task-oriented or goal-oriented?" You can repeat this question for all of the *transferable skills and professional values* that are most important to you.
- "What advice would you give me as a potential manager of _____?"

It is impossible to *manage productively* without first *hiring effectively*, but once a hiring decision is made, you have checked references, and the candidate becomes a new employee, the challenge changes. Now it's about *managing productively*.

SEVENTEEN

HOW TO EMPOWER SUCCESS

Some think that the toughest responsibility in the life of a manager is making hiring decisions, but equally challenging is making your new hires, and all of your reports, consistently productive. Now that you know how to *hire effectively*, let's talk about a few of the most important strategies and tactics you can learn to *manage* those new hires, and the rest of your team, productively.

Nobody sets out to fail; everyone wants to succeed, because succeeding at work is a big part of succeeding in life. Yet at the same time, very few people have ever been taught how to become successful at work. This insight can give you a distinct advantage in achieving a long and successful management career.

As a manager, the success of the people you hire is your success; the failure of the people you hire is your failure. So turning new hires into successful, productive members of the team as quickly as possible is a primary management *responsibility*. The tactics you apply to make new hires successful can also be adapted for productive management of your other team members, whether they are plodders, superstars, or troubled workers.

What Works and What Doesn't

You carefully discussed *deliverables* and performance standards with short-list candidates as an integral part of the selection cycle. Now, the first step in helping a new hire become a productive *team member* is to share the accepted standards of performance as soon as that person is hired, on her first day, when your explanation will have real impact. You'll use criteria that are both achievable and measurable because you want the new hire to experience success as soon as possible, because success breeds more success.

Waiting until you see a new employee failing and then saying, "You have to improve" doesn't cut it. Implicit in such exhortations is the belief that "If you only tried harder you could easily do better." The result? Needless criticism demoralizes new hires who don't know the ropes or have the information or orientation to do a good job.

Comprehensive Performance Reviews

With regular Comprehensive Performance Reviews, known as CPRs, new hires will become productive quickly, your stars will get the recognition they crave, you'll help underperforming employees turn around their performance, and in the rare instances where you have a troubled worker who does not want to succeed, the CPR strategy encourages him to initiate his own departure.

But if most people want to succeed, why do so many managers have dysfunctional, underperforming departments? The answer is simple: Few managers invest the time in showing individual team members—and the team as a whole—how to succeed. They forget that their primary mandate is *getting work done through others*. CPR offers simple steps to building an almost uniformly kick-ass team.

The manager who enables her reports to do a good job and succeed in their work empowers those reports to believe in themselves. They will take pride in themselves, each other, and the group's strength and reputation, and they will go through hell and high water for the manager who supports and encourages them. They will also help, encourage, and insist that new hires rise to the same levels of professionalism and performance.

The result, for you—beyond a superior team that willingly gives of its best and delivers top-line results—is partly the job security this earns, and partly your growth from a manager into a true leader. CPR is the secret ingredient that propels upward mobility on the management ladder. It helps you develop steadily increasing credibility and visibility within your company, and then within the ever-widening circles of your profession (you can learn about expanding professional credibility and visibility in *Knock 'em Dead: Secrets & Strategies for Success in an Uncertain World* and other *Knock 'em Dead* books). This increases your real worth to your current employer, and your desirability in the eyes of other employers. While you may not like the idea of conducting employee reviews, CPRs are different, and once integrated will become your most valuable *productivity*-enhancement tool.

CPR Frequency and Consistency

The frequency and regularity of CPRs remove much of the fear and anticipation that accompanies a performance review given only once a year. The consistency offers the employee a reliable schedule on which to be heard, a standard against which progress can be measured, and with this greater frequency, the employee perception will change from dread of a judgmental experience to anticipation of an empowering one.

On a new employee's first day, you should take him to breakfast or lunch as a gesture of welcome, and if not you, then the most senior and valued staff member—you will do so another day this first week. The meeting's tone will be positive and encouraging, and you will explain that for the first month, you and he will meet for a few minutes every week on such and such a day and time to discuss how things are going, and to identify what you can do to help. Then, if all is going well, you will meet twice a month for the next two months, and then once a month after that as a catch-up.

These meetings do not need to be long once you have the system working, and they will repay you in better *productivity* very quickly. With a gradually implemented CPR schedule for everyone, all your people will feel appreciated, encouraged, and secure in the knowledge that you recognize their efforts, want them to succeed, and are willing to supply the advice, tools, and encouragement to help them become successful in their chosen profession.

Preparing for a CPR

It is impossible to walk into a CPR cold and expect meaningful results; some preparation is in order. Creating an effective procedure is a simple five-step process.

Step One
Establish acceptable standards of performance in every area of the job.

Step Two
Set these new standards down in a document as they relate to each title.

Step Three
Create CPR folders for *every employee*, including the performance standards for both the person and job title. Include a document for "critical incidents" in which, *last thing every day, you note specific examples of demonstrably superior or inferior performance.*

Step Four
Start by having the new employee develop her own job description during the first week on the job. Introduce this idea at your first meeting with her on the first day of work, and then revise it together at your first CPR meeting until there is consensus. You must agree on what the job is, and how performance standards will be met. If you have performance standards from the employee in her own words, there is more ownership and sense of responsibility. If you are already thinking about existing employees who need this, be patient, we'll get to them in a few pages; for now, we're focusing on new hires.

Step Five

Once there is agreement on the *deliverables* of the job (by the end of the first CPR meeting), give the employee a CPR review form to fill out the afternoon before next week's meeting (you can customize one to your unique needs from the following example). Such self-reviews are invariably objective and in fact have been proven more honest and insightful than manager reviews: They give you advance notice of what the employee thinks and feels—information you couldn't possibly get on such short acquaintance otherwise.

Keeping Track of Performance

Part of your management job is to guide individual and group performance every day. When you notice a special effort—or a problem—document it in that employee's CPR folder and discuss it with the worker when you can. Make time for this note taking at the end of every day: It will prove helpful in preventing management headaches down the line.

Those little notes not only become the basis for coaching that employee to success—something almost all professionals want to achieve—but they also document your *commitment* to adhering to a clearly articulated set of performance standards. This foundation gives your people a sense of security. Your reserve of solid examples of good or bad performance (as opposed to vague recollection) tells your reports that they are noticed, they are important to you, and they are being evaluated according to a set of rules and performance standards by which everyone is expected to abide.

Just as driving a car requires you to constantly look ahead and behind, adjust your speed, signal a change in direction, slow, stop, and reverse when necessary, so does developing your staff. Possessing the details of what has happened in the past is a key building block for structuring future action plans.

Here is a sample CPR form:

CPR Form

Performance Evaluation for: _____

Date: _____

Job description mutually agreed upon: _____

_____

Performance   Good _____ Average _____ Needs Attention _____

Critical Dimensions

A

B

C

D

E

Taking direction

Attitude toward coworkers

Attitude toward job

Attitude toward management

Quality of work

Quality output

Overall rating

Areas I would like to develop: _____

_____

How manager can help: _____

_____

Commit to achieve: _____

CPR Guidelines

Recognize good behavior and correct bad behavior, but remember that everyone remembers criticism longer than praise. Your focus is identifying problems and providing solutions; your observations regarding both good and bad behavior should always be accompanied with concrete examples and actual occurrences. Never forget: *People respect what you inspect, not what you expect.*

Make sure the environment is conducive to two-way communication. The CPR is not just an opportunity to get your views across; the employee must feel comfortable expressing her own feelings, opinions, hopes, and fears. You should discuss how current performance compares with established standards. Avoid vague comparisons with some elusive ideal performance level; set specific targets and goals.

How to Conduct a CPR

A CPR meeting follows a simple organizational structure. It looks like this:

Warm-up				
Position Review				
Worker Evaluation				
Examination of Deliverables and Variables				
A	B	C	D	E
Employee Comments				
Planning Development and Goals				
Wrap-up				

Formal meetings with management are always cause for an increase in adrenaline level. So set the right tone with some small talk (and perhaps a nonthreatening question or two) about current positive events with which both parties are familiar.

Position Review

Put the meeting on firm foundations by deciding what is going to be discussed and within what parameters. During the review, you will want to make meaningful comparisons and reach consensus on direction, so be sure you agree on:

- The time period that the meeting will address.
- The structure of the meeting: "Paul, here's what we'll do this afternoon. First of all, I want you to give me your evaluation of the past week. Then we'll find solutions for any areas of concern and make our plans for the next week."

This establishes your mutual commitment to work together to address the problems and opportunities you identify.

Walking Through the CPR

Your next step is to have the employee verbally walk you through his own evaluation of his performance.

As the employee explains his performance evaluation, show that you are listening and understand: "So, if I understand you correctly . . ." or "What you are saying is . . ." Otherwise, listen carefully without interrupting, editorializing, or making value judgments. Being heard is validating for the employee, while working for a manager who doesn't listen is demotivating.

Examination of Responsibilities and Deliverables
A B   C   D E

This is the heart of the CPR. Now it is your turn to speak and guide the employee. One by one, review your opinion of performance with each of the critical *responsibilities* and *deliverables*, citing specific examples from the week that you noted in the employee's CPR folder. (On the CPR form from earlier, they're listed as the letters A through E; you will customize them to the needs of that specific job title.)

1. **Set the frame of reference.** "We are going to review your progress on the following items . . ."
2. **Gather information.** Allow the employee to proceed with his verbal explanation of his written evaluation of progress on each of the topics you have agreed to address in the meeting.
3. **Summarize and confirm.** Restate what you have heard and ask for confirmation that what you heard is correct. This ensures that you have a clear understanding of the status of each of the issues under discussion.
4. **Offer your analysis.** When the employee has spoken and you have confirmed understanding, it is time for your analysis of the status on each agenda item and where matters stand today. Discuss what you feel has gone well and why, and what didn't go as smoothly as planned. Intelligent discussion during a CPR will show that you are interested and that you care; this alone is unusual for most working professionals and will by itself encourage the employee to improve his performance. The questions you ask should be as nonthreatening as possible: The aim of the CPR is to reach consensus and create motivational plans for improvement, not to foster conflict and confrontation.

Be Supportive

You can be supportive in three distinct ways:

1. By the way you listen and the *body language* you use.
2. Verbally, with the tone and the way you phrase statements and concerns.
3. By offering tangible help in the form of training and resources to help the employee grow. You might say, "Let's agree on the areas we need to work on, the tools or training that could help, and the time we will need to make some headway." This reaffirms the worker/management partnership and the employee's sense of being part of the team; we'll address the tools and training part of this shortly.

Employee Comments

After the *responsibilities* and *deliverables* have been discussed, give the new employee an opportunity to add anything she feels is germane to the discussion. Theoretically, there should have been plenty of good *communication* on all the issues, but it is essential to give the employee one last chance to be heard before you proceed to planning.

Planning Development and Goals

Reach agreement on the timing of the next CPR meeting and its content. *"If we meet at the same time next week, what should you be focusing on until then?"* Ask the employee for suggestions on what he believes are the next steps in the skill-development experience, because in so doing you build his *critical thinking skills* and sense of responsibility. At the same time, this all-important planning phase will only be effective if everyone agrees and commits to the same goals; and if the impetus comes from the employee, all the better, because:

1. She will have ownership.
2. If goals aren't met, management can't be construed as unrealistic.
3. This approach creates a paper trail for any future problems.

Encourage the employee to set goals to strive for until the next CPR meeting: *"Where do you think we'll be on each of these items by this time next week?"* If the goals are realistic and agree with what you deem appropriate, all is well. If not, you must negotiate either to raise or lower the achievement levels the employee identifies. Often a new worker will want to impress by promising the moon. However, it is better that less is promised and more is delivered—small successes breed more and bigger successes.

Once everything is agreed upon, get in the habit of reviewing the plans and having the employee jot them down. Then, at the end of the meeting, say, *"Remember to e-mail me the plan at the end of the day."* This way, the employee will twice write down his commitments, and twice give you his commitment to follow the plan—once in person during the meeting, and once when he sends you the written version. This process gives your employees much more ownership and commitment to follow-through, and gives you an employee-generated paper trail.

Tools and Tactics for Skill Development

Putting a coaching plan into play following CPR is where the rubber meets the road. It isn't enough to say that you plan to help employees improve their skills: There has to be a means of implementation. Once a need for skill development is identified—or in the case of a new employee an initial training program is set out—a means of accomplishment must be delineated. This will range from you being available to answer questions to other tactics, including:

- **Job shadowing.** The new employee spends time observing one or more team members accomplished in a particular skill area. For example, the new salesperson might spend a week making sales calls with your top sales people before she goes solo, then alternate between days of shadowing and days of solo performance for another week or two.
- **Mentor/buddy assignments.** The trainee is assigned to an employee possessing superior competency in the skill area. In this development scenario, the trainee performs the job with the ongoing advice and oversight of the senior staffer. You could also integrate a mentor dimension into the second stage of the job-shadowing scenario, with the new employee making the sales pitches and the more experienced team member offering support with pre- and post-sales call advice. This gives the newbie on-the-job training and gets her to know and be known by the best people on your team.
- **Personal study.** The employee improves skills by personal study via books, on-demand training, etc. Many companies maintain formal training libraries situated within HR, to which you can readily gain access. If your company doesn't provide a library, you should build your own; the company will probably pick up the costs. The

Internet is a great resource. If you are still drawing a blank, try one of the resource companies such as Monad Trainers Aide (*www .monadtrainersaide.com*), which has been renting and selling DVDs and online training materials on thousands of topics for more than thirty years; ask to speak to Carol and tell her I said hello.

• **Formal training.** You or a particularly skilled team member can run training meetings on topics specific to the department's *deliverables*. HR may also sponsor formal training programs for your staff, or you can go outside to workshops and conferences. Another excellent resource for training is membership in professional associations, which conduct professional development programs locally on an ongoing basis.

Wrapping Up a CPR Meeting

Conclude the CPR meeting on a positive note with a comment about the good progress that has been made and how you hope to see things develop over the coming days. Then stand up, smile, shake hands, and get on with business.

Rinse and Repeat

Take new employees through this process every week for a month. Then, if all is going well, twice a month for the second and third months. After that, assuming they are up to speed, once a month.

If you then extend this process to include the whole team—the superstars, the troubled workers, and the plodders (with a frequency suitable to their needs)—for a year, you will have a truly cohesive team that knows how to analyze, plan, and execute in almost all situations.

Who's Got Time for This?

In the rough and tumble of a manager's life, it's tough to make the time for meetings, and the last thing you want to do is add another review process to your To Do list. But it is foolish to think that time spent on anything else is more important than time spent coaching your team players on the tools and skills they need to succeed. A manager's job is to *get work done through others*, and *productivity* will only improve when you and your staff share the same understanding of the job, its *deliverables*, and the actions it takes to achieve them. Your performance is based on their performance, measured by how effectively you draw diverse personalities together and inspire individual *commitment* to shared goals. You know that as a manager, providing maximum return on investment is your job. However, you must also recognize that your employees only give what they get, so you must consider the ROI from your subordinate's viewpoint as well as the company's. It isn't so much that there isn't time to do CPRs, as it as that there isn't time *not* to do them—it's the most effective way to meet the *deliverables* of your job.

Making Skill-Development Coaching Stick

You should also assess how each worker is absorbing and applying new skills. There is little point in investing time, money, and energy in training your staff if the training has no impact. Everyone is different in how they learn and the rate at which they can absorb and apply new information and techniques. One person might pick things up after simply hearing a new idea: You should be sensitive to this individual being a fast learner, and not smother her with too much training. Someone else might learn more slowly and need ongoing group and individual training through job shadowing and mentoring until the new skill is adequately absorbed. The approaches you use should reflect the needs of the individual and your group, rather than your personal preferences.

Tell, Show, and Involve

In Training and Development, there is a saying: Tell me and I'll forget, show me and I'll remember, involve me and I'll be able to do it myself. The more involvement you can create in a learning experience, the better and more quickly the information will be absorbed.

All three of these techniques (tell, show, involve) have a place in helping staff develop new skills, and used in concert they will give you the most powerful in-department training tool available. This three-part coaching tool works in the following sequence:

1. You share knowledge about the skill, and have the employee execute under your supervision.
2. You assign the employee to work closely with another staff member well-versed in this skill (either as a shadow or a mentor/buddy).
3. You give the employee assignments that build confidence in the skill.

When you start a coaching process by sharing expertise about the area in which the employee is being coached, don't stop once the mentor/buddy is assigned. You don't withdraw from sharing helpful information, nor is the mentor/buddy suddenly unavailable for help or advice. Follow a sequence to get the process moving, then continue to tell, show, and involve as the learning process moves forward, and stay involved with the employee's development through CPRs as you present more challenging assignments.

Be Available

When a report needs help, you must be available, instilling the feeling that they can come to you with questions. Always try to answer the question "Have you got a moment, boss?" in the affirmative. Listen, acknowledge, give the needed input immediately if you can, and if not, arrange a specific time when you can; the staff member will feel validated and better able to continue in the intervening period. Even if other aspects of your work require significant time commitments, make sure that your door is open on a regular basis, as well as any time a real emergency arises.

Some people find it easy to ask advice; others find it far more difficult. Showing a personal interest in and knowledge of your staff members as people will do a lot to break down barriers of distrust and nervousness. Your coaching must include reaching out as you manage by wandering around. You should stop by everyone's workspace regularly to inquire after professional activities, interests, family, and hobbies, or simply to say hello. Once you know a report's personal interests, the Internet gives you a fast way to show personal interest: Search the topic and come up with some related blog, cartoon, or video, and send it to him (for most impact, hit "send" outside of normal business hours).

Your Team's Composition

If you are like most managers, you don't have the opportunity to build your team from scratch; you inherit a team that is made up of four categories of workers:

1. New employees
2. Plodders
3. Troubled workers
4. Superstars

Every department has these four clearly identifiable groups—the new hires, the supermotivated, the troubled workers who either can't or won't make anything more than a minimal effort, and finally, somewhere in the middle, there's a less readily identifiable group, made up of those who plod along doing a reliable job, but who lack either the *motivation* or the *skills* to grow professionally. We've addressed how to get new hires up to speed; now let's look at dealing with the plodders, the superstars, and the troubled workers.

The Plodders
It is easy to assume that anyone without the same burning desire as you is a slacker and easy to mistake these valuable employees for troubled workers, simply because they are not motivated by professional growth. This is a costly mistake, because so-called plodders,

given the right handling, can become the backbone of your group and your reputation, if only you learn how to handle them productively.

You can quite easily identify these middle-of-the-pack performers from their personnel files. When you inherit a new department, you should spend time in HR going over each member's personnel file. You will find that plodders have often been in the job and with the company for a long time, and usually have good attendance records and steady reviews.

You can also get a heads-up from how they are described by your boss, your colleagues, and the people in HR. You'll hear a plodder described like this:

- Likes the routine
- Reliable but not a superstar
- Doesn't complain
- Gets the job done, but don't expect her to stay past five
- Turned down a promotion

You'll find that many of your plodders are competent professionals who just aren't motivated by professional growth much beyond where you find them today. They aren't losers; they take pride in their jobs, they just aren't driven by the same things as the superstars with whom you have more in common. Very often they have other things going on in their lives that take precedence. Often the job is a way to pay the bills, a means to an end that allows them to pay attention to the things that are important in their lives. This can range from caring for an aging parent to writing the next great American novel. If you can recognize the needs of these workers and don't expect them to be gung-ho zealots, you can secure a valuable asset. Here's how:

- Show them respect for being the reliable professionals they are. Be thankful they are not stabbing others in the back, impelled by an insatiable desire for success at all costs. Recognize them as the company stalwarts they are.

- Appreciate their experience and dependability. Be thankful that they don't need watching every moment of the day. These workers can be relied on to work steadily at their assignments, allowing you to use your time to develop more motivated employees or otherwise further your department's interests.
- Keep their workloads manageable. Remember, a plodder may not be late for work, but he is usually gone by five, too.
- Don't press them to learn skills above and beyond those necessary to do the job unless they want to.
- Recognize that sometimes people lack confidence and are threatened by learning, and as a result they sometimes learn more slowly. When a new skill is necessary, perhaps because of the changing technology in the workplace, allow the time and resources necessary for your plodders to pick it up without being penalized or publicly embarrassed.
- Remember that plodders are often undervalued and may carry a little resentment because of that. Value them, and figure out roles to satisfy their needs. Once you are seen to value their efforts you can often win over a serious supporter for your cause.
- Because they are reliable and steady, they are often very good at the things they choose to do well. Sometimes you can show recognition by assigning a new employee for job shadowing or mentoring, but be sure to clear it with the plodder first: some just don't want the hassle, and this is an extra responsibility that needs to be seen as a sign of positive recognition.

So, assuming they would like the responsibility, when it comes to coaching approaches like job shadowing or mentor/buddying, one of your steady, reliable plodders might be just the person to deliver a solid learning experience. This also works because it provides them respect and recognition within their comfort zone. Because workers who fall into the plodder category aren't often seen leaping tall buildings at a single bound on behalf of their employers, they notice praise most often by its absence. Showing appreciation for plodders—conferring status with job shadowing or mentor assignments—gives you the opportunity to show public respect and recognition for people who rarely receive it.

One last word on plodders: As a manager you are likely to be a driven and motivated person. As such, you will naturally gravitate toward people like yourself, even in relationships with your staff. You need to make just as much effort to get to know and find common ground with plodders who perhaps don't share your particular approach to life. Just as you respond to those who take a genuine interest in you as a person, so do others, and getting to know others different from yourself is enriching and widens your knowledge of human nature—a practice the successful manager and leader studiously engages in.

The Superstars

Your superstars need attention and recognition too. I can't emphasize enough how important it is to meet with superior workers at least once a month. These are going to be easy meetings, and a big part of the intent is to show recognition, respect, and appreciation. Too often we think that people who are doing well know it, and know that we appreciate their efforts. Then it surprises us when they resign.

For these people, the CPR is a chance for one-on-one time with you and formal recognition of their efforts. Not only will CPRs serve as a powerful motivating force, drastically cutting down on those unexpected resignations, they will also help you justify raises and promotions when the time comes. Besides, your superstars will be energized by public shows of respect, and you have to eat anyway, so make it a lunch meeting with someone who is most likely going to give you good news, and who will appreciate the recognition.

Regularly feed back the results of your top members' CPR reviews to your boss and to HR; for example, you can simply copy your boss on an e-mail that praises a team member for a special effort or accomplishment. If you want someone to get a raise or a promotion (especially if you are quietly doing succession planning for your own ascent), put special achievements in writing, and make sure she is getting assignments that help her grow professionally.

For example, you might get in the habit of involving your succession candidate in job shadowing, mentoring, resume screening, telephone interviews, and running training meetings. Just be sure that you don't overload her, and that the assignments are in line with how she wants to develop her *skills* and *responsibilities*. You could even delegate the occasional report-writing duty. Not only does this offer a development opportunity, it also allows you (after appropriate editing) to leave your superstar's name on the report along with your own, which gives the superior performer public recognition with senior management. And never forget it gets you out of most of a crappy job, too.

There are numerous meetings, standing committees, and task forces that occur during the year: Bring key people to these proceedings as part of their professional development.

A consistent campaign that promotes your top people in this manner, when combined with the documentation provided by the ongoing CPR process, will make raises and promotional suggestions that much easier to justify. Furthermore, your ability to consistently develop strong performers demonstrates your own success as a manager, and in turn supports your own raises and promotions. Making your people promotable is a subtle form of self-promotion. Whatever you do, don't leave your stars in departmental isolation. They need, deserve, and thrive on recognition; deny them and they'll go somewhere else to feel appreciated.

Troubled Workers

Just as age is no guarantee of wisdom, longevity with a company is no guarantee of *ability*. It is alarming how some companies readily hang on to long-term troubled, incompetent, and disruptive employees. In my opinion this is a sign of incompetent management, because keeping troubled workers creates motivational blocks for your best workers.

To be successful as a manager and a leader, it is necessary to turn around or trim away those who cannot or will not contribute. If you don't, everyone else in your department will think you are too stupid to notice or too much of a wuss to take action. Either way, they will feel insulted by being lumped in with these people, and they will eventually leave.

While taking a troubled worker through the CPR process will give you a paper trail to satisfy HR about a legal and righteous termination, it also encourages a percentage of them to turn themselves around or read the writing on the wall and make a hasty exit. This saves you the unpleasantness and paperwork of termination, gets rid of the headache, yet doesn't put a stain on the employee's resume or make it more difficult for her to find a new job. It's effective, productive (because the people who do work hard will admire you), and humane.

Instituting a department-wide CPR program is the perfect opportunity for helping these employees improve or decide they might find a better shady tree elsewhere before you replace them with someone who wants to make a success of his professional life.

Helping troubled workers starts with a first CPR meeting, at which you ask them to complete a self-evaluation review of their performance in the critical areas of the job.

You agree to meet the following week, making certain that you will have that review on your desk the afternoon before the scheduled meeting, giving you a night to absorb and strategize.

Continue with the weekly meetings until there are demonstrable improvements in the identified substandard areas. When there are improvements, they need to be recognized and praised, and the meetings can gradually be cut back to twice and once monthly.

With troubled workers, you must demonstrate from the start that there is one set of rules and standards for all. This is the group that will provide the most challenge and require the greatest time and effort. Stick to the program: With some of these workers, you will achieve gratifying, even inspiring improvements, and you should be able to elevate the vast majority of your troubled employees to (at the least) acceptable levels of performance. But when the day is done, you will probably still have intractable performance problems with some troubled workers who continue to pull down paychecks for doing a lousy job, lowering your team's morale, and screwing with your career.

With troubled workers who show no improvement after a month to six weeks, the weekly meeting schedule should continue, but with blunt commentary. For example, "Frank, for the last six weeks you have not met the sales quotas you set for yourself, perhaps because you aren't making enough calls. Yesterday afternoon you didn't pick up the telephone between 2 and 2:40 P.M. You know this is prime time for selling. If you were in my position, what would you do?"

Go through each of the critical *responsibilities* and *deliverables* for that job in the same way, detailing where and why performance is substandard and asking what the employee thinks should be done about it.

- "With this performance and continued lack of improvement, despite all the training and support you have requested, I don't foresee a future for you here."
- "With this performance and continued lack of improvement, despite all the training and support you have requested, I just can't see how I could justify a salary increase of any kind this year."
- "Given the situation and lack of improvement in the necessary performance standards, what would you do with me, if our positions were reversed?"
- "Frankly I am concerned that your performance and attitude are pulling down the other team members."

With intractably troubled workers, biting the bullet and refusing to grant *any* pay increase when the annual review time comes around sends a very strong message, especially when probably everyone else is getting a raise. In such instances, you will of course be in close communication with HR to ensure that you are following corporate and legal standards in applying the disciplinary measures that will encourage troubled, and often troublesome, employees to pull up stakes and move on. Ultimately, if neither carrot nor stick helps generate improvements, you have no alternative to ridding your organization of an incapable or unwilling performer. You have a greater obligation to the team as a whole.

The Upsides and Downsides of Termination

If you don't want to fire anyone, or think it's inhumane, consider this: You are a team coach, and when the team loses, management doesn't fire the team, they fire the coach. If this isn't enough to convince you, remember that if you fail to purge chronic poor performers, your best players will believe that you condone lackluster performance, are too weak to take action, or can't tell the difference between hard workers and slackers. Success-driven professionals only want to associate with equally *committed* colleagues, and they will ultimately leave you if you don't trim the fat. And remember: Good performers leaving your department unexpectedly is a black mark on your managerial record. It is your responsibility to replace employees on your chosen schedule so that they in no way impair departmental performance. Your future is at stake and this simple but effective CPR process is your most effective tool for survival and success as a manager.

The steps we have discussed will have established documentation of performance standards that everyone in your department adheres to and that the troubled worker himself generated and failed to meet. This means you should be able to go to HR early on with established documentation of where, how, and for how long a specific employee has been falling short in critical areas of performance, despite regular communication on the issues and the offer of all the tools and assistance necessary for improvement. If you follow HR's approved guidelines, this documentation should make for a clean termination when the time comes. You have done all you can do for the rotten apple, and you have the wellbeing of your team—your professional family—to consider.

Family Leadership

Every group, familial, professional, or otherwise, needs leadership to survive and prosper over the long haul. Your team—the family you have at work—will always have its problems and challenges. That's to be expected, because they are the people with whom you spend the majority of your waking hours. So, it is important to recognize that you are, indeed, the leader of what in many ways is a family group, and that with that honor come certain responsibilities. Not least among them is to keep everyone on track—for their own benefit as well as for the common good. How you handle this *responsibility* will determine the health and wellbeing of your workplace family.

Leadership in a family and leadership at work are tested when things aren't going as planned, and a family that sees you rewarding good work and performance, supporting their success, and wielding authority wisely and firmly with intractably troubled employees, will be a family that trusts, honors, and follows its leader.

In Conclusion

You know that it is impossible to *manage productively* without first *hiring effectively*, and that this skill is the bedrock of all the skills you must develop as a successful manager. With *Knock 'em Dead: Hiring the Best*, you have learned that employee selection and productive management isn't brain surgery; it is just a series of logical steps and sensible techniques that enable you to make consistently good hires and upgrade your staff's productivity as you simultaneously weld them into a proud and effective unit. Cumulatively, you have learned some valuable lessons, not only in successful management but in how to grow from a manager into a true leader. I hope this book will prove helpful to you over the years. I am always available at *www.knockem dead.com* to help with your career management needs.

INTERVIEWING WITHIN THE LAW

This appendix addresses the legal considerations of hiring. It is intended as a general primer; I am not a lawyer and this is *not* meant to be a legal guide.

State and federal laws involving individual and worker rights have been in a constant state of flux over the last few years; in turn, the letter of the law is constantly interpreted by case law. To cover every detail of employment law as it applies to your situation is beyond the scope of this book. Whenever you are in doubt about a question or an approach, please consult company counsel.

One word of caution in dealing with legal counsel from someone who has been paying lawyers for twenty-plus years: *Get the lawyer's counsel in writing that you understand: the written word is all that counts; the spoken word should not be trusted—it is your career and livelihood at stake.*

The principles applied in *Knock 'em Dead: Hiring the Best* are based on common sense and the imperative of consistently productive hires; they also keep you from discriminating in any way and getting your company sued—the kiss of death to a flourishing management career.

The federal and state laws addressing equal opportunity and discrimination in job opportunity and the workplace began to enter U.S. corporate culture with Title VII of the 1964 Civil Rights Act, whose reach was extended by the Equal Employment Opportunity Act of 1972, the Age Discrimination Act of 1975, and the Americans with Disabilities Act of 1990, etc.

Title VII has since become the foundation of employment law in other countries. In 1990 and 1991, immediately before and after the end of apartheid in South Africa, an earlier edition of *Knock 'em Dead: Hiring the Best* brought me the honor of being the first invited foreign speaker in that country to address competency-based, rather than race- or sex-based selection. I quickly learned that many companies were already basing their hiring protocols on the U.S. laws mentioned above.

Employment Discrimination

The laws, amendments, and court decisions that define and clarify employment discrimination are directed toward the elimination of discrimination in the workplace and the protection of equal opportunity for all. In broad terms, when you hire someone, you may not discriminate on the basis of age, race, national origin, religion, disability, or sex. Many states have forbidden discrimination based on sexual preference, while others have not, but the times are changing, and you do not want a stupid misstep to make your career a test case in the courts. Become the spirit of equality that is the bedrock of America and you will stay on the right side of employment laws.

But what questions are clearly illegal? That is not an easy one to answer. A general measure of the legality of a question is this: Is the question necessary to determine the candidate's *ability* to discharge the *responsibilities* of the job satisfactorily? In other words, if the question doesn't have anything to do with the job, don't ask it. When your objective is simply to find the most qualified person for the job, you don't need to ask questions unrelated to job performance.

As a general rule, questions about height, weight, age, marital status, religious or political beliefs, dependents, birth control, birthplace, race, sexual preference, and national origin are strictly out of bounds.

National Origin

You should not ask:

- About the candidate's or the candidate's parents' or spouse's nationality, ancestry, lineage, or parentage
- Whether the candidate's parents or spouse are native-born or naturalized citizens
- The name of the next of kin
- The candidate's or the candidate's family's birthplace
- How the candidate learned a second language

You can ask:

- Whether the candidate is a U.S. citizen, a resident alien, has a green card or other visas that provide the right to work in the United States—so long as you ask all candidates the same question.

You can usually ask:

- About languages a candidate speaks (as long as the question is relevant to the job)

Religious and Political Beliefs

The Civil Rights Act of 1964 was amended by the Equal Opportunity Act of 1972, and in the latter, all matters relating to the examination of religious and political beliefs and affiliations are designated as impermissible—unless you are a religious organization and your legal counsel has specifically assured you (in writing) that such questions are permissible.

You should not ask about a candidate's:

- Political beliefs or affiliations
- Religious beliefs, affiliations, denomination, church, mosque, or synagogue
- Religious holiday observances

You can usually ask about a candidate's:

- Willingness to work on Saturdays or Sundays (if the job so requires)

Even when it comes to character references, you must be circumspect. I have heard of employers who ask for references from a candidate's pastor or religious leader, and that's absolutely discriminatory. However, churches have some leeway when it comes to establishing religious beliefs compatible with the mission of the religious denomination; if you are hiring for a religious organization you should nevertheless check with your manager, Human Resources, and/or the Legal Department and get their advice in writing.

Race

You should not ask questions regarding a candidate's race, country of origin, complexion, or skin color, or those of the candidate's family. If you still think there's a good reason for asking about nationality or race—if you feel it has anything to do with performance in a job, for example, with international positions for which cultural diversity can be argued to be a "must have" skill—you are advised to clear all questions through legal counsel.

Sex

The bulk of sexual discrimination in the selection process is directed toward women.

You should not ask about a candidate's:

- Change of name, maiden name, or original name
- Current or previous marital status
- Preferred form of address (Miss, Mrs., or Ms.)
- Spouse
- Number, names, or ages of children or dependents
- Method of birth control or reproductive ability

You can usually ask:

- Whether the candidate has ever worked for your company under another name
- Whether any of the candidate's relatives currently work for your company

Age

The Age Discrimination Act of 1975 prohibits discrimination in employment against candidates between the ages of forty and seventy. Ultimately, the only question you should ask concerning age is whether or not the candidate is eighteen years old. If you are ever tempted to discriminate against older workers (as many employers are), ask yourself whether you wouldn't rather hire someone who has already made his big mistakes on somebody else's payroll and who is less likely to job hop.

Convictions

In some states, it is illegal to ask about arrests and/or convictions. Whatever the prohibitions, it is extremely risky to inquire about convictions unless you can prove without a shadow of a doubt that the information has a direct relevance to the job at hand. For example, a company whose employees enter people's homes may well be warranted in inquiring about convictions for violent crimes, but in all cases you should seek company counsel before proceeding.

Military History

Most questions concerning military history are illegal, unless the job specifically requires a military background.

You should not ask:
- In which branch of the military the candidate served
- What type of discharge she received

You can usually ask:
- Whether the candidate has military experience in the Armed Forces of the United States

Education

You should not ask, "Are you a high school graduate?" However, you can usually ask the candidate to detail his educational history.

People with Disabilities

The 1990 Americans with Disabilities Act (ADA) has changed the way hiring of the disabled is viewed.

Although ADA law is exceedingly complex, the tragedy is the attitude of many employers when it comes to taking advantage of the untapped human resource of 43 million disabled Americans. People with disabilities have suffered from discrimination throughout recorded history. Even today, despite the countless studies that document their exemplary productivity and on-the-job attendance, disabled workers remain the victims of shortsighted employers who fail to take full advantage of this vast source of talent and competency.

How ADA Affects You

Simply put, the ADA represents a comprehensive set of guidelines that mandate the end of discrimination against people who, from birth or as the result of injury or accident, have a physical or mental disability that substantially limits a major life activity such as hearing, seeing, speaking, breathing, performing manual tasks, walking, caring for oneself, learning, or working. The ADA also protects persons who have a record of such a physical or mental impairment, and those who are regarded as having such impairment.

If you employ fifteen or more people for any consecutive period of twenty weeks during the year, your company is bound by the ADA, which forbids discrimination against disabled persons in all aspects of employment, including the application process, hiring decisions, promotions, assignments, and termination. Employers must also provide reasonable accommodation in the workplace for disabled employees and job applicants. Reasonable accommodations might include making physical changes to the building in which your organization is located, restructuring jobs, modifying schedules, or providing a disabled employee with special equipment or even a reader or interpreter as an assistant. Additionally, state regulations often pick up where the ADA leaves off. Some states have requirements that are substantially more stringent.

There's one exception to the law, however. If you can show that a proposed accommodation would be "excessively costly, extensive, substantial, or disruptive," or would "fundamentally alter the nature or operation of the business," then your company may be granted an exception based on undue hardship.

There are different ways to approach the many challenges of providing access and accommodation. Before you make any assumptions, remember that the size, structure, function, and financial resources of your company will ultimately determine your ability to make changes— and these factors may exempt you from certain provisions of the ADA altogether. Again, talk to Human Resources and/or legal counsel.

Legal Discrimination

According to the ADA, there are three conditions under which you, as an employer, are allowed to discriminate legally. You may do so when the employee's disability will:

1. Threaten the public health
2. Risk the safety of others
3. Restrict the execution of the essential functions of the job

For example, if your company manufactures food products in open vats, then the law (and plain common sense) dictates that you may discriminate when it comes to hiring people with infectious diseases. Likewise, you wouldn't be in violation if you were to deny employment to a person with one leg who applied for a job as a firefighter, if the resulting lack of mobility might risk the life of an infant trapped in a smoke-filled room.

However, the law is very clear when it comes to judgments based on perceived, rumored, or past impairments. You can't reassign, for example, a receptionist who has controlled high blood pressure to a less stressful position simply because you're afraid she might have a heart attack, or exclude an engineering candidate from consideration due to his past history of mental illness, or because he was at one time misdiagnosed as having a learning disability.

Remember that a disability is defined as an impairment that sub-stantially restricts one or more major life activities. Forms of social expression, minor neuroses, temporary afflictions, and sexual disor-ders, however, are not protected disabilities. For that reason, a can-didate with a broken arm that would eventually heal itself would be excluded from ADA protection.

The Essential Functions of the Job

In any hiring decision, the first and most important question should always be: Is the candidate qualified for the job? Does the candidate possess the requisite skills, educational credentials, work experience, *motivation*, licenses, and/or certifications to be seriously considered for employment? If the answer is yes, so far so good.

If the person also has a disability, you need to go one step further and answer the next question, which is paramount in the eyes of the ADA: Can this candidate perform the essential functions of the job, with or without a reasonable accommodation?

This is where things get complicated, because most of us aren't accustomed to quantifying job duties in such a precise manner. According to the ADA, there are three reasons why a job function could be considered essential:

1. *The position exists solely to perform the function.* That is, if you need someone to transcribe handwritten documents eight hours a day, and that's all the job entails, then transcribing is an essential function.
2. *There are a limited number of other employees available to per-form the function.* This is a corollary situation in that it specifies the need for versatility, especially in smaller businesses with fluctuating demands. If transcribing is the usual job, but peak periods of intensive activity require answering the phone and shuttling out-of-town customers to and from the airport on short notice, then the versatility itself becomes an essential function of the job.

3. *The function requires special expertise.* If the rest of the staff and all the customers only speak Lithuanian, then fluent Lithuanian language skills may be considered an essential job function.

In determining exactly what's essential and what isn't, the ADA suggests that you look for evidence that would either prove that the new hire would actually be required to perform the function, or prove that removing the function would fundamentally change the job. Evidence may come from written job descriptions, observations of past or current employee performance, the amount of time normally spent performing various functions, or the consequences that may arise from not requiring a person to perform an essential function. If neither the requirement nor the removal conditions can be proven, the function has to be considered nonessential.

The Total Hiring Picture with Respect to the ADA

The provisions of the ADA cover a broad range of employment-related activities. If you think that your nondiscrimination responsibilities are limited to the interviewing, offering, and managing processes alone, think again. Your legal obligations extend to every conceivable aspect of the hiring picture, including these:

- *Application procedures.* If you run a job posting on CareerBuilder or an ad in the Sunday paper with a phone number but no address, you must also provide a telecommunications device for the deaf (TDD) or telephone relay service to accommodate inquiries by the hearing impaired. Similarly, you must ensure accessibility to your facility for the purpose of conducting an interview.
- *On-site recruiting.* If your company exhibits at a job fair or visits a college campus looking for recruits, you will want to ensure physical accessibility for those with disabilities who may wish to attend.
- *Personal associations.* If you deny employment to someone because she has a relationship with a disabled person, you run the risk of being held liable under the ADA.

- *Activism.* If you retaliate against someone who has a past, present, or pending ADA-related grievance, or attempt to coerce someone who gives aid to a person seeking protection under the provisions of the law, you could be headed for trouble.
- *Third-party representation.* If the search firm, employment agency, or college placement office you use in your recruiting or screening efforts fails to comply with any ADA provision, then you could *both* be held accountable.
- *Succession planning.* If you're interested in long-term team building, be careful. You can only evaluate a candidate's qualifications based on what the job currently is, not on what it might be in the future.

The ADA and Interviewing

In addition to making sure that disabled candidates are given equal consideration during the selection process, you need to adhere to certain ADA guidelines for the interview itself.

For example, the ADA explicitly forbids you to ask a candidate during an interview whether he is disabled, or to inquire about the nature or severity of the disability. However, it is the candidate's responsibility during the interview to inform you of a disability that may not be noticeable, since you are only required to provide reasonable accommodation for a disability of which you are aware.

Once the disability has surfaced, it's permissible to ask questions about the candidate's ability to perform specific job functions, or allow the person to describe or demonstrate how she would perform these functions. To be on the safe side, though, you should always try to phrase your questions so that they center on "if" rather than "how."

What do I mean? Well, let's suppose the candidate is a quadriplegic, and seems like he might need some sort of special transportation to get to work. You may be tempted to ask, "How do you plan to get to and from the office every day?" A more appropriate (and legally defensible) question would be, "The hours of work here are 7:30 A.M. to 4:30 P.M. If you were an employee of this company, is there any reason you can think of that you wouldn't be able to fulfill your essential duties during those hours?"

Another no-no is asking the candidate to take a special medical exam at any time during the pre-employment process.

The only exception is a standard medical examination given after an employment offer has been made. However, if a standard exam reveals the existence of a disability that was previously unknown and you end up hiring someone else, then you must show that the exam played no part in your decision. Similarly, any skill or aptitude evaluation can only pertain to job-related activities and has to be consistent with business necessity.

To Test or Not to Test

A few words on the issue of essential versus nonessential functions as they relate to testing. If you design a test used to assess a candidate's ability to create illustrated letterhead on Macintosh computers using the latest version of Adobe Illustrator, then you have to make certain that all job candidates are tested in this way, and that the tested skills represent an essential function of the job, not a peripheral activity; in reality, the development of pre-employment tests are best left to testing companies, who have more experience in developing nondiscriminatory tests.

To comply with the ADA, you must guarantee that a disabled person can take all pre-employment tests, even if it means making a reasonable accommodation by providing special access or a trained helper. And above all, you must avoid any type of test that might unwittingly screen out a disabled but otherwise qualified person.

The goal of these guidelines is to ensure equal opportunity for everyone, not to engage in reverse discrimination. As far as the law is concerned, you're under no obligation to employ a person *because* she has a disability. Your duty is simply to not discriminate against that person because of the disability.

To cover all the bases, it's a good idea to keep a written JD on file for each position you plan to fill. Even though it represents only one form of evidence, a clear and accurate job description is a good defense should you ever be accused of discrimination. I advise that you run any job descriptions or job description manuals by your organization's legal counsel.

Hiring Within the Law

The laws in each state differ, and they change all the time. If you are concerned about the wording of your selection strategies or interview questions, consult your own Human Resources department and/or legal counsel, the Equal Opportunity Commission, or your state employment organization.

INDEX